The Lanarkshire Police Chronicles

George Barnsley

Ringwood Publishing
Glasgow

First published in Great Britain in 2022
by
Ringwood Publishing
0/1 314 Meadowside Quay Walk,
Glasgow G11 6AY

www.ringwoodpublishing.com
e-mail: mail@ringwoodpublishing.com

ISBN 978-1-901514-92-6

British Library Cataloguing-in-Publication Data
A catalogue record for this book is available from the British Library

Typeset in Times New Roman 11
Printed and bound in the UK
by Lonsdale Direct Solutions

Contents

PART THREE: FOOD AND DRINK

PART FOUR: THEFT

PART NINE: IN MEMORIAM

PART TEN: THE NEED FOR FORMAL RECOGNITION FOR TWO WHO DIED ON DUTY IN LANARKSHIRE

Dedication

This book is dedicated to Constable George Taylor and Detective Sergeant William Ross Hunt, two brave police officers who gave their lives in the service of their communities.

We will remember you.

Always.

Foreword

Since the history of a Police Force is by extension the history of the communities it serves, George Barnsley's fascinating selection of stories in *The Lanarkshire Police Chronicles* follows the triumphs and disasters of Scotland's industrial heartland. Through war and peace, from the mundane to bloody murder, the narrative perfectly describes the shades of policing over the last two hundred years.

In a wider sense, the tales from Lanarkshire reflect the history of Scottish Policing as a whole, for the mix of heavy industry and rural hinterland are a microcosm of the wider nation. Lanarkshire Constabulary, always Scotland's largest County Force, had a deserved reputation as a tough and effective outfit. As the western neighbours of my old Force, Lanarkshire were always stalwart. In times of need they could be depended upon. Policing the busy Coal and Steel towns of the central belt bred good Police Officers.

No one is better placed to tell this story than George Barnsley, a hugely experienced policeman with deep roots in Lanarkshire. For years, he has tirelessly championed efforts to preserve the history of policing in Scotland.

In these chronicles, the author makes full use of his extensive knowledge as he weaves together stories, from the early enacting police legislation to salutary tales of people at their best and worst.

The underlying theme is timeless. Many aspects of Policing have changed and new threats, like Cyber Crime, have emerged. But behind the new challenges, the fundamentals remain the same. Human behaviour has changed little, and neither has the need for a community-based Police Service that operates with the consent of those it serves.

Fittingly, the chronicles of Lanarkshire's policing are dedicated to the memory of two of Scottish policing's fallen heroes, Detective Sergeant Ross Hunt and Constable George Taylor, both Lanarkshire men, murdered in the execution of their duty. No detail is spared and rightly so, for the truth can be diluted with time.

Ross Hunt's brutal murder in 1983 shocked my generation of Police Officers while George Taylor's death in 1976 stands out for the gallantry with which he faced the deadly assault of two criminally insane murderers.

It beggars belief that both officers' valour has still not been officially recognised, an injustice that must surely be corrected.

The fullest description of these dreadful crimes is an appropriate conclusion to this dedicated piece of work, for it reminds us of the dreadful cost paid by some police officers in the course of their duty.

Lest we forget.

Tom Wood QPM
Formerly Deputy Chief Constable
Lothian & Borders Police
Author of *Ruxton: The First Modern Murder*

Author's Introduction

I was born and brought up in Airdrie, Lanarkshire. From a very young age, I aspired to become a police officer. I still remember watching police procedural series on the TV such as *Dixon of Dock Green*, *Z-Cars*, and *Softly-Softly*, all of which cemented my ambition.

I joined Strathclyde Police in 1978 and became a Police Constable at Coatbridge Police office, where I spent the next six years working the beat and in patrol cars.

I worked in the division until 1998, when I was promoted uniform Sergeant at Maryhill. Between then and my retirement in 2010, I served in every rank up to and including Superintendent in uniform and in the Criminal Investigation Department. One of my more prominent roles was in 2003, when I was appointed Detective Inspector at the Serious Crime Squad, based at Helen Street in the Govan area of Glasgow.

Throughout my working life, I have listened to colleagues relate stories of their experiences in the police. When I first started out in my policing career, there were many officers still serving or awaiting retirement, who had served with the armed forces during World War Two. Their tales were extraordinary and they joined a police force that had very little in the way of equipment, forensic support, or communication. They had to deal with things using their initiative and common sense.

My personal experience in the police service has helped me witness many changes in both the kinds of people who went on to become police officers and the nature of police operations itself. The supply of amazing stories, however, never diminished.

I found these stories and experiences fascinating. Their merit, together with my great interest in policing history and my work post-retirement with Lanarkshire Police Historical Society, the details of which are in Appendix Two, have persuaded me to document them for the wider public: I aim to describe the difficulties in policing and simultaneously honour the many silent heroes who go out to work every day, not knowing whether they will return to their families. Of course, some unfortunately don't.

It is to these wonderful, brave, and dedicated police officers that this book is devoted. They neither seek nor receive proper recognition. They do their job because they want to keep their communities safe and protect the public, of which they, too, are the part.

In addition to my own experiences and the stories told to me over my career, I have had unprecedented access to police reports and other police records over a full period of 150 years of the police service in Lanarkshire.

I was spoilt for choice with the number of stories I could tell. Organising them into a coherent and constructive narrative was a major challenge. I swithered as to whether I should present them in a chronological order or codify them by geographical area. Ultimately, I decided to tell them in categories across ten different parts.

- *Part One: A Sense of Community*
- *Part Two: The Police in Wartime*
- *Part Three: Food and Drink*
- *Part Four: Theft*
- *Part Five: Breach of The Peace*
- *Part Six: Assault*
- *Part Seven: Murder*
- *Part Eight: Scottish Policewomen*
- *Part Nine: In Memoriam*
- *Part Ten: The need for formal recognition for two who died on duty in Lanarkshire*

I have also added three Appendices:

Appendix One: A Brief History of Policing in Lanarkshire

Appendix Two: The Lanarkshire Police Historical Society, for those particularly interested in the changing history of police service organisation in Lanarkshire and cognisant of the need of documenting and honouring the police service over time.

Appendix Three: Glossary of Abbreviations. Throughout the book I have sometimes used abbreviations for some police titles eg. PC instead of Police Constable. This Appendix provides the full title for all such abbreviations.

I hope you enjoy reading these real-life stories of policing in Lanarkshire, some of which conclude with very serious and wretched endings. The purpose of my book is to raise awareness of the role of a police officer, give a glimpse into the dangers they encounter, underscore the importance of community spirit, and, finally, emphasise the kind and humane aspects of their jobs.

Most importantly, my book seeks to highlight the failure of our government in recognising the bravery of police officers who lost their lives to protect their communities and supporting their bereaved families who faced enormous loss with little or no assistance. The very least our government can do is properly recognise the bravery and sacrifice of these officers and, in doing so, extend support to their families.

PART ONE:

A SENSE OF COMMUNITY

The police and the community are one and the same. Without the support of the public, the police cannot operate. In years gone by police officers worked and lived in the same community, thereby building essential local knowledge and intelligence. It has often been said that the local policeman would immediately know if a crime was committed and who the culprit was; the matter would be dealt with swiftly and effectively, not through the courts.

There was mutual respect between both. The local communities knew who their police officers were and approached them with vital information as and when required. Police officers were visible and walked the beat. That is the policing that I joined and enjoyed.

Unfortunately, today's policing, in my opinion, has lost that connection. We don't know who our local officers are and rarely see them walking the beat. Perhaps the majority of police officers rarely get the chance to fully engage with their local communities. In any case, with declining visibility and communication, we are losing a vital connection and understanding of community needs.

Chapter 1:

THOSE DARNED SOCKS

Unlike nowadays, murders were dealt with very quickly. This case is an example of how fast and efficiently the police worked years ago. There was limited forensic capability. Large murder squads to provide assistance with resources didn't exist. It was down to the local officers, usually lead by the Detective Superintendent, who would be in charge of overall decision making. Everything was very much 'hands on' for the local officers. Their local knowledge of criminals, the geography of the area, and their contacts in the community were vital in such investigations.

Notably, back in the day, there was great public interest and, undoubtedly, a great fear in the community if a murderer wasn't arrested quickly. The local rumour factory would go wild, causing great pressure from senior officers and the media to 'get a result.' These factors continue to persist. The police still need the assistance of local communities to investigate crime because the general public constitutes the eyes and the ears of the local 'goings on.' Quite simply, the police cannot function without public support. The following case from 1952 is a perfect example to illustrate the significance of public cooperation.

Michael Conly, or Michael Connelly, known in the Lanark area as 'Old Mick', was a seventy-nine-year-old homeless man who lived in a hut located in a field at Huntlygate Farm, Lanark. Old Mick was well-liked by the locals; the older generation was particularly sympathetic to him. The younger generation, however, looked down on him. To them, he was the subject of ridicule and abuse for they failed to understand his struggles when they encountered him.

His hut was a ramshackle affair, measuring about four feet high and eight feet long. He built it himself with the landowner's permission. It was built with linoleum, old wood, rags, and sacks, and held together by a barbed wire that was lashed to the various parts of its structure. His bed was a bundle of rags on the bare ground. He cooked outside using old pots and pans, and used the barbed wire to hang his washing. The hut could be seen from the seventh tee of Lanark Golf Course. It may not have been the most spacious or homely, but it was all the shelter and space he found himself needing. He once refused a place in a local Old Folks Home in 1951, telling people that he was happy with his lifestyle.

Old Mick never caused any trouble to anyone. Originally from Ireland, he was a former miner and was well known and cared for in the area; some local people and businesses provided him with food and drink. For example, every Tuesday when the baker's van travelled across the town, a local woman named Agnes Innes, who had known Old Mick for several years from wandering the town, from Whitelees Road would meet him outside her house and have a chat with him. The baker would give Old Mick free bread and Agnes would buy him whatever else he needed.

On Friday the 15th of August 1952 Old Mick drew his pension and was last seen in the town on Sunday the 17th of August by some local people out for a walk. He had not spent any of his pension and the lady from Whitelees Road did not see him at the baker's van on Tuesday the 19th. A week later, at about noon on Sunday 24th of August, two men walking their dogs near to the golf course, thought they would pay Old Mick a visit to see how he was.

They walked to his hut and shouted that they were outside but got no response. They grew concerned and eventually looked inside the hut to find Old Mick lying on top of his bed of rags, his head covered in blood. He was fully clothed with his boots on the ground beside him and several other bloodstained items lay on the floor.

The men walked to Huntlygate Farm to contact the police and Sergeant Duncan McLew was quickly on the scene. When he saw the scene, he immediately sealed the area off and contacted headquarters. At this stage, there was no obvious motive for the crime.

Detective Superintendent Hendry took charge of the case and informed the CID (Criminal Investigation Department). Professor Allison, the pathologist, attended the scene and made a detailed examination of the body at the locus, although due to the height and restriction of the hut, some of it had to be removed to allow proper access. Early observations were that Old Mick had been murdered. The body, that had undergone horrific facial and body injuries, was removed to the mortuary at Law Hospital for later examination where it was confirmed that he had been murdered. The cause of death was a fracture to the skull, laceration of the brain and intracranial haemorrhage.

A search of the area around the hut revealed several clues. Footprints at the entrance and to the side of hut were obtained using plaster casts and it was clear from the impressions that these did not belong to Old Mick. Constable James Clark of Lesmahagow, found the broken neck of a bottle, a blood-stained towel and a blood-stained iron bar nearby that were later found to have Old Micks' blood on them. The search of the hut revealed only a few personal belongings of Old Mick and there was no money from his pension.

Local enquiries started at the farm and surrounding area. The baker who provided Old Mick with bread indicated that he had previously told him that he had sufficient money to give him a decent send-off if anything happened to him. Old Mick did not have a bank or savings account and no money was found on his body or within his hut. There was also no trace of his pension book. So, where had it gone?

Other enquiries revealed that a local man had been seen spending money in bars and the cinema. This was unusual as he did not normally have money and had recently lost his job as a farm labourer. It transpired that on the 17th of August, this man, George Francis Shaw, had given his estranged wife £2. She found this strange as he had been out of work for the previous two weeks. It was also noted that Shaw was seen with another male by the name of George Dunn in the Clyde Valley Hotel, Kirkfieldbank, on the afternoon of Sunday the 17th of August buying people rounds of drinks. In total, he had bought sixteen whiskies, pints of beer, and a tray of bridies. Shaw was also seen to have a bundle of pound notes in his possession.

Three witnesses were traced who recognised Shaw and Dunn near to Huntlygate Farm on Sunday the 17th of August. They could easily identify the pair, which they later did, as they had spoken to them for some time. Shaw and Dunn were then traced and taken into custody by Detective Superintendent James Hendry and DC Archibald Nicolson. They denied any involvement in the murder.

Shaw was twenty-five years of age and provided an address at Kenilworth Road, Lanark. It was his father's address as he himself slept rough. Dunn was twenty-one years of age and was a local, coming from Ravenstruther, sometimes living with his father there.

Impressions were taken of their footwear and their clothing was seized. A pair of socks worn by the accused Shaw were identified by the lady from Whitelees Road, and her son, the original owner of the socks, as a pair that she had given to Old Mick. She could identify them because of the colour of darn that she had used to repair them – *it is amazing how many times the simple or small things are the key to serious crime investigations.*

Most notably, both of the accused's footwear also matched the plaster casts taken at the locus and neither could account for the money in their possession. They were arrested and charged with the murder of Old Mick as well as the theft of those 'darned socks' and an unknown amount of money. They were remanded in custody, maintaining their innocence.

Old Mick was identified by two nephews from Bathgate. His funeral was held at St. Mary's Roman Catholic Church in Lanark on Tuesday the 26th of August, the same day that the two accused were arrested. It was a simple affair, attended by his nephews and some people he knew from Harthill. Superintendent John Anderson of Lanark was also in attendance.

The trial started on Tuesday the 2nd of December 1952 at the High Court in Glasgow, (*they did not mess about in those days!*) the presiding Judge was Lord Carmont.

There were sixty-five witnesses on the indictment. The trial heard evidence until Saturday the 6th of December and was adjourned until Tuesday the 9th of December. During four hours of evidence in the witness box, DS Robert McNeill of the Lanarkshire Constabulary provided the devastating evidence of the boots.

During the trial, it became apparent that the accused Dunn, in the words of a doctor, was 'feeble minded, with a mental age of only eight or nine' as he did not appear to understand the gravity of the charges or the proceedings in court. With this, the jury was instructed by Lord Carmont that they could not find Dunn guilty of murder.

Following closing remarks and direction from the Judge, the jury retired for one hour and forty-five minutes. They returned with guilty verdicts, with a Majority of eleven to three; one juror had stood down earlier. Dunn was found guilty of culpable homicide and sent to Carstairs State Institute, a short distance from his home, without limit of time. Shaw was found guilty of murder. Lord Carmont donned his black cap and sentenced Shaw to Death by Hanging, to be carried out on Tuesday the 30th of December 1952 at Barlinnie Prison. The court was silent during sentencing and a female juror openly wept as sentence was passed. An appeal was lodged and heard, on the 8th of January 1953 in Edinburgh, by Lord's Thomson, Patrick and MacIntosh. They refused the appeal having found this to be an 'Anxious case'. A new date for execution was set for Monday the 26th of January.

Shortly after 8 a.m. on Monday the 26th of January 1953, George Francis Shaw was executed at Barlinnie Prisoner. His executioner was the famous Albert Pierrepoint. George Dunn remained in the State Hospital, Carstairs, until 1983, when he was transferred to Hartwood Hospital. It is not known what happened thereafter.

As we mentioned at the beginning of this case, without the help of the local community, their awareness of their surroundings, their caring and attentive nature and indeed, let us not forget, the town gossip, this case may have been far more difficult to solve. Being aware of someone spending unusual amounts of money and passing this information to the police provided the Detectives sufficient cause to look closely at Shaw and Dunn. Adding to that, one woman's kindness — that is, grant of a pair of darned socks to Old Mick — was enough to provide the police with the proof that they had their men.

But let's not forget that Old Mick was found because of the caring community and how they thought about his welfare. People went out of their way to check on him, which is a rare thing nowadays with regards to the homeless, not just because he was well-liked, but because they genuinely cared for one another. And that is why communities are so important.

Chapter 2:

THE CHAPELTON CONTEST

Not all incidents that the police investigate or deal with are related to dishonesty or unnecessary violence. Some can be interesting and have surprising outcomes.

In the early hours of the morning, on Monday the 16th of January 1871, large crowds began to gather on the roads leading to Chapelton, a small village near to Strathaven. People of all classes were in large luxurious carriages, simple donkey carts and on foot milling around the area.

On the cold January morning, Chapelton was to be the location of a prize fight between Jem O'Brien, an Irishman, and Joe McDonald, a Glaswegian, who were both living in Glasgow. They were accomplished bare knuckle boxers, having taken part in several fights. They had met previously when O'Brien was the victor. This was the revenge match.

The fight had been organised about two months previously with a prize of £25 to the winner. Word was spread around local pubs and hostelries, and the venue agreed upon. It was to be at Rutherend Toll, near Chapelton.

The crowds began to make their way there from about five o'clock in the morning. They travelled from Hamilton, Motherwell, East Kilbride, Lanark, Larkhall, and many of the other surrounding towns and villages. The crowds reached more than one thousand at one point. Many of the crowd were being sold alcohol from a nearby tavern, enjoying their libation, which was warming them from the cold.

A nearby field was identified for the fight and they began to erect the ropes to make the ring. About an hour elapsed before they finished marking the area and creating a viewing platform for the spectators.

The police intelligence system had identified that the fight was to take place. Superintendent Christison, along with five constables and sergeants, made their way to the area. At about 8 a.m. they saw a large crowd at the Toll. They stood back to see what was happening.

A shout went up from the crowd: 'It's the slopes, the coppers.' It was a reference to the group of police officers who could be seen approaching from the direction of Strathaven. Some police reinforcements had also arrived, doubling their number to twelve. The police moved forward, dispersed the organising group, and removed the ropes.

Captain Mackay, the chief constable, also arrived in his carriage. On seeing him, the group ran to nearby houses and spoke to the main organisers, claiming that the Riot Act was to be read. A false claim as this had not been mentioned by the police!

A large group of about sixty rough looking individuals emerged from the nearby tollhouse and outbuildings. All looked as if they had been engaged in bare knuckle fighting as they had the appearance of hardened fighters. The group and organisers walked out to confront the small force of officers. CC Mackay stepped in front of his men and ordered everyone to disperse.

As you can imagine, the sight of thirteen police officers in front of a group exceeding one thousand was not a particularly worrying sight for them.

The CC called to his men to close ranks and gave the instruction to 'Draw Batons.' Incredible as it may seem, the large group of spectators turned and ran or drove off to avoid arrest and injury. This was an incredible outcome, considering the police were significantly outnumbered.

The scene was described as 'comical' since the police officers were unable to give chase as they were in fits of laughter at the sight. It would initially have been a scary moment for the officers and no doubt their nerves were on edge up until the point the crowd ran away.

The two competitors, O'Brien and McDonald, then, emerged from a Public House and ran off when they saw the police. McDonald made his escape over fields.

O'Brien was not so lucky. He was guided into a carriage by his friends, which made off, in an attempt to escape the scene. However, the horse was not of racing stock and the police carriage quickly overtook it, bringing it to a halt after a short distance. O'Brien was arrested after perhaps the first police vehicle pursuit in Lanarkshire. He was then removed to Hamilton and charged.

Meanwhile, the spectators all headed in varying directions, despondent that their entertainment did not take place but certain that it would in the near future. On their way, there was some mischief on their part. They set fire to a house under construction and stole two 'mutchkins' of whisky from a public house, both in Limekilnburn. (A mutchkin is a Scottish unit of capacity equal to a quarter of the old Scottish pint, or roughly three quarters of an imperial pint.)

O'Brien appeared before the Sheriff at Hamilton that afternoon and remanded in custody. He was released on Saturday the 21st of January on £10 bail. His friends had raised the money to release him for a further fight. Apparently, the pawn shops in Hamilton had a roaring trade that day.

O'Brien and McDonald met on Friday the 27th of January, near New Kilpatrick in Bearsden, where their fight, advertised as the 'Prize Fight for the Championship of Scotland,' took place. It lasted for an incredible five hours and seven minutes. Both were in a particularly bad state and the fight was declared a draw.

This time, McDonald was arrested and O'Brien made his escape. McDonald received sixty days imprisonment. O'Brien was later arrested on the 13th of March and was also sentenced to sixty days.

Both appeared at Hamilton Sheriff Court on Wednesday the 19th of April. They pled guilty and were sentenced to a further twenty-one days imprisonment.

The use of good police local knowledge and speaking to members of the public certainly paid off in this instance. The police were well aware in advance of the fight and had put their operation in place. However, perhaps they had not quite realised the size of the crowds that were to attend.

A police officer will never have two days that are exactly the same. Duties differ considerably, from tackling the most serious of crimes to performing school crossing duties. There's never a dull moment.

Chapter 3:

AN ARMED POLICEMAN

At around midnight, on Wednesday the 15th of April 1874, Constables Thomas Derrick and James Menzies were on duty on Main Street, Overtown near to the Caledonian Railway Station, walking toward Waterloo. They encountered an elderly woman, in a drunken condition, and decided to walk her to the safety of her home in Overtown.

As they walked along the road, they met a group of about twelve men. The group had been drinking and took exception to the officers dealing with the elderly woman. Constable Derrick attempted to explain that they were taking her home when one of the group lashed out, punching his face and bursting his nose into a bloody mess.

The other members of the group decided to join in the attack. Both officers were knocked to the ground and tried to defend themselves as best they could, however, they were heavily outnumbered. At this point the old lady decided she was better off walking herself home!

The officers were taking a terrible beating and one of the men, Patrick McCall, knelt on Constable Derrick's chest reigning blows on his face and upper body. Constable Menzies was in a similar position with at least three of the men punching and kicking him all over his body. A terrifying position for the officers to find themselves in.

Constable Derrick tried to fight McCall off as best he could and reached into his coat pocket. To the surprise of all concerned, he removed a revolver and fired a shot into the leg of McCall, causing him to fall over. He then fired a second shot in the air.

This caused the group to disperse in an instant. Constable Menzies scrambled to his feet; he was not as badly injured as Constable Derrick. He whipped out his baton, striking two of the assailants. Menzies then helped Derrick to his feet and the two made their way, as quickly as they could, toward Overtown Police Station. The injured man was left lying in the street, being assisted by his friends.

The group had re-assembled and followed the officers, keeping their distance, no doubt wary of Constable Derrick and his revolver. They had armed themselves with large wooden poles, lengths of wood and stones, which they threw toward the officers. Their numbers had also increased to about twenty as others had joined in the fight. Clearly the officers were well outnumbered and decided it was time to head for safety.

The two officers made their way back to the police office and bolted the doors. The officers were also currently living in the police barracks so they were not only protecting the police office, but also their homes. The crowd gathered outside and threw a wide range of wooden and brick missiles at the windows and doors, breaking several of them.

An occupant of a nearby house had seen what was happening and ran into Wishaw to alert the officers stationed there. Several officers were awakened from their sleep and hurried to the scene. On seeing them approach, the group ran off in all directions.

A doctor was called to attend to the two officers. Dr Mitchell had to insert several stitches to cuts on Constable Derrick's face and neck. He was in a very poor condition and had to be attended to at home for several days. Constable Menzies had some minor cuts and a number of bruises on his body.

The officers were able to identify some of this group and in the morning the round-up began. Four men were quickly arrested at their home addresses, their names were:

- *William Muirhead*
- *Robert Hannah*
- *James Robertson or Porteous*
- *Patrick McCall*

When the police called at his home, McCall was found lying in his bed with a gunshot wound to his left leg. A doctor was called, and the bullet removed as evidence.

All four men, who were miners, were arrested and appeared at Hamilton Sheriff Court where they were remanded in custody to await trial.

On Saturday the 10th of October 1874 the four accused appeared at the High Court in Glasgow. All four pled 'Not Guilty'.

Constable Derrick was the first witness called. He entered the witness box and described the incident in detail. The Advocate Depute did not dwell on the officer's possession of a revolver, as would be expected, but the defence did!

The defence QC asked Constable Derrick if a revolver was standard issue equipment for a police officer. Constable Derrick stated that it was not. He was then asked the obvious question, 'Why were you in possession of a revolver on that night?'

Constable Derrick calmly replied that this was the fourth time that he had been attacked by a mob whilst working in Overtown. He was concerned for his safety and decided to always carry a revolver with him when on duty.

When asked why he discharged the revolver into the leg of the accused McCall, he replied, 'I thought that he was going to kill me and decided to shoot him in the leg, to frighten him off.'

No further questions were asked. A very strange situation and not something that would happen today!

Constable Menzies was called and corroborated the circumstances of the attack. Both officers identified all four accused as being part of the group that attacked them.

Lord Young, the presiding judge, addressed the jury and said, 'I will provide no expression or opinion about Constable Derrick being in possession of a revolver and neither should you. That is a matter for the consideration of his superior officer.' The jury retired for a very short deliberation and returned with a unanimous guilty verdict. Lord Young, on passing sentence, said, 'This was a cowardly attack on the police, especially when they are in the execution of their duty. I will take into consideration that you have been in custody since your arrest and will, therefore, limit your sentence to one month imprisonment each.'

This was indeed a bizarre case, with Constable Derrick carrying a revolver and using it during the incident. Lord Young was extremely generous to him in his address to the jury and perhaps the sentence passed was in some way due to this.

Were there repercussions for Constable Derrick from his superiors? We will never know.

It must be remembered that the firearms legislation was very minimal at that time, with no requirement for a licence and the carrying of weapons was not uncommon. However, I think that perhaps Constable Derrick was being just a bit overzealous!

Shortly after the incident he was transferred to Shotts, and by 1881 he was the Keeper of the Sheriff Court House and Sheriff Officer in Lanark. He held this position for over thirty-five years until his retirement. He died in 1928 at home in Albany Drive, Lanark at seventy- seven years-old.

It just goes to show how times have changed significantly. It does also emphasise the dangers faced by police officers at that time, with no access to communications or appropriate resources to assist them in these circumstances.

There were many strikes and disputes in local areas where the police and community came into conflict. From the response given by Constable Derrick, he clearly felt that there was a threat to his life and he carried the revolver to protect himself. However, that really is not a proper excuse.

In hindsight, and being aware that we are not in possession of the full circumstances, it may have been better to approach his senior officers to explain the situation and perhaps get a transfer to another station? What do you think he should have done?

This is a really unusual case, even for a time so long ago. For a police officer to carry an unauthorised firearm was quite startling, however, as mentioned he did have some fear for his and his family's safety. This was of course, prior to the extensive firearms legislation we have today. Indeed, if a police officer today carried a weapon in this manner he or she would face quite serious charges and consequences and no doubt a significant jail term!

Chapter 4:

CASHING IN ON TRAGEDY

Fraud is a very common problem and has been for centuries. Greed is a common factor in this crime and seeking to gain some form of advantage over others, the driving factor. Notably, fraud is investigated by many agencies, including the police and is a long, involved and time- consuming process. On many occasions no-one physically sees the crime take place as it is committed by letter or other form of writing. The following story is just one example of such a crime.

At about 11:40 p.m. (ships time) on the 15th of April 1912, during her maiden voyage from Southampton to New York City, the RMS Titanic, a British passenger liner operated by the White Star Line, sank in the North Atlantic Ocean having struck an iceberg. She was approximately 375 miles south of Newfoundland at the time.

Sadly, of the estimated 2,224 passengers and crew aboard, more than 1,500 died. At the time this one was of the worst sinkings of a single ship and the deadliest peacetime sinking of a superliner or cruise ship. With much public attention in the aftermath, the disaster has since been the subject of many books, movies, television programmes and speculation.

One of the crew members on board that fateful night was James Marks, who was born in Wishaw on the 10th of October 1884. He was one of the seven children (with three brothers and three sisters) of Irish parents, Robert John Marks and Mary Jane Ferguson, who came from Londonderry and Tyrone, respectively. The family appear on the 1891 census living at East Park Street in Cambuslang and James' father was described as a steel worker. The family later moved to Munro Place, Mill Road, Cambusnethan in Wishaw being listed at that address on the 1901 census. James was described as an iron worker and his father as a travelling sewing machinist.

At the age of twenty, James moved to the south of England and enlisted in the Royal Marine Light Infantry's Portsmouth division on 1 November 1904. He then joined the Royal Navy as a stoker on 12 January 1906, his first ship being Nelson. He also served aboard *Victory II* and *Sapphire* and made several voyages aboard *Canopus* which would prove to be his last ship with the Royal Navy. Evidently, his conduct whilst in service left much to be desired. He spent at least one spell in the cells for misconduct, including abandonment, and several spells of hard labour on account of his behaviour. His poor record led to his eventual discharge on 25 March 1909.

Prior to his discharge, James was married in Portsmouth on the 25th of April 1908 to Minnie Renyard, who came from the City. They had one child, a son named Ronald James, born on the 19th of October that year. James and Minnie were reportedly estranged from each other by the time of the *Titanic* disaster and current-day family attest that the marriage between James and Minnie was a 'shotgun' wedding and once James was let go from the Navy in 1909, he abandoned his wife and child and there was little contact between them. This is suggested by the 1911 census as James was absent from it, but his wife and child are listed as living at 14 Landport Street, Landport, Portsmouth, the home of Minnie's father William George Renyard.

James, instead, returned to Wishaw, where he lived with his parents. One of his brothers got him a job with an insurance agent (which did not last long) before he was employed in a steel works. He then left Wishaw again in October 1911, without telling anyone and returned to Southampton. He did not visit his wife or contact her.

James signed on to the Titanic, on 4 April 1912, giving his address as 93 Livingstone Road, Southampton and noting that his last ship had been the Avon as an assistant pantryman.

Sadly, James Marks' story ends here as he is reported as having died in the sinking of the Titanic and his body, if recovered, was never identified. His parents later benefitted from the Titanic Relief Fund as Class 'G' dependents.

In February 1917, a letter was received at Lanarkshire Constabulary Headquarters in Glasgow, from Minnie Marks, which was handed to Superintendent Easton, who in turn instructed the Detective Department to make enquiry. In the letter, Minnie explained that she was married to James, who came from Wishaw, however she had not heard from him for almost six years. She was writing to enquire if he was known to them and if so, was he still alive. It isn't clear why she contacted the police after six years, perhaps she was struggling for money and as the child was getting older, felt that he should be involved in the child's upbringing. What her inquiry did do however, was start a series of events which resulted in the conviction.

It wasn't long until DI Syme and Detective Anderson made enquiries with the family. They spoke to the parents at which time they were informed that James Marks had died in the sinking of the Titanic. The officers asked if they were aware that James was married to which Robert Marks replied that he knew there was a girl in Portsmouth who had a child to his son but did not know if they were married.

The Detectives also interviewed other family members, including Mrs Reid, a sister of James. She provided some very interesting information that her parents were aware of the marriage and had been in correspondence with Minnie several times. She also said that her parents had photographs of Minnie and the child and that they had received a slice of wedding cake after the wedding.

The most interesting aspect of her statement was that she had heard rumours that her parents had applied to the White Star Line for compensation on losing their son in the disaster. She said that she had spoken to her parents about this, unhappy that they had done so when he had a wife and child who should benefit from any claim. They denied making any claim to the company. It was only recently that she had heard that a claim had been made and they had received payment. She was also aware that her parents had recently received more letters from Minnie but had not answered them.

Provided with all Mrs Reid's information, Superintendent Easton replied to Minnie Marks explaining that her husband had died in the Titanic disaster and it was believed compensation had been paid to his parents. He advised her to communicate with the shipping company and so, Minnie Marks wrote to the White Star Line who confirmed the claim and forwarded her letter to their solicitors, Hill, Dickinson & Co of Liverpool. It was agreed that they would pay her £50 in compensation.

Superintendent Easton also communicated with the CC at Portsmouth, making him aware of the circumstances. This led the police at Portsmouth to make their own enquiries, establishing that Mr Robert Marks had received £150 from the White Star Line and £20 from another relief fund. All the money had been spent.

Meanwhile, the Lanarkshire Detectives had also made enquiry with the firm of solicitors, speaking to Mr John Gibney, who informed them that a claim had been made by the father of James Marks. The claim indicated that Mr Marks was the next of kin with no mention of a wife and child. If there had been, the circumstances would have been investigated to establish the rightful claimant. The claim also mentioned that whilst residing with his parents, James had contributed £1 per week to the household.

The solicitors wrote to Mr Robert Marks offering him £100 in compensation. He replied that if they offered £150, he would advise his wife and family to accept it. This was agreed by the solicitors and the money deposited with the Liverpool County Court who in turn transferred it with Hamilton Sheriff Court and the money paid periodically to the accused.

A statement was obtained from Mr Gibney and the investigation set in motion. Minnie Marks was interviewed and a full statement taken, including the fact she had written to Mr and Mrs Marks several times since she met and married James. She could also produce letters from his mother acknowledging the marriage and birth of their son. Minnie added that since she last saw her husband in 1909, she had written to his parents on numerous occasions, marking her letters 'If undelivered return to sender.' None of the letters had been returned.

As a result of their enquires Lanarkshire Constabulary officers charged Mr and Mrs Marks with 2 crimes:

- *That they falsely represented and pretended that they and their six children were dependents of their son*

- *That they falsely represented and pretended that their son always contributed £1 per week to their support and falsely induced the company to pay £150 and did defraud the White Star company.*

Both Mr and Mrs Marks strenuously denied the charges and pled Not Guilty. Their trial took place between Tuesday the 16th of April and Wednesday the 17th of April 1918 at Hamilton Sheriff Court in the presence of Sheriff Shennan and a Jury. Evidence, as provided to the police, was heard from the sister of James Marks. The defence attempted to discredit her by saying she had a grudge against her mother. In response, she admitted that she had been obtaining credit in her mother's name and that her mother had taken out an advert in local papers informing shop owners not to extend her credit. However, everything she had said was the truth. Minnie Marks gave her evidence as did the police officers and agent of the solicitors' company. On the first day the court sat until 8 p.m. having heard twenty-nine witnesses for the prosecution with a total of fifty-seven productions shown in evidence.

The defence commenced on Wednesday the 17th of April, producing four witnesses, family members and friends. They all stated that James Marks had mentioned a girl in Portsmouth but never mentioned marriage.

The accused Robert Marks was then called to the witness box where his defence solicitor tried to show his good character. He gave his occupation as Sub-Postmaster at Wishaw West Cross and said that he had previously worked with the Singer Sewing Machine Company for over 20 years. He also listed several associations he was a member of, none of which he could have joined if his character were in question. He denied knowledge of Minnie Marks and her son. When shown the many letters written by her, he said that he knew nothing of them until the case was called.

In response, Robert was shown a letter, written by his wife and co-accused which said, *'Dear Daughter, you are not to say I wrote to you and any answer to my letters should be written c/o Mrs Reid, Low Main St, Wishaw.'* This was her own daughter.

Robert Marks was asked to comment on this and replied, *'It must have been her intention to conceal the correspondence from him.'*

He eventually admitted making the claim for compensation but again denied that he knew anything about his son's marriage. He was adamant that the first he knew of a marriage was at the time of the police investigation in 1917.

Sheriff Shennan interjected, 'At the time the news of the disaster came, you knew there was talk of your son having a wife and baby?'

The accused replied, 'I never heard of a baby.'

Sheriff Shennan then asked, 'Did you make any effort to communicate with the wife after your son's death?'

'No because I did not know there was a wife.'

'You knew there was a rumour of a wife and you knew the wife was living if there was a wife?'

'No, I did not know.'

'Did you ask your wife?'

Robert simply replied, 'No.'

'You did not even think it your duty to ask your wife about the rumour of marriage?'

'No.'

'And you made no effort to trace her?'

'No.'

This exchange ended the case for the defence as Mrs Marks did not give evidence.

The Procurator Fiscal and Defence addressed the Jury and the Sheriff summed up the case. The jury retired for an hour. On returning, the Foreman stood and pronounced that they had unanimously found both accused guilty of both charges.

The defence, by way of mitigation, pointed out how serious this was for the accused, especially Robert Marks in his position as Sub-Postmaster. He would practically be ruined. He had suffered great pain and anxiety and although brought on by himself it was through ignorance and a wrong conception of what he was entitled to. The defence also alluded to the ill-health of Mrs Marks and the pain this had caused her.

Sheriff Shennan turned to both accused, addressing them, 'After a trial in which the jury had given them every consideration, they had unanimously found them guilty of that very serious charge. I will certainly differentiate between the two of you, because I cannot leave out of account, in a matter of this sort, that the husband must accept responsibility.

'I have frequently pointed out in such cases that injustice was not done so much to corporations or employers defrauded in that way, as to the vast mass of men who were entitled to compensation. Unfounded claims like this were what put employers on their guard and made them less ready than they otherwise would be to settle compensation claims at once.

'I cannot regard this otherwise than a serious offence. At the same time, I am sorry to see a man in the accused's position in the dock.

I must impose a sentence of imprisonment in your case and the lowest I can impose consistent with the circumstances is three months.' Turning to Mrs Marks he said, 'I recognise that you have acted under the influence of your husband, it would never do to let you go scot-free. In the circumstances I will give you the benefit of a fine of £10 or twenty-day's imprisonment.'

The fine was paid.

Mr and Mrs Marks continued to live at 208 Main Street, Wishaw until Mr Marks died in 1918 and his wife in 1934. The widow of James Marks,

Minnie, remarried in 1921, becoming Mrs William Butler. She had a son named Anthony John the following year. She died in Gosport, Hampshire in 1971.

James' son, Ronald, later joined the RAF, working in communications and spent much of the time between the two Wars in Palestine. The outbreak of the Second World War saw him serving in Malta during the period that the island was blockaded by German forces. He later returned to the UK and was reportedly involved in the D-Day Landings in 1944. During peacetime he returned to England and was married in 1947 to Sheila Catherine Laura Irvine, a native of Oxfordshire, and the couple had two children. Ronald retired from the RAF in 1963, having risen to the rank of Wing Commander, and he then joined the allied Radio Frequency Agency, part of NATO, in a civilian capacity. He died in Brussels, Belgium in 1972.

This was an investigation into one of the most famous shipping disasters in history, that went virtually unknown until I found it in the local newspapers. Indeed, the Titanic historians were unaware of the case until I contacted them and provided them with the details.

An investigation of this nature, in the early part of the 20th century, would be complicated due to locations involved, the various agencies and the lack of proper communication systems.

The fact that Mr Marks used the death of his son as a result of this disaster to gain financial advantage leaves a bad taste. Denying knowledge of his daughter-in-law and grandson perhaps gives an insight into the type of character he was.

In my opinion, his punishment was quite lenient in the circumstances.

Chapter 5:

A BRAVE GIRL

Most people will try not to get involved where they see a crime being committed. However, there are some that do. The 1900s was no exception.

Nowadays, there is more concern about getting a good photograph or a video to post on social media rather than try to stop the crime being committed. In the 1900s, women did not commonly involve themselves in any way if a crime was committed, but there were some who did and displayed great courage in their endeavours. The following story highlights the bravery of a young girl in the early 1900s, something that was not a common occurrence but was recognised by the police.

At about 10 p.m. on the 6th of January 1904, a young woman, Jeanie Foster of 104 Airbles Street, Motherwell was taking a break from her job as a Bakers Assistant at 'Bryce's' Bakery, Brandon Street, Motherwell. She decided to go for a short walk and locked the rear door of the bakery. She was away for about ten minutes and returned via the common close when she became aware of a young male on the boundary wall of the bakery and adjoining property.

He did not see her, and suspicion and intrigue had her watching to see what he was doing. He went behind the stair near to the rear door of the bakery, disappearing out of sight, and she quietly followed. As she got closer to his hiding spot, she saw a second young male join the other. It appeared that one was trying to open the door of the bakery with a key whilst the other kept look-out. Not very well obviously!

On seeing her, the male with the key threw it away and the look-out bolted. She grabbed the one at the door and kept hold of him, screaming at the top of her voice, 'Police, Police!' A local beat man heard the shouts and ran to the premises where he saw Jeanie struggling with the boy. He immediately grabbed and restrained him. Jeanie picked up the key which she handed to the police. Jeanie managed to raise other people in the building and other police officers were contacted.

The boy was removed to Motherwell Police Station where DS Frank Robbie was on duty and took over the investigation. The key was found to be a roughly made 'skeleton' key which was later found to open the doors of 5 shops in the Motherwell area, all of which had property stolen. These types of keys were common in those days. The boy was 'interviewed' and initially gave his name as McGregor, later admitting this was false and his real name was James Buddy. Indeed, the Buddy family were a well-known criminal family in the Motherwell area and no doubt he 'acquired' the key from other family members.

DS Robbie also noticed that the boy was wearing what appeared to be a new pair of trousers. He recalled a recent housebreaking at the premises of Jackson the Tailor, Brandon Street, Motherwell in September 1903 and the trousers were later identified as having been stolen from the premises. Due to this connection, Buddy was immediately cautioned and decided to tell all, admitting to being involved in a series of housebreakings and named one of his accomplices as Alexander Henderson, the boy who had run off when confronted by Miss Foster.

DS Robbie, Sergeant Strachan and Constable MacLeod then visited the home address of Buddy at Roman Road in Motherwell. A search of the house found a veritable Aladdin's cave of stolen property from a large number of housebreakings of shops in Motherwell over the previous few months. Alexander Henderson, who was accused of being involved in all the Housebreakings was found in the house and arrested. It was also established that the other occupants were sisters-in-law, Christina Buddy or Henderson and Mary Ann McDonald or Buddy and Donald Buddy who were arrested and charged with Reset. The housebreakings took place between the 29th of August 1903 and the 6th of January 1904 at various premises in Brandon Street, Muir Street, Scott Street, Windmillhill Street, Calder Street and Hamilton Road, Motherwell.

The list of property stolen was extensive and included:

- *Boots*
- *Buttons*
- *Trousers*
- *Jackets*
- *Fur cape*
- *Socks*

23

- *Braces*
- *Caps*
- *Hair Pomade*
- *Mufflers*
- *Ties*
- *Slippers*
- *Cutlery*
- *Diamond necklace*
- *Brooch*
- *Comb*

The five were detained in custody, three pled guilty (James Buddy, Alexander Henderson and Christina Henderson) whereas the other two maintained their innocence. James Buddy and Alexander Henderson pled guilty to nine charges of Housebreaking and Christina Henderson pled guilty to reset of the ill-gotten gains. On Thursday the 25th of February 1904, the trial took place at Hamilton Sheriff & Jury Court with Sheriff Thomson presiding. Evidence from all the witnesses was heard and the jury adjourned for a very short time, returning with unanimous guilty verdicts. In summing up Sheriff Thomson thanked all the witnesses, especially Jeanie Foster for her courage and bravery.

With the case of sentencing, the Sheriff described the house as 'A veritable den of thieves', and sentenced Mary Ann and Donald Buddy to one month in prison. With this, Mary Ann Buddy's solicitor asked if her sentence would run from the date of her arrest to which Sheriff Thomson replied, *"No, certainly not. I think she is the ruling spirit of the house and responsible, to a large extent, for everything that went on!"* The Sheriff's other sentences concluded with Christina Henderson released due to having pled guilty and having been in custody since she was arrested and James Buddy and Alexander Henderson receiving fifteen months imprisonment.

On Monday the 8th of February 1904, the gallantry of Miss Foster was duly recognised. CC Despard, on behalf of Lanarkshire Constabulary, had purchased a gold mounted umbrella, with engraving, for Miss Foster, which was presented to her by Provost Findlay at the Burgh Court in Motherwell. Superintendent Moir and the officers of the Motherwell division also showed their appreciation by presenting Miss Foster with a handsome dressing case to recognise her bravery. This was presented by Baillie Brown. If she hadn't acted in the way she did, those housebreakings could have gone on indefinitely, however, because of her actions they were stopped and a large number of items recovered and returned to their rightful owners. Miss Foster replied that she appreciated the gifts and she added, 'I think I have only done my duty as a citizen of the town and if I were placed in the same position, I would do the same again.'

She was a courageous young lady, properly recognised for her bravery and courage, something that was and is still not a common occurrence. If she hadn't acted in the way she did, the housebreakings could have gone on indefinitely.

Chapter 6:

THE GLASGOW COUNTERFEITERS

Another recurring crime that was thwarted by a woman is discussed in the following story.

During 1918 and early 1919, businesses in the Central and Eastern areas of Scotland were suffering badly due to the large amount of counterfeit bank notes being passed in shops and pubs. The notes were particularly difficult to detect unless they were given scrutiny. It was especially difficult during busy periods.

Late in the afternoon on Saturday the 4th of January 1919, a young female sales assistant was working a Drapers shop in the Dykehead area of Shotts. A man entered and made a small purchase, handing her a £1 note, and she gave him the necessary change. He turned and left the shop, as he did so he appeared to speak to another male in the doorway, who then entered the shop. He too made a small purchase and handed the girl a £1 note. He was also given his change and left the shop.

As she was placing the notes into the cash register, she noticed a peculiar feel to them. On closer examination of the printing, she determined that these were fake. She was aware of the bogus notes in circulation as there had been widespread coverage in the newspapers and the local police had also visited shops to advise them to be alert when handling bank notes.

She went to the front door and into the street but could not see the men. She called a young boy over and asked him to go fetch the police quickly. The boy ran off and returned with two local policemen, Constables Bruce and Henderson. The girl explained what had happened and that the men were strangers; she had never seen them before.

The officers decided that the first port of call would be the local railway station, which was about half a mile away. They entered the station and casually looked around the west bound platform to see if she could identify the men. Unfortunately, she could not recognise anyone.

However, the officers noticed two men paying particular attention to what they were doing. They moved toward these men who immediately moved off. The officers followed and the men quickened their pace.

They then burst into a run, heading for the entrance to the station. As usual on a busy Saturday the Station Master had closed the gates so that only one person at a time could enter or leave. On seeing their escape route blocked both men threw items away against the corner of a building.

The officers closed in on their men and arrested them. They recovered the discarded items which were found to be more fake bank notes. There were sixty-one £1 notes and fifty-four 10-shilling notes.

The men were taken to Shotts Police Station and interviewed, identifying themselves as:

- *John McVey (24) of 38 James Street, Shettleston*
- *Joseph Trainer (25) of 29 Walkinshaw Street, Bridgeton.*

The CID were made aware of the arrests and the circumstances. Communication was then made with the Eastern Division of the City of Glasgow Police and the home addresses of the two men were raided by the police.

In McVey's house the police found an interesting array of items, including:

- *One Printing Press*
- *One Lithographic machine*
- *One-hundred-and-sixty Scottish Bank Notes*
- *Seventeen Ten Shilling Notes*
- *Twenty-two £1 Notes*

A search of Trainer's house also recovered a large amount of Bank Notes. The wives of the two accused were also arrested and they too were found in possession of counterfeit notes.

Constables Bruce and Henderson made enquiries with the local shops in Shotts and Dykehead and discovered that ten notes had been passed by the two men. These were all seized by the officers.

The arrested men were removed to Hamilton Police Office and later to the Eastern Division of the City of Glasgow Police for further enquiries to be made. The men appeared at the Glasgow Central Police Court on Friday the 10th of January where they were remanded pending further enquiries.

These enquiries resulted in one-hundred charges being libelled against the accused between the 1st of February 1918 and the 4th of January 1919. The charges included forging the bank notes and uttering them as genuine. The location of the incidents included Ayr, Stirling, Edinburgh, Leith, Hamilton, Coatbridge, Airdrie, Falkirk, Paisley, Dunoon, Rothesay, Helensburgh, Clydebank and Glasgow.

The forged notes were of the Bank of Scotland, Royal Bank of Scotland, Treasury Notes, Clydesdale Bank, The Union Bank, The North of Scotland and Town and County Bank.

A large number of goods were recovered that had been purchased using the notes, however many had been sold on to willing buyers, which unfortunately is the typical result in counterfeit crimes.

The two men appeared at the High Court in Edinburgh on Friday the 31st of January 1919 where they provided a guilty plea. Their wives had the charges against them dropped.

The Lord Justice Clerk, Lord Scott Dickson presided. He heard the prosecution and defence submissions. It was clear that both men had an accomplice in the making of the notes. They were both miners and the forgeries were particularly intricate. However, they maintained that they were solely responsible for the forgeries. I would doubt, however, that this was the case as these types of crimes require specialist equipment, which is not easily sourced.

The method of forgery was to place transparent paper over a genuine note and trace the outline, the colour was then added by hand. Then passed through the press and lithograph to produce the quantity desired. This was a common method of forgery at the time.

His Lordship commented, 'These forgeries are exceedingly clever and showed a delicacy of hand which I would have thought the rough work of a miner would have rendered impossible. This is a serious offence necessitating severe punishment. For practically a year you have been making forged bank and treasury notes and passing them as genuine. The artwork has been skilfully done and shows that you are a dangerous couple. I sentence you both to fifteen years Penal Servitude.'

Constables Bruce and Henderson were Commended by the CC and awarded 'The Merit Star' for their 'clever and astute' work in capturing the counterfeiters.

This case is a perfect example of the police and community working together.

Had it not been for the shop assistant, these crimes may have gone unnoticed for some time. Her attention to the details of the notes is not something that is commonplace. Many people just accept what is given or indeed said to them without challenge. In addition, even if challenged, the criminal would have rehearsed what to do in circumstances where they have been identified or caught and try to talk their way out of it by claiming that they are an innocent party.

When the police officers were made aware of the incident, they used their knowledge of the local area to trace the men responsible and arrest them. By quickly communicating the crime to senior officers and Detectives, they set in place a series of events which identified and stopped extremely serious criminal activity throughout a large area of Scotland.

Had this not been stopped, the criminals could have continued for a significant time and perhaps not been caught and brought to justice.

Chapter 7:

TWO POLICE FORCES AND A DOG

In the early part of the 20th century there were sixty-four Burgh, County and City police forces in Scotland, compared to the one current national police force. Communication was difficult, as telephone and telegraph systems were the only official way to do so, other than written communication.

Officers working in forces that neighboured each other, would meet regularly and build up good relationships, sharing intelligence and information. It was in their own interest to do so, as criminals do not work within boundaries.

April and May 1920 saw several housebreakings, at good quality houses, reported in the Mount Vernon and Baillieston areas of the Airdrie Division of Lanarkshire Constabulary. These were allocated to DS Jordan of the Criminal Investigation Department.

At the beginning of June another housebreaking took place in Bargeddie and DS Jordan attended the scene to check for fingerprints or other traces left by the culprit. As he checked the house, he saw a small piece of paper lying on the floor. Curious, he picked it up and opened it. The paper was a wage slip for a man named Thomas Egan and the company issuing the slip was the Airdrie Colliery. The owners of the house had no idea who this person was or how the slip came to be there.

DS Jordan contacted one of his counterparts at the Airdrie Burgh CID, DS Jolly. He asked that enquiries be made at the colliery to trace the man named Egan. DS Jolly began his enquiries. He visited the colliery and ascertained that an Egan did indeed work there as a fire pit operator. Egan had previously worked with the Merchant Navy as a ship's fireman and he was living in lodgings in Hallcraig Street, Airdrie. DS Jolly returned to the police office, and obtained the services of a uniformed officer and the Burgh police pet dog 'Paddy.'

Together, they walked from the police office on Anderson Street to Hallcraig Street and entered the lodgings, enquiring as to the whereabouts of Egan. They were told that he had went out earlier and had not yet returned and so, the officers left the lodgings by the front door, which faced on to Baillie's Lane.

As they walked on to the street, they saw a young man stop on the pavement opposite who, upon seeing the officers, he turned on his heels and ran off along Baillies Lane toward Graham Street. The officers and 'Paddy' gave chase. It was quite a short pursuit. A passerby had seen Egan run off and the police officers chasing him. As Egan reached him, he extended his leg and tripped Egan, causing him to fall.

'Paddy', being naturally faster than the officers, stood guard barking until DS Jolly and the Constable captured their man. The fact that Detective Jolly had his own dog with him is quite interesting and the fact that the dog was engaged in the arrest is amusing as there were no official police dogs at that time. There are a few stories of dogs accompanying officers on their lonely beats and providing them with company and indeed much needed assistance.

Egan was taken to the police office in Anderson Street and DS Jordan informed. When searching Egan, DS Jolly recognised the coat he was wearing as similar to one stolen during a housebreaking in Airdrie. He seized this and later had it identified by the owner. DS Jordan immediately attended at Airdrie where he was updated by DS Jolly. Both then attended the lodgings and searched Egan's room.

On entering, they found a treasure trove of items including watches, jewellery, cameras, watches, thermometer and keys. These were all seized and taken to Airdrie police office. From the property recovered in the search, the Detectives identified a total of 10 housebreaking and one Theft by Opening a Lockfast Place, between the 22nd of April and the 10th of May 1920.

It was quickly established that Egan was English, therefore enquiry would have to be made with forces south of the border to ascertain if he was known to them. From his interview, it transpired that his first housebreaking, in Scotland, was at a house in Mount Vernon, where he stole a gold pocket watch and bangle. He then turned his focus to Airdrie, where he committed six housebreakings. He then returned to Mount Vernon where he broke into a Minister's house, stealing a silver cigarette case and some other small items. He also stole the Minister's daughters'

31

WW1 medals, including the Red Cross Medal and 1914-15 Star. After this he resumed his crime wave in Airdrie and Bargeddie. However, the question remained, why was a young man from England breaking into houses in Lanarkshire?

He enlightened the Detectives by telling them that he had committed several crimes in England, receiving a lengthy prison service. When released he decided to straighten himself out and joined the Merchant Navy. On shore leave in Glasgow, he had met a young lady and had fallen in love with her. He returned to sea and at the end of his term of service had saved £75 with the plan to return to Glasgow to marry her.

When he arrived back in Glasgow he stayed with the lady for a month and found out that she was in fact already married. However, he found this out a bit too late as she had made off with his £75 savings, leaving him destitute. He then came to Airdrie, where he was employed in the colliery, however this didn't provide the income required to keep him in the lifestyle he enjoyed. Therefore, he decided to return to what he knew best – criminality.

Enquiries with the Metropolitan Police revealed that Egan had begun his criminal career as a young boy in 1900, receiving 9 strokes of the birch for his troubles. Since then, he had accumulated ten previous convictions for dishonesty. With the last one gaining him three years of penal servitude. Egan appeared at Airdrie Sheriff Court on the 6th of June 1920 where he pled 'Not Guilty.' He was remanded in custody to allow further enquires to take place and on his next appearance he pled guilty to all charges.

Due to his previous convictions and previous custodial sentence, he was remitted to the High Court for sentencing. On Monday the 19th of July 1920 Thomas Egan appeared at the High Court in Edinburgh with the Lord Justice Clerk, Lord Dickson presiding. His Lordship stated, 'Your criminal record is a bad one, starting in 1900 as a young boy. Since then, you have accumulated 10 convictions, for the last of which you received three years Penal Servitude. Therefore, I must sentence you to five years Penal Servitude.'

These cases where there is collaboration between police forces, in those days, are significant. There were few telephones, no email, no internet to make life simple and investigations easy to conduct. Officers had to use their initiative and common sense, making physical contact with colleagues in other forces and hoping you got the right person who would be willing to help.

The investigating officers also went above and beyond this case, identifying his crimes in England and reason for being in Scotland. It is worth noting that in those days a large amount of crime was committed merely to stay alive and perhaps feed families. This case is a good comparison as to what people these days deem to be poverty compared to the era when this case occurred.

Today, police forces collaborate on an ongoing basis, making the detection of crime and sharing of intelligence, information, techniques, and day-to-day occurrence. Computerised systems and combined training courses make this much easier than it used to be in the early 20th century.

Chapter 8:

'HOUSEY HOUSEY'

During the 20th century one of the most common crimes for the police to investigate was illegal gambling and betting, from small groups at street corners to more organised events involving many otherwise law-abiding citizens. The police would keep a watch on these events and on occasions had to gather large groups of officers to 'raid' premises where the illegal events were being held.

The small village of Whiterigg, near Airdrie, was the scene of a 'sensation' on the evening of Sunday the 4th of April 1948.

At about 9 p.m. officers of Lanarkshire Constabulary raided the local village hall, where a card game of 'Housey' was taking place. The police had received information that illegal gambling was at the center of the game, which was a regular occurrence in the hall at weekends.

Officers had been taking observations on the hall and watched as the location filled during the evening. Once it appeared that the game was underway the officers signaled to their colleagues and the raid began.

Dozens of police officers were drafted into the area and arrived in the village in an assortment of cars and vans. So engrossed in their game, the attendees were unaware of the police entering the building and surrounding the tables where they were all sitting.

The games were halted and all the participants rounded up. It was a strange scene as they all calmly walked in line outside and were placed into the vehicles being used by the police. In total, there were 159 arrests made. £222 5s 9d was seized from the tables. Also arrested were the organisers of the event, Charles Brady, William Quinn and Thomas Fitzpatrick, all office bearers of Airdriehill Shamrock F.C.

The suspects were mostly women, pensioners and teenagers. They were all taken to the County Police Office at Rawyards where the police checked their names and addresses until one o'clock the following morning.

Once verified they were all released for report.

The scenes at Airdrie Sheriff Court on Thursday the 20th of May 1948 were a sight to behold, with all the accused packed into the Courthouse. The accused all pled guilty and Sheriff Stevenson fined 156 of them £1 and admonished three, who were elderly pensioners.

On hearing the admonishments, the other accused all rushed forward causing mayhem and chaos, all claiming that they too should be admonished, for varying reasons. Additional police resources had to be called in to the court and six of the accused removed to a smaller adjacent court room. Two of them had their cases re-considered and were also admonished.

The cases of Brady, Fitzpatrick and Quinn were heard separately. They were charged with using the Hall as a Gaming House and were each fined £5.

At the same time as the Whiterigg raid, similar raids were made in Greengairs where thirty- one miners were taken into custody for playing pontoon for money in the Greengairs Homing Pigeon Club Hut and £12 was seized during the raid.

When the police approached the hut, they could hear shouts of 'Dollar on,' 'Half Dollar on' and 'Quid on' indicating that money was being played for.

The miners appeared at Airdrie Sheriff Court on Monday the 17th of May 1948 where they all pled guilty. Thirty were fined £2 and one, a sixty-six-year-old retired miner, was fined £1.

The secretary of the club, William Miller, was charged with allowing the hut to be used for the purposes of gambling. He pled guilty and trail was fixed for the 28th of June. He was found guilty and fined £5.

By coincidence, the local Constable had only just retired in February 1948, having spent thirty-two years in the village. During that time, he never made an arrest! It was also rumoured that he enjoyed a game of cards! For money perhaps?

I wonder if perhaps the local Constabulary wished to send a message to the inhabitants that things were about to change?

It is well known that the British love to gamble and place bets, on virtually anything! They also don't like paying tax on their winnings, which is why so many illegal gambling and street corner 'bookies' were in business. Times have changed and it is so much easier now for people to have their little 'flutter', with appropriate warnings attached!

35

Chapter 9:

A DOORSTEP CRIME

In general, the public are very trusting by nature and take people at face value. This makes most people very vulnerable to opportunist criminals.

Tuesday the 17th of July 1951 was just the same as any other day for Jane Tweddell, the wife of the local Inspector of the Royal Scottish Society for the Prevention of Cruelty to Children, at 45 Union Street, Motherwell.

Jane was performing her daily household chores when she heard a knock on her front door. On answering this, she found a woman standing on her doorstep who asked if Jane's husband was home as she wanted to speak to him about her own husband leaving her destitute. Jane told the woman that her husband was out at work, but the woman was insistent that she wanted to make a complaint about her husband and his treatment toward their children.

So, Jane asked the woman to come inside, and she would take a note of her complaint and pass it on to her husband. She took the woman into her living room and asked her to take a seat, whilst she noted the details of the complaint.

Jane then remembered that she had left some things cooking in the oven and told the woman to wait whilst she went to the kitchen to deal with it. The woman cheerfully agreed. After a couple of minutes, she heard movement in the living room. She called through to ask if everything was alright to which the woman replied that she was feeling sick and Jane said, 'Perhaps you would be better going outside in that case.'

The woman agreed and shortly after Jane heard the front door opening and then closing.

At this point Jane remembered that she had left her handbag hanging on the sideboard in the living room, inside was a wallet containing over £8 in cash. She ran into the living room and could see the handbag still there although it was hanging by only one handle instead of the two. She looked inside and her wallet was missing.

Realising what had happened she ran to the door, down the garden path and onto the street. She could see the woman running down to the street and called to her to come back.

Unsurprisingly, the woman ignored the request!

Jane went to a female neighbour and explained what had happened which had the neighbour also running along the street, shouting at the woman to come back. Again, the pleas were ignored. At the same time, Jane had returned to her house and called the police. A car was quickly dispatched to the location.

Meanwhile, a young thirteen-year-old girl had been watching events unfold and she took up the pursuit of the woman following her in the direction of Merry Street toward Jerviston Road. The girl lost sight of her but shortly after a police car arrived on the scene. The girl stopped the police and told them what she had seen, she then jumped in the police car and headed for Jerviston Road.

As they drove onto Jerviston Road, the girl shouted out that they had just passed the woman. The police car swiftly turned and the girl pointed her out. The arrest was made. In the woman's possession was the purse and contents, which totalled £8 17 shillings and 6d. If it hadn't been for the help of the young girl the police may never have found the culprit, as she would have just blended into the surroundings, perhaps looking for another victim.

The woman was taken to Motherwell Police station where she identified herself as Jeanie McKie or Kelter or Blair (forty-seven years of age). When questioned she said that her husband had received money from the Assistance Board the previous Friday, however, on the Saturday he made off with the remaining money and had not returned. She had been advised to report her husband to the Child Cruelty Inspector, which she intended to do. However, when she saw the handbag, the temptation was too much. She looked inside, saw the wallet and stole it. She said, 'Money is what I needed most, so I took it.'

She appeared at the Burgh Police Court on Wednesday the 18th of July 1951 in front of Baillie McNamee, pleading guilty to the theft. Baillie McNamee said that this was a serious offence and it was his duty to impose a custodial sentence. Jeanie was sentenced to twenty days imprisonment.

This story provides an example of how trusting people can be and treat others based on their own personal standards. This was not an uncommon crime, tricking one's way into a house for the purpose of stealing things. In fact, it is a crime that the police still investigate today. Criminals are always on the look-out for vulnerable victims and show little care or respect for their age. The story also shows how even young children appreciate what is going on around them. The young girl in question showed great initiative in following the woman and stopping the police. We sometimes don't give our children enough credit.

Chapter 10:

A POLICEMAN'S LOCAL KNOWLEDGE

On many occasions, criminals are caught because police officers know their local area, the lanes, shortcuts and the like, that many of the criminals are unaware of. For example, when I joined the police, the more experienced officers would show you all the property on your beat, all the important places, shortcuts, lanes, nooks and crannies that were very important local knowledge. In fact, it used to be the case that police officers had to check the property, shops, and businesses on their beat, twice every nightshift which included pulling door handles/padlocks and checking windows and any other possible points of entry. Additionally, if a housebreaking went undiscovered, the beat officer had to explain why it had been missed and provide times when they checked the property. It was a big thing. The police no longer do this, nor do they have regular beats, which is why a lot of local knowledge has been lost. The following story emphasises the importance of local knowledge, not only of crime, but of your surroundings.

On Monday the 2nd of May 1955, seventeen-year-old Peter Paterson, a parcel boy with the Central S.M.T. Bus Company, left their premises on Graham Street, Airdrie. He had a bag containing £200 cash, which he was to deliver to the Commercial Bank in the Town Centre.

It was a Bank Holiday and deposits were not being routinely taken, however, special arrangements had been made to receive the money. It was only a short walk for Peter, and he knocked on the door, attracting the attention of staff inside. As he waited, he became aware of a man that he didn't recognize, leaning against the door of the bank.

All of a sudden, this man and another attacked him, pulling him to the ground and snatching the bag from his grasp. The two men ran off along Buchanan Street toward Hallcraig Street, but the surprise attack didn't stop or weaken Peter's awareness as he recognised the second man from the village of Bargeddie, where he lived. Within seconds, Peter was up and ran the short distance back to the S.M.T. office and told his colleagues what had happened. They telephoned Airdrie Police Station and reported the incident whilst Peter headed back out to see where they had gone.

When the report was received at Airdrie Police Station, a message was circulated to police cars in the town and officers on the beat were also alerted via the police phone boxes located at several parts of the town. One such officer was Constable Chris Johnston who was on the beat at the top cross on East High Street, Airdrie. When he saw the light flash on the police call box he contacted the office. He learned of the theft within minutes of it happening and headed toward Chapel Street, which he knew would be a possible direction of the culprits.

Meanwhile, on mobile patrol was Inspector Gordon McConnachie and Sergeant William Danskin. They headed in the direction of Mill Street, stopping at a railway bridge where they saw two men on the railway line. On seeing the police, the two ran off, forcing the Inspector and Sergeant to exit their car and chase them along the line toward Chapel Street. The police officers split up as they knew, from the direction the robber was heading, where he was likely to appear. Inspector McConnachie saw one of them drop the money bag, which he later recovered.

Peter Paterson met Constable Johnston on Chapel Street, he identified himself and they started searching for the men. They both headed toward the nearby 'Standard' works where they met Inspector McConnachie and Sergeant Danskin. It was clear that the two were in that area.

They began to search the works and eventually cornered the two hiding behind some machinery. Both were arrested and taken to Airdrie Police Station. The money bag and its full contents were recovered. The whole incident was over within fifteen minutes due to the prompt actions of Peter Paterson and the police.

The two culprits were identified as Leslie Hutchison (19) of Motherwell and John Smith Davidson (17) of Bargeddie. On searching Davidson, the police officers found a hand drawn map of the Bank, S.M.T. offices, Buchanan Street, Mill Street, and the escape route taken by them. It also showed the police office, which was temporarily located on Buchanan Street at that time. Obviously, the crime had been well prepared by both.

Both also admitted to two other crimes:

> • *On the 5th of April 1955, breaking into the shop occupied by William Donnelly at 2 Coatbank Street, Coatbridge and stealing*

150 cigarettes

- *On the 28th of April 1955, breaking into the same premises at Coatbank Street and stealing 800 cigarettes, a jar of sweeties and 5 shillings.*

Hutchison and Davidson worked together in premises next to the shop on Coatbank Street, where they hatched their plan to break into the shop. It transpired that Davidson knew Peter Paterson, who was also from Bargeddie, and that he delivered the takings for the S.M.T. to the bank. Paterson was not involved in the crime.

Both appeared at Airdrie Sheriff Court on Tuesday the 5th of July 1955, pleading guilty. Incredibly both were fined for committing the crime with Hutchison fined £15 or 60-days imprisonment and Davidson £12. Sheriff H.W. Pirie explained that in normal circumstances he would have sent both to prison, however, due to submissions by their defence agent Mr W.H.M. McWhinnie and the Probation Department, he was prepared to give them a chance. He hoped that they would take this opportunity to reflect on what they had done and take advantage of the chance that he had given them.

A very generous chance that they were given indeed!

Did they appreciate the opportunity they were given? One of them certainly didn't! In September 1957 Hutchison was sentenced to 30 days imprisonment for the Breach of the Peace, two charges of police assault and attempting to rescue a prisoner following an incident at the 'Halfway' Bar, Main Street, Bellshill.

Although the monetary fines in this case were quite severe, for the time, the punishment does not, in my opinion, fit the crime. There was crime of violence, the taking of a significant amount of money and the forced entry into premises by committing the other crimes. Was the punishment a deterrent? I think not.

Re-offending is still a major issue. There can be many reasons for this. Some may be financial or to support certain habits and addictions. However, quite simply, some people are just habitual criminals who cannot help or stop themselves when the opportunity arises to commit a crime.

The story also highlights the effectiveness of good teamwork in the police and knowledge of the local area. Historically, police officers worked the same area for many years, building up a knowledge of the physical surroundings and those who inhabited the area. Police officers became well known in the community and people would speak to them and pass on important information about events happening in the area.

Unfortunately, this style of policing has gone and officers no longer have the time to build their local knowledge and many do not have the opportunity to forge strong links with the community. To be effective, the police need the support and trust of their communities. It is becoming increasingly more difficult to contact the police through call centres and the closure of local police offices. Although we sometimes look back through rose tinted glasses, perhaps the local style of simple policing we had wasn't such a bad thing.

PART TWO:

POLICE IN WARTIME

During both World Wars crime continued to be committed, however police forces were struggling to maintain their numbers due to police officers, who had previous military service, being recalled for active service. As the war progressed, other police officers volunteered or were called up for military service.

To supplement police numbers, Special Constables were appointed for the duration of the war to replace the officers who were fighting for their country.

War also created the opportunity for new crimes, associated with rationing and the 'Black Market,' to have a significant impact on policing.

Chapter 11:

LANARKSHIRE POLICE IN WARTIME

It is not clear how many police officers from the small Burgh forces were killed in active service. A record was not kept of these numbers.

However, Lanarkshire Constabulary maintained a comprehensive list of officers that served, died and were wounded during WWI. The list of officers is a reminder of the service they gave to their country and for some the ultimate sacrifice. Eight officers resigned due to wounds or other reasons which made them unable to continue their police duties.

The following indicates the impact on the officers that served:
- *Ninety officers served in H.M. Forces*
- *Twenty-four killed or died of wounds*
- *Twenty-nine wounded or gassed*
- *Eight resigned*

Twenty-seven-percent lost their lives. However, when we add those that died and those that were wounded or gassed, it relates to fifty-nine-percent of the total number that served. Thirty-five-percent of those that served did not return to the force.

Some of the officers were also in receipt of specific honours, in addition to the campaign medals issued:
- *Eight Military Medals*
- *One Distinguished Conduct Medal (Constable Matthew Steele was also awarded the Military Medal and was unfit to resume police duties)*
- *One Military Cross (Constable Robert Thomson)*

Those that lost their lives are remembered at the Lanarkshire Constabulary Memorial, erected at the then police headquarters in Beckford Street, Hamilton. This is now part of Hamilton Sheriff Court.

At the end of WWII, a further ten police officers were added to the memorial.

Chapter 12:

RECALLED TO WAR

At times of conflict, police officers are regularly called up to serve in the armed forces. Indeed, many are former military personnel who may already be on the 'reserve list,' which means they will be the first to be recalled. The Boer War was one of the first major campaigns where this was the case, with the First World War seeing thousands of police officers being called up.

One of those police officers, who was recalled for military service, was Jeremiah Kelly Shannon who was Killed in Action on the 1st of August 1918. At the time of his death, he was a Lieutenant serving with the 7/8th Battalion of the Kings Own Scottish Borderers in France.

Jeremiah was born on the 13th of February 1885 at 18 Boyd Street in Kilmarnock and his father, Ambrose Shannon, was a Farm Servant. Jeremiah was educated in the town and the family lived at various addresses including Glencairn Square and Titchfield Street. He had ten brothers and sisters however, three died shortly after birth.

When it came time to leave school, Jeremiah found employment working on the local farms, but in 1895 he appeared at the Police Court in Kilmarnock. The charge was theft of a pair of boots, entrusted to him by a traveller. Jeremiah unfortunately pawned the boots and spent the money. Although the traveller withdrew the charges, Jeremiah was sent to an Industrial School for five years, a reformatory school where juvenile offenders were sent to see the error of their ways!

However, his aspirations lay elsewhere and on the 1st of March 1904, at Kilmarnock, he joined the 3rd Battalion, Scots Guards with the Regimental Number 5324 at the age of nineteen. He travelled to London where he was stationed for a substantial part of his service. On the 30th of September 1906, he left the army, remaining on the 'Reserve' list, and he returned to Lanarkshire where he joined Lanarkshire Constabulary, initially stationed at Motherwell. He involved himself with the sports sections of the force and was particularly skilled at Rifle shooting.

On Saturday the 6th of November 1909, he was on duty on Airbles Street, Motherwell with his colleague, Constable Charles McIver (who later went on to be the CC of the Winnipeg Police), when they had occasion to arrest a young man for Breach of the Peace. As they did so, another youth ran toward them and began inciting others standing nearby. They rushed both officers, knocking them to the ground, punching and kicking them, so much so that they lost their hold of their prisoner, who easily escaped.

Fortunately, the officers managed to regain control of the situation and arrested the main protagonist, William Watts, who was charged with Breach of the Peace, Assault on the officers and rescuing a prisoner from police custody. Watts pled guilty and was very fortunate that two new judges were on the bench. As this was their first case, they decided to fine him 20 shillings or 14 days imprisonment. They did declare that he was getting off verylightly. *This is not unusual as there has always been a great inconsistency with rulings in court cases. As police officers, you just have to accept this as you have no control of the decision making.*

Jeremiah was later transferred to Shawsburn and then to Cambuslang, where he was serving when the First World War began. He immediately volunteered for service and on the 6th of August 1914, he was mobilized at London. Notably, many police officers served their country during both wars and without doubt the first world war was the most brutal and violent experienced.

Very quickly, on the 29th of August, he was appointed as an unpaid Lance Corporal with the 2nd Battalion and on the 7th of October the Battalion arrived in France. Even quicker, they were in the thick of the first battle of Ypres, in mid-October.

One of Jeremiah's colleagues in the 2nd Battalion, Constable William Bain, who worked in Lanark, wrote home:

'I have been wounded in a bayonet charge. I was in three charges on the one night and we have sustained heavy loss. I was wounded in the little village of Zonnebeke, about 7 miles from Ypres. One night, we fought in the pouring rain all night. I shall never forget that night in all my life. It was our Division against 250,000 Germans and we had to hold them back for four days before we got relieved. I believe there were times when we were hanging by the skin of our teeth. Jerry's (Jeremiah Shannon) company has lost more than half its men and 30 of my company got buried alive in the trenches, which were blown in by the Germans. The enemy must have lost thousands. I only wish the Allied reinforcements had come up sooner. The Germans had come up to our firing line and wanted to surrender, but we could not take them in.'

Jeremiah was also wounded in this action, receiving a gunshot wound to his left arm on the 23rd of October and returning to the United Kingdom for treatment. He was allowed furlough from the 30th of October to the 20th of November 1914. During this period, he returned home and was involved in the recruitment of volunteers at Cambuslang. On his return to his battalion, he remained in London until the 22nd of April 1915, when his battalion once again returned to France. On the 3rd of June 1915, he was promoted Corporal and on the same day appointed unpaid Lance Sergeant.

Jeremiah was involved in several engagements and on the 8th of October 1915 he received another gunshot wound to the right arm at the Battle of Loos. He was sent to a convalescent camp to recover and returned to duties on the 16th of October.

In November 1915, Jeremiah was granted home leave and he returned to Glasgow, where he married Jane Bryson Thomson, a Tailoress, of 208 Cumberland Street, Glasgow. However, he did not have long to celebrate his marriage until he returned to active service.

Jeremiah also had a lucky escape during WWI, when, during some action, he was struck in the back by a bullet. The Daily Record & Mail described the incident at the time of his marriage:

DAILY RECORD AND MAIL

30 November 1915

'SAVED BY HIS RAZOR'

LUCKY SCOTS GUARDS MAN MARRIED

An interesting military wedding has taken place by special licence in Glasgow, the happy couple being Sergt. J. Shannon. 2nd Scots Guards, and Miss Jane Bryson, Glasgow, daughter of the late Mr Arthur Thompson, North Lodge, Mauldslie.

Sergt. Shannon, prior to the outbreak of War, was a member of the Lanarkshire Constabulary stationed at Cambuslang. He was popular as an athlete, and was a frequent prize-winner at constabulary sports. He has been at the autumn of last year and has been twice wounded.

A few days prior to his marriage he had a narrow escape from death in France. A bullet pierced his knapsack and shattered his razor, but for which he must have been shot through the back.

One of the gifts which Sergt. Shannon's bride cherishes most is the broken razor which saved her soldier-lover's life. The honeymoon was necessarily brief as Sergt. Shannon was under orders to return to the fighting line within twenty-four hours of the marriage ceremony"

On the 5th of June 1916 he was appointed Acting Lance Sergeant and on the 1st of November 1916, Acting Company Sergeant Major. Clearly, Jeremiah's capabilities were evident and in May 1918, he was granted a permanent commission as 2nd Lieutenant. He was posted to the Kings Own Scottish Borderers, joining the 7/8th Battalion on the 26th of May.

The Battalion was in reserve near the Arras-Lens Road. On the 9th of July the Battalion relieved the Royal Scots and Canadian troops at Fampoux near Arras. They later moved on to the Soisson-Riems salient where they prepared for an attack near Villemontoire. The Battalion was supporting a French led offensive in the Battle of the Marne.

The Battalion was weak due to heavy losses in recent engagements. They were heading into battle with ten officers and two-hundred-and-sixty other ranks. One of the officers was Jeremiah Shannon. Zero hour was at 0900hrs and was indicated by means of lights dropped from an aeroplane.

The Germans were maintaining machine gun fire from tanks which were supposed to have been destroyed by earlier artillery fire, this had obviously failed and as a result the attack broke up. It was decided to make another attack at 3:30 p.m. The Battalion moved into action once again, receiving heavy machine gun fire from the Germans, which ultimately meant their withdrawal from the attack.

This came at a great cost with almost twenty-five percent of their men killed, including 2nd Lieutenant Jeremiah Shannon who was killed by the machine gun fire. Two other officers were also killed. The bravery of Jeremiah and his comrades is quite clear from the circumstances of his service and sacrifice. His Battalion were relieved later that evening and moved back to the trenches at Chaudun.

Jeremiah is buried at the Vauxbuin French National cemetery where 9,229 Germans, 4,898 French and 273 British soldiers are buried.

He is also mentioned on the Lanarkshire Constabulary War Memorial in Hamilton and memorials at the Cambuslang Old Parish Church, 3 Cairns Road, Kirkshill, Cambuslang and Kilmarnock.

Many soldiers received Field Commissions due to the number of officers killed in action. The authorities tried to identify those that had shown good leadership skills and perhaps had been regular soldiers prior to the war, as their training was more evident. Clearly Jeremiah was one of these soldiers.

Like many he did not have much time with his new wife. It was common-place for sweethearts to marry in haste as they may not see their loved ones again and they wanted to be permanently reminded of them, should the worst happen.

Chapter 13:

THE DANGER OF RESTRICTIONS

During WWI, several restrictions were imposed, throughout the country, including the rationing of food, early closure of pubs, movement of Aliens (Foreign Nationals) and a restriction on lighting during the evenings.

Street lighting was also heavily restricted due to the belief that the Germans were planning air raids and there was also the issue as to the cost of running streetlights having an impact on local budgets.

In early 1916, CC Despard had made the council aware of his intention to restrict street lighting in Motherwell. The council had asked that streetlamps in the busy throughfares and street be left in place, specifically at Knowetop, however, the CC refused the request, leaving only one 32 candle power lamp at that location.

At about 8 p.m. on Sunday the 2nd of April 1916, a detachment of soldiers billeted in Motherwell, were parading through the town prior to being posted to one of the theatres of war. They were marching on Windmillhill Street and heading toward Knowetop.

As word spread of the parade, members of the public emerged from their houses and lined the streets to wave their heroes off. At the same time CC Herbert Despard and his chauffeur were driving from the police office on High Road to Wishaw, on urgent Lanarkshire Constabulary business. Their route also took them along Windmillhill Street.

Meanwhile, two women, Elizabeth Morrison and a Mrs Kennedy, had heard the commotion on the street and ran from Mrs Morrison's house at 207 Windmillhill Street (near to the present police station).

Excited by the buzz of the parade, the two ladies dashed behind a tram, travelling from the direction of Wishaw, to ensure they could see the soldiers. In too much of a hurry and minds on the other side of the road, the ladies forgot about road safety and as they emerged from behind the tram, they ran into the path of the car, occupied by CC Despard, with no time for either party to avoid impact. The vehicle, unable to stop in such a short space of time and with the poor lighting the driver may not even have seen them, drove over the top of the bodies of the two women. The tyres on vehicles, at that time, were solid and coupled with the weight of the car, would have caused great pain to the women.

The chauffeur stopped the car and he and Mr Despard hurried to the aid of the ladies, who appeared to be severely injured. They had cuts and bruises with blood streaming from the injuries to their faces, arms and legs. The women were lapsing in and out of consciousness and they were carried back into the house of Mrs Morrison and a Doctor called to attend them. The Doctor tended to Mrs Morrison for over an hour but unfortunately, she succumbed to her injuries. She died of serious internal injuries and shock. She was only thirty-seven- years-old.

Thankfully, Mrs Kennedy only suffered from minor head injuries and fully recovered.

The funeral of Mrs Morrison took place on Wednesday the 5th of April and was attended by many people in the town. Also in attendance was CC Despard, his chauffeur and a large detachment of Lanarkshire Constabulary officers.

The accident was a tragic set of circumstances, brought about by several factors: the military marching through the town, the streetlighting and tram cars. Though, notably, there was very little coverage of the accident in the newspapers. Whereas if this had happened today the press would have had a field day and the incident subjected to incredible scrutiny. Perhaps the events of WWI overshadowed this tragic event.

There was no punishment for CC Despard or the driver as it was believed that this was just a tragic accident, that could not have been avoided, due to the various factors mentioned.

In comparison to similar incidents that may take place today, there would now be full scale investigation, with all sorts of experts called in to analyse the collision and contributory factors. Whether the driver would be prosecuted would depend on the outcome of the investigation, and at the very least there would be a full Fatal Accident Inquiry held at the Sheriff Court.

How the times have changed.

Chapter 14:

A NARROW ESCAPE

It is amazing how police officers, over 100 years ago, investigated and detected crimes. They had to have some ingenuity and foresight to work out where criminals would go after committing crimes, especially in remote areas. Communication systems were very basic and indeed in their early years. Police officers had to get into the mind of criminals to work out their movements and actions. This is one such case.

At about 10.30 a.m. on Sunday the 10th of September 1916, a young girl, Alice Mitchell, was cycling from Dunsyre to Blyth Bridge, via Dolphinton. As she turned on to the Dolphinton Rd (now the A702) to head for Blyth Bridge she became aware of a male riding a lady's bicycle. It was unusual as he was also wearing a sailor's uniform. He was cycling from the direction of Dolphinton station, and he disappeared around a corner ahead of her.

As she cycled round the corner, she could see that he had dismounted his bike and was lying on the grass. What really drew her attention was the revolver that he was holding in his hand.

He pointed the gun in her direction and fired it toward her, narrowly missing her. He fired a second shot as she passed him, which hit the road and when she was about ten yards past him, a third shot. All three shots missed her.

This must have been a terrifying ordeal for the young girl, cycling along quiet country lanes and roads, when, for no reason, a gun is discharged toward her! Goodness knows what went through her mind.

She cycled on furiously to Newmills Farm where she stopped and told the famer what had happened. He telephoned the police and then went back to where Alice had seen him, but there was no trace of the shooter.

Superintendent Grace and Inspector Milne attended at the farm and interviewed the girl, obtaining a full description of the sailor. Local officers were alerted, and enquiries made with the Royal Navy.

It transpired that one of their sailors had absconded from Edinburgh. He had been on duty in motor patrol boats but had made off with a revolver and cartridges. It was reported that he had also stolen a lady's bicycle from Upper Gray Street in the St. Leonard's area.

The sailor's name was Ernest Sellars. A full description was circulated.

A Lanarkshire officer in Newbigging had been making enquiries following the circulation. He spoke to a young boy who told him that he had seen a sailor on a bicycle and had sold him his cap for a halfpenny. The sailor had told him he was heading for England. This information was relayed to Superintendent Gracie.

The police forces covering the border were notified, whilst a search of the Lanarkshire and Dumfriesshire area went on.

At around midnight that same night, police officers in Carlisle had seen a figure on a bicycle going through the city with no lights on. They had followed it to a bus stop on the outskirts.

In a bus shelter, they found Sellars lying on a bench. When questioned, he said that he was delivering urgent dispatches for his admiral. He was searched and the revolver, cartridges and bicycle were recovered. Sellars was taken to Carlisle Police Office and the Lanarkshire office was informed.

Superintendent Gracie attended and arrested Sellars, returning him to Hamilton where he was charged with the theft of the revolver and cartridges, theft of a lady's bicycle and with the assault of Alice Mitchell by firing three shots at her. He was remanded in custody.

On Tuesday the 31st of October 1916, Sellars appeared at Lanark Sheriff Court in front of Sheriff Scott Moncrieff and a jury. He pled 'Not Guilty'.

The court heard the evidence of all the witnesses and then Sellars took to the witness box. In his evidence, he admitted stealing the revolver, the cartridges and the bicycle. He denied shooting at Alice Mitchell. He maintained that he was shooting at rabbits and she just happened to cycle past at the same time.

The Procurator Fiscal and Defence agent summarised their cases and the jury retired. They had only been out for a few minutes and returned with guilty verdicts on the theft of the revolver and bicycle and, surprisingly, 'Not Proven' on the assault charge.

Sheriff Scott Moncrieff sentenced Sellars to sixty days on each charge to run consecutively from the date he was taken into custody in September.

This case emphasizes, once again, the lack of resources and communication systems for the police at this time. However, one good factor to be taken from this case is the public co- operation in providing the police with crucial information on movements and descriptions.

The basic, yet efficient, way in which the description of the suspect was circulated throughout the country, and that in a quiet area of Carlisle, police officers had the sense to link the man they found to the shooting is amazing. There was no use of emails, photographs or social media, yet the suspect was found.

Today, firearms officers, helicopters and lots of resources would be deployed to the area. Gold, Silver and Bronze commanders would be appointed to take charge and the radio system would be buzzing. However, this case was solved by good simple policing.

Two things about this case surprise me. Firstly, why was Sellars not charged with attempted murder? Secondly, why was he not indicted to the High Court?

Perhaps this can be put down to strange times, and the fact that a war was raging – Sellars would likely be returning to active service at some point. I suppose we will never know.

The case leaves more questions than answers ...

Chapter 15:

THE CASE OF THE SABOTEURS

We often hear of sabotage during WWII and immediately our minds drift to Commando raids or similar acts. However, such acts often took place closer to home.

On Thursday the 13th of June 1940, three men, Joseph Brady (18) and Francis O'Neill (19) of Airdrie and William Johnson (17) of Glasgow, appeared at Glasgow Sheriff Court on charges under the Emergency Powers (Defence) Act 1939 and other defence regulations.

The circumstances were that all three had been working at a West of Scotland Brick Works. The exact location was not disclosed to the public; however, it was most likely in the Airdrie area.

Other workers had suspicions about the pair for some time and were keeping a close eye on them. The suspicions had risen as they had been making references to the war and were being negative about the British armed forces and Government.

Brady was seen to place a piece of broken bolt into one of the brick machines whilst O'Neill threw a shovel full of iron into the same machine, whilst it was in motion. The outcome was that the rotating knives of the machine were seriously damaged causing the machine to stop operating. The pair were reported to management who in turn contacted the police. CID officers attended and interviewed the witnesses. As a result, both accused were arrested.

When interviewed both further admitted that whilst acting together, they impeded other machinery being used in the production of bricks. These machines were described in court by James Adair, the Procurator Fiscal, as ' ... being essential to the life of the community namely the manufacture of bricks for the construction of Air Raid Shelters.'

Johnson, who worked in the Transport Department, was found to have been tampering with the haulage schedules and was disrupting the supply of essential materials. This was only discovered when the police officers investigated the case.

All three admitted that their acts were intentional in an effort to disrupt the war effort.

When they appeared at court, they pled guilty to the charges. Sheriff Haldane passed sentence of eighteen months imprisonment on both.

It was important, during the war, that such acts were dealt with quickly by the police and other authorities, to maintain public confidence. The police officers in this case dealt with the investigation promptly and with professionalism, quickly identifying the culprits and bringing them to justice.

This prevented suspicion falling on the wider community and perhaps causing unrest and reprisals on innocent people.

Chapter 16:

FIVE GO TO WAR

During times of war, police officers are generally amongst the first to step forward and volunteer for active service. This was the case in both world wars. It is likely that a sense of discipline and working in a uniformed service were two of the reasons for joining up. This could also place a heavy burden on police forces as many had small establishments and the loss of experienced officers had quite an impact.

On Friday the 22nd of August 1941, five members of the Motherwell & Wishaw Burgh Police left town to begin their service with the Royal Air Force.

The five were:

- *Constable Gilbert Barclay with eleven years police service from Coatbridge*

- *Constable John A. McKillop with six years police service from Johnstone*

- *Constable Murdo Mackay with three years police service from Skerray in Sutherland*

- *Constable Alexander Yuill with three years police service from Bothwell*

- *Constable Adam Watson with three years police service from Newmains*

They belonged to a small police force with approximately seventy-three full-time police officers employed. These officers would be replaced by part-time Special Constables and War Reserve Police officers, this was the same for all forces. Numbers were increased dramatically with the part-time officers due to civil defence responsibilities and possible invasion scenarios, where the civil authorities would require a large resource to call upon.

Whilst Constable Watson was stationed at Wishaw, all others were based at Motherwell.

On Wednesday the 20th of August their colleagues held a social gathering in the police gymnasium at police headquarters in High Road, Motherwell. There was a large turnout of regular officers, War Reserve, Special Constabulary and local dignitaries.

The CC, George Lamont was the master of ceremonies and was accompanied by Mr J.C. Patterson, Procurator Fiscal, Commandant James Haig M.C. of the Special Constabulary, Mrs Fotheringham, Commandant of the Women's Auxiliary Police Corp and Inspector G.P. Thomson, Deputy CC.

An excellent tea was provided by the Co-operative, Wishaw Branch, with the City of Glasgow Police Choir providing musical entertainment.

At the interval, CC Lamont presented each of the officers with a shaving kit in a leather shaving bag from their colleagues, and Mrs Fotheringham presented them with a fountain pen from the Women's Auxiliary Police Corp.

CC Lamont wished the officers every success during their military service and a safe return home at the end of hostilities. He said that they should continue their RAF service as they had done whilst serving as police officers, as gentlemen, and to remember that they represented the Scottish Police Service. The CC said that he was certain that they would give a very good account of themselves.

Constable Barclay replied on behalf of the five officers, saying:

'There are several ways of knocking a person speechless. Your kindness and thoughtfulness in these gifts and the CCs speech is one of them. If you were in my position, speaking for my four colleagues and myself, you would realise how elusive words can be.

One is tempted to say "Thank you" over and over again and leave it at that, but such brevity would completely fail to do justice to our real feelings and would not be an adequate acknowledgement of your good-will and well wishing.

We are delighted with the spontaneous way in which the move to recognise our joining the Royal Air Force came about and the generous manner in which it has been supported.

These gifts will recall many happy memories and will assure us of your continued regard throughout what we hope will be a very short separation. During the period of our absence our thoughts are certainly to turn frequently to those of you who are being held on the home front and to the pleasant times we have had together.

From the bottom of our hearts, we thank you.'

The evening ended with a very loud rendition of 'For they are jolly good fellows.'

At the end of the war, four of the officers returned safely. Unfortunately, the officer who did not was Constable John McKillop who was killed in action. His Halifax, LL588, took off at 1430hrs on Friday the 6th of October 1944, from RAF Breighton in the East Riding of Yorkshire. His crew were on a bombing mission to Germany.

The aircraft collided in the air with another Halifax (MZ310), both machines falling on or near the Dutch Reform Church at Oude-Tonge (Zuid-Holland) on the island of Overflakken. All the crew were killed outright.

John lies in grave 20. B. 6. at Bergen-Op-Zoom War Cemetery, Netherlands with his comrades.

John McKillop was born on the 5th of October 1913 at No 2 Thorn Street, Partick. His father, Alexander McKillop, was a steel worker. John was raised in the Partick area where he also received his education.

John enjoyed sports and he loved boxing, winning many trophies in his younger years. On leaving school, he worked bedside his father as a steel worker. His boxing career was extremely successful, and he toured Norway on two occasions and represented Scotland at the 1934 British Empire Games in London.

However, John decided that work in the steel industry was not for him.

In 1935 he joined Motherwell & Wishaw Burgh Police. John continued his boxing career whilst in the police and in total, he won fourteen amateur championships, including four welter weight and middle weight Scottish and three Scottish Police titles.

On the 7th of February 1941 John married Motherwell girl, Elizabeth Thomson, a typist from Orbiston Street. John was residing at the Police Barracks in Motherwell. They married in the South Dalziel Church. They had a son, John, born in 1942, at Cambusnethan in Wishaw.

It is thought that Elizabeth re-married in 1947.

In 1946 his colleagues from Motherwell & Wishaw Burgh Police Club gifted to the Scottish Amateur Boxing Association (Western District) a silver cup in the name of John A. McKillop. The first competition for the cup was at St. Andrews Hall, Glasgow on the 19th of December 1946.

The cup, which cost over £100, was engraved:

'Presented by the members of the Motherwell & Wishaw Police Club to the Scottish Amateur Boxing Association (Western District) for Annual Competition for the Middleweight

Championship in Memory of Flt.Sgt. John A. McKillop, Killed in Action, 6 October 1944.'

All five were young men who no doubt had horrendous experiences through their involvement in the war. It would have been a terrible day when the news of Constable McKillop's death was received as he would have been known to many. Obviously, a popular member of the force and community through his boxing activities he was remembered in some small way by the donation of the cup.

PART THREE:

FOOD AND DRINK

Chapter 17:

THE WHIFFLET SHEBEEN

The word 'Shebeen' dates back as far as the 1700's. 'Shebeens' are privately set-up, illegal places for drinking alcohol. The attraction was obvious for many reasons, such as being cheap and avoiding taxes. The alcohol was of varying quality and generally the location of a 'Shebeen' was a closely guarded secret between a few people, it could be a house, shop or anywhere at all. The only problem was that people always talk and aren't good at keeping secrets.

In mid-August 1884, when Coatbridge was still policed by Lanarkshire Constabulary, the local officers received information that Catherine Craig or McShane, from the Coatbank area of Coatbridge, was running a 'shebeen' (an unlicensed drinking establishment for the consumption of alcohol) at her house located at Penman Row, Coatbank, Whifflet, Coatbridge. She also ran a small grocer's shop from her house. The activities usually took place during the early hours of the morning.

The family were known to the local officers as her husband, a miner, was serving a fourteen- day prison sentence for assaulting her on the 14th of August.

It was decided that a watch would be kept on the shop to monitor the activity and establish whether the information they had received was accurate. Constables Lockhart and Lamont were allocated the task.

The officers established their observations from a nearby building, just after midnight on Sunday the 17th of August. They were there for about an hour when they saw two men approach and enter the house. Silently, the officers crept closer to the building and noticed that one of the windows of the house had a broken pane of glass with a small piece of cloth covering the gap. Constable Lockhart gently moved the cloth aside and both officers looked inside.

They could see the two men and Mrs McShane standing inside. One of the men was heard to ask McShane for whisky. The officers watched her walk to her bed and from under the covers remove what appeared to be an almost full bottle of whisky. She took the bottle to the table and poured the whisky into two glasses.

One of the men said that he would pay for the whisky and placed his hand in his pocket, thereafter, handing something to Mrs McShane, which she put into her pocket. She was heard to say something like 'It's alright.' It was too dark for the officers to see what was actually handed over.

The officers, on seeing this transaction, moved to the door, which was insecure and walked inside. One of the men tried to make a run for the back door but was quickly stopped by Constable Lamont. Mrs McShane was seen to grab a gallon jar and head for the sink. She was stopped by Constable Lockhart. The jar was later found to contain 14 gills of whisky.

Once everyone was secured and their names noted, Constable Lockhart searched the area of the bed. He found a quart bottle which was later found to contain 3 gills of whisky. Mrs McShane was found to have two shillings in her pocket. The officers seized the evidence, including the glasses and some other items. Statements were taken from the two men and Mrs McShane charged with running a 'Shebeen.'

Mrs McShane appeared at Airdrie Justice of the Peace Court on Friday the 29th of August in front of Justices Murray, Wilson and Aitken. She pled 'Not Guilty.' Evidence was heard from the two men and the police officers, and the productions presented in court. Mrs McShane declined to give evidence. After a very short deliberation, Mrs McShane was found guilty.

She was fined £1 or ten days in jail. She was also ordered to pay £1 17 shillings and 6d in expenses.

She declared quite vocally that she wasn't for paying and was duly removed to prison.

Ironically, her husband was released from prison on the same day that she started her sentence.

Chapter 18:

LOCKED UP FOR A LOCK IN

As many will recall, the licensing hours in Scotland were quite strict until more recent times with ten o'clock closings and little or no Sunday openings.

In 1905, it was no different, ten o'clock closing was the norm.

On Saturday the 8th of July 1905, The Central Vaults Public House on Main Street, Cambuslang, was open for business. It was a busy day with locals enjoying their short time off. On approaching 10 p.m. the pub, as usual, became very busy with people scrambling for their last drink of the weekend, big queues at the bar and everyone gulping down their last drink.

The staff eventually managed to clear the premises and close the doors. They cleaned up the empties, checked all the toilets, bars and saloons of the premises and finally locked the doors, turned off the lights and pulled down the blinds until they started their shift on Monday.

Throughout the day, on Sunday the 9th of July, there was a lot of gossip in the neighbourhood about strange noises coming from the Central Vaults. People thought they were hearing things and dismissed it.

However, at about 8 p.m. on the Sunday, the family living directly above the pub thought they could hear movement and things being knocked over. One of the family was dispatched to the local police office to make them aware that something may be wrong.

Sergeant George Gordon, Constable William Nicol and Constable Donald McNeil attended at the home address of Mr McLaughlin, the owner of the premises, explaining the reports of noises within. They were handed the keys and went straight to the pub.

On opening the doors, they were met by a man, covered head to toe in saw dust rolling about on the middle of the floor. He was completely senseless with alcohol. The officers couldn't walk him to the police station and the drunk cart was called to the scene.

The man was literally 'legless' and had to be placed on the cart several times as he continually rolled off. Eventually he was under control and strapped to the cart. Off he went to the police station.

The scene on the way to the police station at Clydeford Road was quite incredible. Families were returning home from the evening church services to be greeted by the singing, shouting and swearing of the drunken man. Their faces must have been a sight to behold.

He was in the cells for several hours before any sense could be obtained out of him. When searched he had a bottle of whisky in his jacket pocket. He was identified as Michael Hart, a miner, of Smithfield Terrace, Park Street, Cambuslang.

It transpired that he had been out drinking for a considerable part of the day and became quite drunk. He decided that his last port of call would be the Central Vaults, just before ten o'clock, for a quick drink. He ordered two, a beer and a whisky, which he quickly consumed. Prior to leaving he headed to the toilet to relieve himself before the walk home.

When he came out of the toilet, he went to the top door to find it locked. He found himself between the external door and the internal door. He decided to sit down and wait for someone to come and open the doors, it would appear, however, that he fell asleep and was missed by the bar staff who had already checked and secured that area.

When he awoke, he found the pub empty. *Perhaps he couldn't believe his luck?*

To keep himself occupied, for the next twenty-two hours, he set about tasting the contents of the bar until he was in such a state that he started to knock over the tables and chairs, alerting the upstairs occupants.

The decision then was what to do with him. He was eventually charged with theft of the bottle of whisky and kept in custody. Sometimes it isn't easy to identify the appropriate charge, especially in circumstances such as these!

On appearing at Hamilton Police Court on Monday the 10th of July, he pled 'Not Guilty' and was released on a pledge of £2.

On Monday the 17th of July he appeared at the Police Court for trial. He maintained his 'Not Guilty' plea and was defended by Mr Cassels, a local solicitor.

The witnesses were called and the evidence heard. In summing up, Mr Cassels submitted that the case had not been proven, the Procurator Fiscal had not established that his client had intended to commit theft and had been locked in by accident.

The Judges considered the evidence and agreed with Mr Cassels. The case was found 'Not Proven' and the accused dismissed. In the bigger scheme of things, it really wasn't such a bad outcome!

It was probably the best night he had ever had and totally free of charge!

Chapter 19:

UNATTENDED KEYS

In 1905, a series of strange thefts from a shop in Strathaven were causing concern in the town. Mr Quintin Santini, owner of the ice-cream shop at The Cross, Strathaven, had noticed that from the 10th of November, some money and confectionery had been going missing from the shop. However, there had been no break-ins. He had, unfortunately, lost some keys.

The items stolen maybe provided a clue, other than the money. Five dozen bars of chocolate, two boxes of Swiss chocolate, large quantities of various sweets, four cigars and a small number of cigarettes were stolen.

There had also been several attempted housebreakings at other shops in the area and other premises entered by using true or false keys, but nothing was stolen on these occasions.

The police were made aware of all the circumstances and started their investigations. It was clear that someone was using the keys to enter the shop after it had closed. The local officers kept a close watch on the local youths in the area and particular attention was given to shops in the town whilst checking their property in late evenings and on nightshift.

Just after midnight, on Monday the 26th of November, two police officers were patrolling Strathaven Town Centre, checking the property to ensure that all was in order. They spotted two teenagers walking on Kirk Street. Clearly suspicious at that time of the morning, the officers approached the youths, who ran off on seeing them. The officers were off their mark and quickly captured the boys after a short chase.

The teenagers gave their details as:

- *Hugh Campbell aged thirteen, of 29 Castle Street and*
- *William Knowles aged twelve, of Lethame Road.*

They were searched and Knowles was found to have eleven keys in his possession. Campbell had a small amount of change in his pocket.

They were asked where they had been and Campbell immediately admitted that they had just entered the shop of Fleming the fishmonger and stolen some money. The officers and teenagers walked to the shop, which was secure. The keys found in Knowles possession were tried in the lock and one successfully opened the door.

Inside, the officers could see that the shop had been ransacked and the till was lying open. Campbell said that the money in his pocket came from the till, a total of 2 shillings and 1 penny.

The shop was secured and the teenagers taken to the police station, and their parents summoned to attend. Both came from decent families. Campbell's father was the local water inspector and Knowles father was a miner.

Both also admitted the housebreakings at the ice-cream shop and offered to show the officers where some of the items were hidden. Only a small amount of chocolate was recovered.

The keys were tried in the ice-cream shop and again, one was found to open the lock of the front door. The boys told the officers that they had picked the keys up from the counters of various shops in the town during the day when they saw them lying unattended. All the keys fitted the doors of several local shops.

The boys were charged with the housebreakings, between the 10th and 25th of November 1905 at the ice-cream shop and fishmongers and released into the custody of their parents.

On Monday the 11th of December 1905, the boys appeared at Hamilton Justice of the Peace Court, pleading guilty to all charges. The justices showed leniency, due to their age and the fact that they had not previously offended. Utilising the First Offenders Act, sentence was deferred for six months pending their good behaviour.

Unfortunately for William Knowles, he did not get the opportunity to make another appearance at the court.

On Sunday the 24th of June 1906, he was with two friends, bathing at the reservoir at the Pomillon Burn just outside Strathaven.

William decided to go in for a swim, however, he was quickly caught by the strong current and struggled to stay above the water. He called for help and one of his friends, named Law, went to his assistance, grabbing Knowles hand, he too began to struggle.

The third boy jumped in and could only get to Law and pulled him to safety. William was swept away by the current and under the water. The

71

other two boys stood on the wall at the reservoir, shouting and waving their arms.

Mr Robertson and his wife, from Glasgow, who were spending the weekend in the area, spotted the boys and went to see what was wrong. Mr Robertson, on finding out what happened, stripped off his jacket and dove into the water. He swam under the surface and managed to get a hold of William. However, his body was lifeless and he could not pull him to the surface. He tried several times without success.

The police were called and attended at the reservoir. It was another two hours before William's body could be removed, by clearing some of the water and allowing it sweep through. William was still only twelve-years-old.

A tale of opportunity and tragedy. The boys took the opportunity, when they saw the keys, for a small crime spree. Typically, in this type of circumstance, they do not think of the consequences or impact on the wider family. The local gossips would have had a field day and the parents embarrassed with the gossip and coverage in the local papers.

Sadly, one of the boys lost his life in tragic circumstances, which again, would have had a major impact on the local community, especially their friends and schoolmates. No doubt the same police officers dealt with both incidents, as there would only be three or four of them working in that area.

Chapter 20:

A QUIET SATURDAY LUNCH

Over the years, gun control has improved wherein, the carrying and use of firearms is strictly controlled by numerous amounts of legislation. However, times haven't changed that much, as no amount of legislation is going to stop the illegal carrying and use of firearms.

Many years ago, it was common for people to carry firearms as a matter of course. Indeed, during and after WWI thousands of weapons were in circulation, brought back from the war by returning soldiers as souvenirs. These were also used, on occasion, for criminal purposes.

On Saturday the 28th of April 1917, in a restaurant on Union Street, Hamilton, people were enjoying a quiet lunch, engaged in conversation.

At one table two men sat opposite each other. They were strangers forced to share a table as the restaurant was so busy. As you would expect they engaged in conversation, one was a local miner and the other was an 'Ostler' (a person who looked after other people's horses when they stopped at a Hotel or Inn). Their conversation turned to the war. The miner, Bernard Malloy, informed the other man that he had three sons all in the army at various theatres of war. The 'Ostler' was comparatively young and Malloy asked if he had served in the Army and the man replied that he had served in France.

Without any provocation or other words, Malloy became extremely aggressive, calling the other man a liar and shouting and swearing. The other customers in the restaurant were shocked by the behaviour and a great commotion started. Malloy sprang to his feet and from his jacket produced a revolver, pointing it at the other man, threatening to shoot him if he did not admit to being a liar.

As you can imagine, this caused even more of a commotion with customers and staff running for the doors and clambering under tables. One member of staff ran out of the rear door of the premises toward

Hamilton Town Centre. Fortunately, he spotted two Hamilton Burgh police officers, walking on Brandon Street and stopped them, informing them of what was happening. All three returned to the restaurant.

Fortunately, the officers had an advantage. Malloy had his back to the front door and the officers could see him in the restaurant pointing the gun at the other man and shouting at him. Malloy could not see them. The officers quietly opened the door and entered the restaurant, jumping on Malloy's back and forcing him to the floor. A struggle took place and one officer managed to get a hold of Malloy's wrist and shook the gun free from his grasp. They eventually overpowered him and got him under control. On checking the revolver, they found that it was not loaded.

Today this would have probably ended up in a hostage style incident with the café being cordoned off, negotiators called to the scene, full firearms teams, senior officers in charge, etc. It would take ages for such an incident to be resolved, however, here we have two officers showing total courage and bravery by facing the armed man and fighting him to the floor. Bravery medals would now be issued to the officers, but back then they would not receive even a 'thank you!'

Malloy was arrested and taken to Hamilton Police office where he was kept in custody. Statements taken from people in the restaurant were sufficient to charge Malloy. It is worth noting that at that time there were not the same firearms regulations as we have now and possession of a firearm was not an uncommon occurrence. I suppose with the timing being during the war, it meant that soldiers would have brought back all sorts of things, including guns and other weapons.

Due to this, the charge libelled against Malloy was a Breach of the Peace by 'shouting, swearing and presenting a firearm in a threatening manner to the terror and alarm of the lieges.' Malloy appeared at Hamilton Burgh Police Court on Monday the 30th of April 1917, with Provost Moffat presiding. Malloy pled guilty to the charge and was fined £5- or thirty days imprisonment.

As simple as that, the case was solved and justice served in a matter of two days! This case shows how attitudes have changed as the misuse of firearms have increased over the years. I can only imagine how that incident would be dealt with today! We would have the scene contained for some distance around the restaurant, traffic diverted, media crawling everywhere, all levels of Incident Commanders, a full firearms team, negotiators, etc.

The case would certainly not be held in a local Justice of the Peace Court but in the High Court in, at least, a years' time, with all sorts of psychiatric assessments and reports being produced on Malloy. The fact that the response to firearms has drastically changed proves that times have changed, just a little, but crime really hasn't changed that much!

Chapter 21:

AN INSPECTOR CALLS

A police officer develops a certain instinct through their experience of dealing with varying situations, observing people's behaviour, and generally dealing with members of the public. An astute police officer will notice things that people in general will not, leading to some very interesting arrests. The career criminals also build their own instincts, opposite to that of the police. That's how an interesting battle of wits emerges.

At about 11:45 a.m. on Saturday the 19th of March 1927, the Temple Bar at 55 Graham Street, Airdrie, closed as were the regulations for mid-day licensing laws. The owner, Mr William Buchanan Robertson, had locked the doors and headed home.

The Temple Bar was located opposite the L.M.S. Railway Station on Graham Street, near to where the large Boots the Chemist now stands. Graham Street was and still is the main thoroughfare through the town.

It was a busy Saturday, as usual for those days. Tram cars were travelling up and down the Graham Street and the Railway station was a hive of activity. However, three men managed to avoid the notice of the people on the street as they slipped off the Tramcar heading east, which had come from Glasgow. They got off just a few yards away from the Temple Bar.

They walked to the front door of the premises and whilst two of the men provided cover, the third, Thomas Gillespie produced a 'jemmy' from his coat and quickly forced the padlock from the outer door. The three moved inside the door out of public view.

The lookouts kept an eye on a Constable who was standing a little further up the street from the Railway Station. However, what the lookouts did not see was Inspector James Turner walking along Graham Street from the direction of Airdrie Cross. They were clearly limiting their observations.

As Inspector Turner approached the Temple Bar, he could see that the outer door was slightly ajar, and the padlock was missing. With his suspicions aroused, he quickly pushed the door inward, startling the two lookouts.

On seeing the Inspector, the two took flight and bolted across the street and into Baillies Lane. The Inspector grabbed Gillespie, who was crouched down, still busily trying to force the inner door of the pub. The jemmy fell to the ground as the Inspector hauled him to his feet by the shoulders of his jacket and informed him that he was being arrested.

Inspector Turner called to the Constable further up Graham Street who ran to his assistance. Gillespie was promptly removed to the nearby police station where he was very quickly persuaded to divulge the names of his accomplices.

Other officers made a search of the Town Centre and eventually found the other two, Harris and Mackay, trying to conceal themselves in the railway station awaiting a train to Glasgow.

As is usually the case, the three had multiple names and unsurprisingly multiple convictions, they were:

- *Thomas Gillespie aka Thomas Gilmour and John Clutchey. No Fixed Abode.*

- *John Harris aka Jacob Harris and Jacob Katavoanick of Glasgow.*

- *Archibald Mackay aka Alex Mclean of Glasgow.*

All three were remitted to the Sheriff Court where they appeared on a charge of Attempting to Break into The Temple Bar, 55 Graham Street, Airdrie, with intent to steal.

Gillespie pled 'Guilty.' The Procurator Fiscal moved for sentencing, describing Gillespie as 'A thief and nothing but a thief.' He asked for the maximum sentence to be imposed. Sheriff Shanks agreed and expressed his annoyance with people from Glasgow coming to Airdrie to commit crimes. Even worse, he went on, having the audacity to commit such crimes in the middle of the day. Gillespie was sentenced to six months hard labour.

Harris and Mackay opted to plead 'Not Guilty,' which was probably not the best decision they had ever made!

Following a trial at Airdrie Sheriff Court, again in the presence of

Sheriff Shanks, they were found guilty as charged. The Sheriff again expressed his annoyance at travelling criminals and even worse, wasting the court time when they were quite clearly guilty!

They both received twelve months hard labour. This was, no doubt, due to the fact that Gillespie had decided to plead guilty whilst the other did not and, in his opinion, wasted the time of the court. The same principal is applied to sentencing today.

Inspector Turner later went on to become the CC of Airdrie Burgh Police in 1933, serving in that role for eighteen years. He was a prolific 'Thief Catcher' throughout his service and well known to everyone in the town. Even in his later years in his service as CC, the local press reported his involvement in arrests.

Chapter 22:

BUSY BOYS

Criminals generally do not just commit one crime and stop. They commit a series of crimes, some of which result in them being arrested and some which go undetected by the police, through lack of evidence and information as to the culprits. This is through no fault of the police.

The job of a police officer, historically, on the nightshift, was to make a detailed check of all property on their beat. This meant checking windows, doors and pulling padlocks. Working on a regular beat meant that officers would get to know the area, unusual movements or lights burning on premises.

It was an important function of the police, to protect property in their area on their night shift. Indeed, I have personal experience of this, failing to find a housebreaking on your beat would result in reports as to why it was missed, perhaps even being called out of your bed to answer a senior officer as to why you had missed a housebreaking. Therefore, I can assure you that every part of your beat was subject to very close scrutiny, it was personal and it was your territory.

On the evening of Saturday the 5th of May 1934, Benjamin Smith, the Assistant Manager of Austin's Bakery, North Road, Bellshill, near to Bellshill Cross, counted the days takings and secured them in the office safe. There was a total of £300 cash and insurance and postage stamps to the value of £33.

He then locked the premises and walked to his home on Lynnburn Avenue.

In the early hours of the morning of Sunday the 5th of May, a police officer, checking the property on his beat, noticed that a light was burning within the premises, which was unusual. He checked the doors and windows of the building, however, everything appeared to be in order. The officer noted the incident in the station logbook at Bellshill Police office prior to going off duty.

When the dayshift came on duty, the keyholder, Mr Smith, was contacted and it was arranged to meet him at the bakery. Upon arrival, they found the external doors were all secure. He and the officers went inside. The place had been ransacked with flour and butter scattered over the floor and walls.

As they approached the general office, they noticed that the padlock on the door had been forced. They went inside and immediately looked toward the safe. The lock on the safe door had been blown off, leaving a gaping hole and the door hanging at an angle, however, the safe itself was intact. Lying next to it was a jack and brace.

The police officers looked closely at the safe door. It was clear explosives had been used and that they had been packed with large amounts of butter. The explosion had covered every surface of the office – walls, floor, ceiling and furniture – with the greasy substance. This must have been a horrible sight and of course a waste of very good butter in days when such commodities were in great demand. Indeed, safe blowers used all sorts of substances to pack explosives, in another story we describe how mince was used in such an instance!

There was also a fuse wire leading from the safe out of the office door and upstairs to another office. They followed the trail and found a flash lamp battery with the end of the wire attached to the connectors.

A further examination established that entry had been gained by climbing to the roof and breaking a skylight window. They had left the same way. There is no doubt that they had checked out the property or even had some insider knowledge about the layout of the premises. It is very rare that such crimes are committed on a whim.

The CID were asked to attend, which they did, and a thorough Scene of Crime Examination was carried out by DI Frank Crowe. He found fingerprints at the point of entry and on the safe. These were forwarded to the City of Glasgow Police fingerprint department for comparison, however, the search of the records proved negative. Investigations into the crime continued even though it went undetected.

Many months later, on the morning of Saturday the 1st of December 1934, the cleaner opened the 'Nile Billiard Saloon' at 102 West Nile Street, Glasgow. When she walked inside, she could see that the premises had been ransacked and she called the owner, James Williamson, who immediately made his way there.

He was shocked at the mess and hurried to check his stock, finding that 5340 cigarettes, seventy-two bars of chocolate, a pair of opera glasses, a billiard table brush, a cardigan vest, a pair of eyeglasses, seven bottles of aerated water and £2 and 9 shillings had been stolen.

James and the cleaner also found a door on the ground floor, leading onto a lane, lying open but there was no damage. The cleaner was adamant that it had been locked when she arrived. The police were called and attended.

DC Simpson checked the premises and established that the persons responsible had probably secreted themselves on the property prior to it being closed by hiding in a cavity above a lavatory door on the first floor and left the premises via the ground floor door, just after the cleaner arrived for work and phoning Mr Williamson.

The details of the crime and stolen property were circulated to all Glasgow Divisions. Later that afternoon, Detective Lieutenant Paterson and a colleague were on duty near to Anderston Cross, in Glasgow. A tramcar, travelling east, approached them and they noted a somewhat peculiar sight. Two men were on the foot plate at the rear of the tram, one of them pulled a suitcase from under the stairs and the second picked it up. They then jumped from the tram.

Suspicions raised; the two officers made their way toward the two men. They identified themselves as police officers and were about to ask who they were, when one of the men bolted. Detective Lieutenant Paterson grabbed the remaining youth whilst his colleague sprinted after the other. After a short chase, he caught him on Washington Street.

Both were taken to a nearby Police Box, where the two identified themselves as Charles Lang and James Rennie from Glasgow. The police officers checked the suitcase to find that it was packed full of cigarettes. Remembering the earlier circulation regarding the Nile Billiard Saloon, Detective Lieutenant Paterson cautioned both men. Lang replied, 'I have never seen that man in my life before.' Rennie said nothing.

Transport was summoned and the men and suitcase were taken to the Eastern Police office. There they were photographed, fingerprinted and kept in custody.

Mr Williamson was asked to attend the police office where he was shown the cigarettes, which he identified by pencil marks that he had instructed his employees to put on every packet in stock. All of the packets in the suitcase had these marks. None of the other property was recovered.

The two men were charged with the housebreaking and remanded in custody when they appeared at Glasgow Sheriff Court the following day.

Meanwhile, their fingerprints were sent to the fingerprint department where they were examined by Lieutenant Bertie Hammond on the 4th of December. Lieutenant Hammond did not identify the fingerprints from the Nile Billiard Saloon crime; however, he did identify the fingerprints of Lang as being those found at the scene of the housebreaking at the Bellshill Bakery.

He identified sixteen ridge characteristics in two corresponding fingers. There was no doubt that Lang had left these prints at the scene of the crime. This information was forwarded to Lanarkshire Constabulary.

On Monday the 10th of December 1934, DI Crowe and a colleague, interviewed Lang whilst he was being held at the Eastern Police Office in Glasgow. He denied the crime and when charged, replied, 'I would prefer to say nothing about that meantime.' The circumstances were reported to the Procurator Fiscal.

On Wednesday the 20th of February 1935, Lang and Rennie appeared from custody at the High Court in Glasgow. The prosecution led their evidence and when Lieutenant Hammond was challenged on the fingerprint identification, he stated that he was one-hundred percent certain that the prints left at the scene of the Bellshill housebreaking were made by the same fingers, those of the accused Lang. He added to this by saying that over 500,000 fingerprints were examined each year in his department and in his experience different fingers had never produced such similarity.

The defence produced the sister of Lang who provided an alibi, that her brother had lived with her and her husband for over a year and had never been out all night. A second defence witness, unemployed riveter John Porterfield, said that he had been with Lang on the night that the Billiard Saloon had been broken into, between 8 p.m. and 11:30 p.m. when Lang had left him to go home. *This did of course pose the question as to where Lang went thereafter, and one must wonder why this witness was called?*

Both accused gave evidence, denying the crimes. Lang could not explain why his fingerprints were found at the Bellshill Bakery and denied ever being in that area. He could not recall where he had been on that particular date. He also denied knowing Rennie and said that he was with Porterfield before going home to his sister's house.

Rennie also denied knowing Lang and could not adequately explain where he was on the night the Billiard Saloon was entered. He claimed it was pure chance that they were on the same tram and denied that he picked up the suitcase.

At the conclusion of the trial the judge, Lord Wark addressed the jury, who retired for less than twenty minutes. They unanimously returned a verdict of guilty on both accused.

Turning to the accused Lord Wark said, 'You have been found guilty of serious crimes and provided unbelievable defences. Your saving grace is that you do not have many convictions. I sentence you both to twelve months imprisonment.'

It is difficult to believe that the accused had not committed other crimes, especially Lang, in the period between these two crimes. As previously mentioned, with many habitual criminals they sometimes get away with more crimes than they are caught for.

Chapter 23:

SOMETHING'S FISHY

Working the nightshift in the police can be an unusual and eerie experience. Walking or driving about the streets or countryside, continually looking for unusual movements or people being where they shouldn't be. It was amazing what could be encountered or seen.

On a quiet night shift in June 1975, two Motherwell Police officers were on the wind down and ready to finish their shift. It was 6:15a.m. on Thursday the 5th of June, their property had been checked and they were making their final drive around their area, before heading to the office, hand in their radios and head home for a well-earned sleep.

They were driving along Muir Street when they saw two youths, one wearing a full Motherwell Football kit and the other carrying a box. On seeing the police, the youth carrying the box threw it away and both made a run for it. Nightshift could be a very busy shift, whilst everyone is sleeping, others are out taking the opportunity to steal whatever is there and so, the officers clearly thought something was afoot and chased the two youths. It didn't take long until both were safely in custody.

This was a regular occurrence especially on a nightshift when delivery drivers would drop their deliveries to the local shops and stores and leave them for the occupiers to arrive.

Another regular theft was milk from the doorstep! The box was also recovered and was found to contain fifty fresh haddock! *People will literally steal anything, if it moves, they will take it.*

The two master criminals were quick to admit what they had done. They had been wandering about the town all night and when walking on Brandon Parade saw the boxes being delivered to the Fishmongers Shop. Thinking that no-one would notice, they decided to have one of the boxes for themselves and no doubt make a small profit selling the fish to friends and neighbours. Although it might seem strange to steal fish, there will be a buyer for literally anything. Everyone is looking for a bargain.

The two then identified themselves as Thomas Hannah (seventeen) and Alexander Dallas (seventeen) from Motherwell. Curious, they asked why Hannah was wearing the football kit and were very surprised by his response. He admitted breaking into the Fir Park Shop, 150 Windmillhill Street, Motherwell on the 15th of May that year and stealing the strip.

The officers checked the crime reports and sure enough, the shop had been broken into with £116 worth of kit and £110 in cash having been stolen. Both were charged with the theft of the fish and Hannah with the Housebreaking at the Fir Park Shop.

On Tuesday the 8th of July 1975, both appeared at Hamilton Sheriff Court in front of Sheriff Nigel Thomson. They pled guilty to the charges and their previous convictions were read by the Procurator Fiscal. Sheriff Thomson remanded both until the 23rd off July at which time both were sent to Borstal to be educated in 'staying on the straight and narrow!'

Hopefully, they learned their lesson.

This case is another perfect example of the vigilance of police officers, knowing their local area and using the instincts they had built during their service. They ultimately cast their line and made a good catch.

PART FOUR:

THEFT

Crimes of dishonesty, such as theft, theft by housebreaking and robbery have been and still are one of the most common occurrences for the police to investigate. They can range from the most basic shoplifting to more serious and organised cases of housebreaking or robbery.

The police as investigators have to apply their detection skills and training to solve these crimes, sometimes having to adopt unusual techniques to do so. Forensic science has also played an important part in the detection of crimes and is now so advanced that evidence, sometimes invisible to the eye, can solve cases.

Chapter 24:

A LIFE OF CRIME

An unfortunate aspect of criminal activity is the amount of people who follow in their parents or siblings' footsteps. Police officers will regularly find members of the same family, over many generations, living a life of crime.

Similarly, many sons and daughters of police officers will follow their parents' career path and join the police.

Michael Clinton was born in 1874 in Motherwell. His father, John, was a coal miner and the family lived at Watsonville Rows situated in the centre of Motherwell Burgh. The houses were in a terrible state even though they were built just before he was born so the family later moved to Scott Row in Craigneuk, Wishaw.

Notably, in addition to being a coal miner, John Clinton was no stranger to the local Constabulary. He was a prominent housebreaker and quite a violent individual, being arrested and imprisoned on numerous occasions.

Michael unfortunately followed his father into a life of crime. Having been lucky to receive several warnings and admonitions, he eventually felt the full weight of the criminal justice system. In April 1887, he and another local youth, both aged fourteen, appeared at the Wishaw Police Court on several charges of Theft by Housebreaking. They were found guilty and sentenced to ten days imprisonment. At the end of their sentence, they were to be confined to a Reformatory school for five years. It was the desire of the judges that this would put an end to their criminal activities and set them on the road to a good and law- abiding life. Perhaps this was wishful thinking!

Having spent his time at the Reformatory, Clinton was released back into the community and returned home to Craigneuk. He did not take too long to return to his old ways, making numerous appearances at Court throughout 1892, some of which are described below.

In February he was charged with throwing a pail full of water over a man at Scott's Row. He was fined five shillings or three days in prison. The fine was paid.

On the 12th of May, he was caught poaching, using catapults, on the Dalzell Estate. He was found guilty and fined £1 12s and 6d, which he again paid.

Later that same year, on the 10th of September, four members of the Clinton family, including Michael, were involved in a dispute with a local family, resulting in the Clinton's being charged with Breach of the Peace and Assault. They pled not guilty and went to trial. They were found guilty and again fined £3 3s or thirty days imprisonment. The fines were once more fully paid.

On the 3rd of December 1892 he appeared at the Burgh Police Court along with his friend John Kelly. They were charged that on between the 1st and 2nd of December they had broken into the Caledonian Bolt & Rivet Works and stolen a spirit level. The police arrested them near to Dalzell Colliery in possession of the stolen item. When in custody their homes were searched and a violin and bow was found. Enquiries revealed that these items had been stolen from an engine room at No. 1 Colliery at Carfin. They were remanded in custody to Duke Street prison. They later appeared at Hamilton Sheriff Court and were sentenced to thirty days imprisonment.

Would the New Year see a change in his behaviour?

Not really. He again started where he left off once released from prison.

On Saturday the 29th of April 1893, Constables Leslie and Maxwell were on duty in Craigneuk, when they had occasion to speak to a noisy crowd of young men and ask them to move on, one of whom was Michael Clinton. As the officers walked away, some of the group followed them. Clinton began verbally abusing the officers and as they turned to face them again, Constable Leslie felt a blow to his chest. The officers could see that Clinton had in his hand a catapult from which he was firing iron punchers. Several missed the officers.

They ran forward and the group ran off in various directions, however, the officers had their eyes on Clinton, whom they caught after a short chase.

Clinton appeared at Wishaw Police Court on the 11th of May, denying the charges of Breach of the Peace and Assault. The case went to trial and the police officers gave their evidence. The defence called some of the other youths whose evidence amounted to a denial of the charge, however, many of their versions differed dramatically. Clinton was found guilty and sentenced to thirty days.

1893 saw several minor convictions for Clinton, most resulting in fines. In 1894 he continued his ways. In February he was arrested for Theft by Housebreaking at Farmside Place in Craigneuk, along with another local man. They stole a silver watch and lady's jacket. They attempted to pawn the watch in Glasgow, however, the owner of the shop sent an assistant for the police as he suspected the watch had been stolen. Officers attended and apprehended the pair, who were handed to Lanarkshire Constabulary.

The watch was identified by the owner, and both charged. They denied the charges and were remanded in custody. When they appeared at Hamilton Sheriff & Jury Court on the 31st of March 1894, they pled 'Not Guilty'.

Sheriff Davidson presided and the jury listened to the evidence, which was overwhelming, and they took no time in returning a guilty verdict. Sheriff Davidson told Clinton that until now he had been dealt with leniently, to no effect. He had no option other than to sentence him to four months imprisonment, which at that time meant the full sentence.

Over the next few years there were numerous convictions, mostly for violence and breach of the peace. He received numerous fines and short terms in prison. On one occasion Clinton was attacked by a man in Craigneuk who stabbed him in the head.

On Tuesday the 21st of February 1899, Constable Guthrie was on nightshift in Motherwell. It was shortly after midnight when he was checking the premises of Jesson's Butchers at No.110 Windmillhill Street. As he made his way to the rear of the premises, he could hear voices. As he exited the common close, he saw two men, one of whom he knew as Michael Clinton. Clinton was in possession of a pickaxe and the other man a shovel. Constable Guthrie approached the men and Clinton swung the pickaxe at the officer, striking him on the face, causing a large bleeding cut and smashing his teeth.

Clinton lashed out continually and when the officer had the better of him, he bit him several times on the hand.

The other man ran off leaving Clinton and Constable Guthrie engaged in a long and fierce struggle. The man was arrested nearby, as he was seen running from the rear of the shop. When the arresting officer went to see why he had ran away, he discovered Constable Guthrie and Clinton in a violent struggle, and both managed to overpower Clinton.

Constable Guthrie had several stitches placed in his wound and had to have his teeth repaired, however, he was on duty the following evening. A possible factor could be that police officers did not receive any pay if they were off sick, or he had a tremendous dedication to duty.

It should be said that when Clinton appeared from custody his head was bandaged and his face severely bruised and swollen. Clearly, he had violently resisted arrest.

On Friday the 24th of February Clinton was sentenced to sixty days imprisonment for Attempted Housebreaking with Intent to Steal and Assault on Constable Guthrie.

In 1900, Clinton became involved in more serious crime, resulting in an appearance at the High Court in Edinburgh on the 28th of October. He and some accomplices had been arrested following a housebreaking at East Calder on the 7th of October. When arrested he provided false particulars, giving the name John Flynn.

A month later, Clinton was further charged with Housebreaking at Hurst, Nelson & Company Iron Works in Flemington, Motherwell, for stealing a large quantity of brass bushes to the value of £40.

Following a trial, Clinton was found guilty and sentenced to five years penal servitude. He was starting to pay a more serious price for his criminality. He was sent to Peterhead Prison.

In May 1905, Clinton was given a ticket of leave from prison, six months before the end of his sentence. He was soon back to his old ways.

At about one o'clock on the morning of Friday the 7th of April 1905, he was caught by the police having broken into a plumber's shop at Flemington Bridge in Motherwell. Constables Riach and Brechin caught him forcing open the rear door of the premises and as before, he made a fight of it. Constable Riach suffered cuts to his face and Constable Brechin gained some bruising.

Due to being released from prison early, he was detained in custody and later remanded until his court appearance. He appeared at the High Court in Glasgow on Wednesday the 10th of May, pleading guilty and was sentenced to an incredible eighteen-months imprisonment. The reports state that he jumped up in the dock and punched the air on hearing the sentence. He expected a much heavier one. Once again the courts had failed to provide an appropriate punishment to the crime.

True to form, he had only been released a matter of weeks when he was up to his old tricks. On the 7th of March 1908, Clinton and another man, violently attacked a miner as he walked on Roman Road, Motherwell. They struck the man about the head and body and stole his silver watch, fob and a sum of money.

The man reported the matter to the police who made their enquiries. Suspicion soon fell on Clinton and his companion and they were arrested.

Due to Clintons previous convictions, the two appeared at the High Court in Glasgow on the 7th of May. Once again, he pled 'Not Guilty,' and the case went to trial. The jury found the evidence overwhelming and convicted both of the crime.

Clinton was sentenced to seven years penal servitude and as he left the dock, shouted at his friends in the court, 'Don't worry lads, I'll fetch it alright.'

Thankfully, Clinton was now out of the way for a considerable time, but of course, he had to re-appear at some point! That he did in 1914.

On the 5th of February 1914, the Globe Store Public House, Globe Buildings in Motherwell was broken into. Nine bottles of whisky and a sum of money was stolen. Shortly afterwards Michael Clinton was arrested for Breach of the Peace. In his possession were two bottles of whisky, which were identified as coming from the housebreaking at the Globe Public House.

Clinton was charged with the housebreaking and following an appearance at court, remanded in custody pending trial.

He appeared at the High Court in Glasgow on the 22nd of April. He maintained a 'Not Guilty' plea and the trial took place with Lord Anderson presiding. Once again, the evidence was overwhelming, and a conviction followed. Lord Anderson said, 'You have been, for a very long time, engaged in criminal enterprise. In my opinion you are a particularly dangerous criminal and I sentence you to six years penal servitude.'

Clinton was released from prison early in 1920, returning once again to Motherwell. He lived in one of the local Craigneuk Workmen's Home where a young local girl, Mary McGown was working. She became infatuated with him, much to her parents' annoyance and they began courting.

During this time Clinton was also drinking heavily, and on the 21st of April 1920 he was arrested following a large-scale disturbance in Craigneuk. He, unusually, pled guilty and was sentenced to thirty days imprisonment.

When released he returned to the Home and continued to see Mary McGowan. In fairness to Clinton, he stayed off the drink and tried to persuade Mary not to continue seeing him, explaining his criminal and violent background. She would not be moved and in December they travelled to Glasgow, where they married at Blythswood. Mary's parents were unaware that this had happened until she told them sometime later.

Mary and Clinton went to her parents' house to collect some clothes, however, this did not go well. An argument started and a fight took place between Clinton and her father. Clinton was alleged to have produced a large stick from the sleeve of his jacket and struck Mr McGowan on the face before McGowan's sons intervened, separating both parties with Clinton and Mary walking away.

Mr McGowan contacted the police and when they located Clinton the following day, they found him in possession of the large stick. He was duly arrested.

On appearing at the Police Court Clinton maintained a 'Not Guilty' plea. The trial took place and he admitted being in an argument but not the assault. He also explained that he had tried to persuade Mary not to continue seeing him, but she was determined that they marry.

Although he was found guilty the court and the procurator fiscal did show some sympathy for him. The Judge showed leniency and imposed a fine of £5 or thirty days imprisonment. The fine was paid immediately.

The couple decided to leave the area and they set up home in Leith, where they had two children. It would be nice to be able to report that Clinton had seen the error of his ways and turned his back on crime. Was that the case? Unfortunately, not.

At about 8:30 p.m. on Saturday the 14th of October 1922, two plain clothes Detectives in Edinburgh observed three men enter the area between Fountainbridge and Bread Street. They appeared to be acting suspiciously.

The officers kept watch for several hours, at some points of the watch they heard the sound of a horn blowing. Just after midnight, the three exited the close. The Detectives approached all three and identified themselves, uniformed officers also joined them.

The three were searched and found to be in possession of several items including, jemmies, gelignite, detonators, keys, a brace and bits, keys, an electric torch, woollen mitts, hacksaw blades, catapults, stones and a blow horn. One of the men had a canvas belt around his shoulders containing a variety of housebreaking implements. One of the co-accused was Thomas Wright Reid of Edinburgh, an infamous high-quality housebreaker. It is possible that they all served prison sentences together and formed a partnership in crime, learning from each other and planning future crimes.

All three were charged with Theft by Housebreaking, Housebreaking with Intent to Steal and the Explosives Substance Act 1883. They appeared at the police court, however, were remitted to the Sheriff Court and remanded in custody.

The charges dated between the 21st of July and 15th of October 1922. They included blowing open a safe at a public house in Elm Street, Edinburgh and breaking into a draper at Bread Street. When Clinton's home at 37 Shore, Leith was searched, the police found explosive substances, skeleton keys and several housebreaking implements.

The trial took place on the 15th of January at the High Court in Edinburgh. Eventually the charge of housebreaking at the public house was dropped. The jury retired for only seven minutes, returning guilty verdicts against all accused.

Lord Alness said that their crimes were aggravated by their long list of previous convictions. He then passed sentence of ten years penal servitude. Clinton replied, 'You have the iron heart of an Oliver Cromwell.' He turned to the gallery, where his wife Mary was sitting, and said, 'Cheer up, I will get through it.'

Clinton was granted early release at the end of 1930. He returned to Leith, living at 267 Easter Road, as his wife Mary did not want him back at home. He also found a job with a local electrician and by all accounts he was a good reliable worker.

Unfortunately, his old habits returned. Clinton had identified a house in Trinity Road, Leith that was unoccupied as the residents were on holiday. Between the 22nd and 29th of August 1931, he and an accomplice, John McLaren, broke into the house, returning on several occasions to steal property.

They stole a silver cigarette lighter, gold fountain pens, three watches, a gold ring, two strings of beads, opera glasses, field glasses and a quantity of bed linen.

On the last occasion they entered the house, on the 29th of August, they climbed the perimeter wall into the garden. Unknown to them, the police were lying in wait, as they had been made aware of the break ins.

As Clinton lowered from the wall a Detective grabbed him. Clinton was holding a hammer and lashed out wildly, striking the officer on the head and shoulder. The cuts were severe with blood pouring from the wounds. Other officers overpowered Clinton and he and his accomplice were arrested.

McLaren gave up without a fight, this was his first serious arrest.

They appeared at Edinburgh Sheriff Court on the 15th of September where, unusually, Clinton pled guilty. Due to Clinton's convictions, the pair were remitted to the High Court for sentencing.

On the 24th of September they appeared before Lord Blackburn. Clinton was asked if he had anything to say before sentencing. He said that it was not his intention to assault the police officer, he was taken by surprise and he hit out wildly.

Lord Blackburn said that his record was a singularly bad one, dating back to his early years in the 1880's. Taking all of this into account and his early release from the ten-year sentence he imposed a sentence of six years imprisonment. He was sent to Peterhead prison.

McLaren was dealt with more leniently. He was a married man with four children and had never appeared in the High Court previously. Lord Blackburn said that he hoped he hoped would not follow in Clintons' footsteps and sentenced him to fifteen months imprisonment.

Just after 2 a.m. on the 10th of December 1934, in Peterhead prison, Michael Clinton suffered a cerebral haemorrhage and died almost immediately. Doctor Forrest, the prison doctor, attended and certified death.

A Fatal Accident Inquiry was held at Peterhead Sheriff Court, presided over by Sheriff Dallas. A verdict of death by natural causes was returned. The head warder, Alexander Stewart advised the court that Clinton was a regular at Peterhead prison, having served four custodial sentences ranging from six to ten years each. His wife Mary had been offered the body of Michael for burial, however, the Procurator Fiscal read a letter from her stating, 'I have not seen or had any contact with my husband for twelve years and I do not wish to claim his body for burial or have anything to do with him.' It is not known where he was buried.

Michael Clinton led a life of violence and dishonesty. This story only covers some of his exploits and no doubt there were many other instances when he was not caught for his crimes. He had become so used to his life of crime that it was impossible for him to change his ways.

I am sure we all know families or individuals, similar to Michael Clinton, however, he surely surpasses many of them, apart from the fact that he never took anyone's life, as far as we are aware!

Chapter 25:

A ROBBERY GONE WRONG

Street robberies were and are a regular occurrence. Robbery is essentially the aggravated crime of theft and to constitute the crime there must be actual violence or the threat of violence toward the victim. Sometimes weapons are used and at other times pure brute force is all that is necessary to commit the crime. On occasions there are terrible consequences to this crime.

At about 11 p.m. on Saturday the 31st of August 1901, the residents of the quiet area of Blairhill, in Coatbridge, were roused from their houses by the sound of screams and shouting from the street outside. They could hear two raised voices, one of them shouting, 'Murder,' several times.

Mrs McIlwee ran to her front door and looked out into the darkened street. She could see two figures further down the street, one of them lying on the ground. She walked out on to the street to get a better look and could see that an elderly man was on the ground and a younger man standing over him kicking him several times on the head and body. She called out, 'You brute, why are you doing that?'

The younger man replied, 'I'm trying to get him home.'

Mrs McIlwee said, 'You are no friend, or you would not abuse an old man like that. You are some kind of keelie.' 'Keelie' being local slang for a thief or a cut-throat.

Also alerted by the cries were Jane Boyd and Matthew McGuiness, in their separate homes in nearby Albany Street, who also came out to see what the commotion was. They too saw the older man lying on the ground and Jane Boyd counted that the younger man kicked him on the head at least eight times with fierce heavy blows. Jane had a whistle on a chain around her neck, blasting on it several times, which brought other people from their houses. She was clearly ahead of her time having an early warning system in the form of a whistle on her at all times!

McGuiness shouted to the younger man to stop, but he replied, 'I'm no robber, I'm getting him home.'

However, the old man could be heard in a weak voice saying, 'He's robbing me.'

The older man struggled to his feet and engaged the younger man in a fight, he was no match for the strength of him and once again fell to the ground in great pain, blood pouring from injuries to his face and head.

Matthew McGuiness ran over and took hold of the younger man pulling him away from the injured man on the ground. McGuiness detected the strong smell of alcohol from both and thought that this was just some kind of dispute and released his hold on the younger man, who immediately took to his heels, heading toward King Street and the West End Park.

Some of the women followed the man and as they did so, saw a policeman on Blair Road. One of them ran to the policeman whilst the other followed the man. The policeman hurried after them and stopped the man, who gave the name of James Miller of the 'Model Lodging House', Rochsolloch Road, Airdrie. When searched he was found to have a broken silver 'Albert' chain and pendant. He could not give a proper account for having this. When the policeman took Miller to the streetlights he could see he had blood on his hands and what appeared to be blood on his boots. He was immediately arrested and assistance summoned.

Miller was then taken to Torrisdale Street where the witnesses and the elderly man identified him as the person responsible for the attack. This was sufficient proof for the police officer.

Other police officers arrived at Torrisdale Street and an Ambulance wagon summoned. The elderly man was found to be George Durham, fifty-three years of age, of 52 Deedes Street in Airdrie. Dr Andrew, who lived nearby in Blairhill, gave medical aid to Mr Durham who was then taken home in the Ambulance and given into the charge of his wife. In those days there were no local hospitals accessible for injured persons. If taken to hospital, it was generally in Glasgow.

The following morning, Michael McGuiness found a broken piece of the silver Albert on the ground where Mr Durham had been assaulted. He handed it in to Coatbridge Police Station.

Mr Durham's condition worsened, and the police arranged for a Doctor to examine him at his home. Dr Kirkland found him to be in a very serious condition and close to death.

The Procurator Fiscal, Mr Lindsay, was informed and he made

arrangements for Sheriff Mair to attend the home of Mr Durham to obtain a 'Dying Deposition.'

On Sunday the 1st of September, The Sheriff arrived with Inspector Sommerville of the County Police, Mr Lindsay – Procurator Fiscal and Mr Dixon-Gray, Sheriff Clerk Depute.

Sheriff Mair noted the deposition of the dying man, as follows:

'On Saturday night, I met some friends in Coatbridge and we had some liquor. I was a little worse for drink and left them at about ten o'clock. I lost my road and found myself in a darkened street. I then met a man that I have never seen before who came up to me and said, "You old bastard," and then punched me in the face, knocking me to the ground. He then kicked me on the face and ribs a few times and grabbed my silver albert chain, which I wear across my vest. I tried to hold on to it, but it snapped. He swore at me and kicked me again on the head and body. Some women came forward and took the man away from me. The man the police showed me is the man who did it.'

Mr Durham sadly died at 5 a.m. on Sunday the 8th of September 1901. Bizarrely the Post- Mortem was conducted at the home address of Mr Durham. The cause of death is recorded as 'Colitis, the result of injuries accelerated by the Deceased's state of the heart.'

Although Miller was charged with Murder and Robbery, this was reduced and his Indictment read:

You are charged that, on the 31st of August 1901, on Torrisdale Street, Coatbridge, you did:

- *Assault George Durham, fifty-three years of age, residing at 52 Deedes Street, Airdrie, by striking him with your fists, knock him down, kick him on the head and body in consequence of which he died on the 8th of September 1901*
- *Rob said George Durham of an Albert Chain and Pendant.*

He stood trial at Glasgow High Court, Jail Square on Friday the 29th of November 1901. Miller appeared from custody and pled 'Not Guilty.'

Lord Kinnear and the jury heard the evidence of all the witnesses, who without hesitation identified Miller as the person responsible for the attack on Mr Durham.

Doctors Kirkland and Tudhope stated that the injuries contributed to the death of Mr Durham, however, if he had been of better health, it would have been unlikely that he would have succumbed to them.

Miller did not give evidence on his own behalf.

The jury did not have to retire, their decision was agreed as they sat on their benches, a unanimous verdict of 'Guilty.'

The Advocate Depute presented seven previous convictions for theft and dishonesty recorded against Miller.

Lord Kinnear addressed Miller, saying, 'You have a history of offending and conducted a cowardly attack on Mr Durham. I sentence you to five years penal servitude.'

It is a strange coincidence that George Durham and James Miller lived in close proximity with Deedes Street and Rochsolloch Road being in the same area. Yet the assault took place in a quiet residential part of Coatbridge.

Was it pure chance that they met at this place or not?

Chapter 26:

AN EXPLOSIVE CASE

On the 7th of April 1904, an interesting ceremony took place within the Burgh Court Room in Hamilton. The purpose of the gathering was initially to 'swear in' the Burgh Constable's who were working at a forthcoming election in the town. However, there was a secondary and more interesting purpose.

Following the 'swearing in,' Acting Sergeant Smith was called forward to receive a 'Merit Certificate' and award of one Guinea. The award was in relation to an excellent piece of Detective work on the part of Sergeant Smith in March of that year. A merit certificate was a commendation from the local council to thank a police officer for outstanding work, which also came with a monetary reward. So why did Acting Sergeant Smith deserve such an award?

Just after midnight on Monday the 29th of February 1904, Constable Bruce was on duty at the New Cross in Hamilton when he saw smoke appear from the cellar of the Stationer's shop on the premises of W.W. Haddow on Quarry Street.

Fearing that the shop was on fire, he ran to the nearby police station (which at that time was located at the New Cross.) He raised the alarm and called out the Fire Brigade. Mr Haddow had also been contacted by telephone and made his way to the premises.

The shop was opened and Mr Haddow and Constable Bruce made their way inside, ready to deal with anyone they found. They did not find the premises to be on fire but did see that the smoke had been caused by blowing open the safe.

A search of the shop was made but the culprits were nowhere to be found. There was no obvious sign of forced entry to the shop and a careful examination was carried out. It was eventually established that entry had been gained by climbing over the outside water closet descending under the stair of the upper flat attached to the shop. This led to a small space beside the outer wall of the shop and an adjoining public house.

It appeared that unsuccessful attempts had been made to force through the wall of the pub and attention then turned to the Stationer's Shop. Entry was successful and once inside they dragged the safe to a cellar hatch, which they opened, and threw the safe into the cellar, causing a large indentation on the floor.

The safe then had two holes bored in the door and blasting powder placed into them. A piece of drum wire was placed in the holes and the door blasted open. Once inside the thieves removed £20 in cash which was in a small leather bag.

They had left several items behind, including a topcoat, brace, bits, a large crowbar, a flask containing blast powder, a piece of bread and a cold chop. No doubt the bread and chop were to keep them going in the event they were there for some time!

An examination at the point of entry recovered a white shirt front, a collar, two drill bits and a three bladed pocketknife.

The officers on duty were all alerted to the break in, and a search of the area started. Communication was sent to all police offices in the area between Hamilton, Glasgow, Motherwell and Larkhall to be on the lookout for any suspicious activity or movements, especially any incoming trains.Local officers were dispatched to the train stations in the Town. It was now later in the morning and Sergeant Smith, who was stationed at Burnbank, made his way to Burnbank Railway Station. He could see several men standing on the platforms waiting to depart in various directions to their work.

Having worked the area for twelve years he recognised most of the men by name or sight, however, his eye caught one man in particular. He stood out from the others as he was dirty whereas the others were comparatively clean. He also appeared to be wearing a sock around his throat in place of a collar!

Sergeant Smith walked up to the man and asked where he had come from. He said that he had travelled from Glasgow to meet a man at the Old Cross, as the man wasn't there, he was returning to Glasgow. He produced a half Caledonian Railway ticket to substantiate his story.

Sergeant Smith did not accept this story as there was no way the man could have come from Glasgow, even on the earliest train, walked to the Old Cross and then to Burnbank at that time of the morning, which was now approaching seven o'clock. The other deciding factor was that the Caledonian Railway station, for which he had a ticket, was in Hamilton Town Centre, when the Burnbank Station was run by the North British Railway!

The decision was made, Sergeant Smith was taking his man back to the police office. There the man gave the name Joseph Wilson of No Fixed Abode. He said that he sometimes stayed in the Lodging Houses in Glasgow, the last one being in Great Hamilton Street.

The topcoat left at the scene of the crime was found to contain an invoice for an ironmongers at Glasgow Cross. The invoice indicated that a brace, a bit, a screwdriver and a chisel had been purchased in the previous few days.

Sergeant Smith was sent, with the prisoner, to Glasgow to ascertain if City Detectives could identify him as Joseph Wilson. They were unable to confirm his identity.

Sergeant Smith had, by this time, been joined by Inspectors Cheyne and Clark. The officers decided that they would visit the Ironmongers to see if the staff in the shop could identify the suspect as the person that purchased the items. On overhearing the conversation, the suspect said that there was no point in doing that and admitted buying the items on the Saturday. He obviously realised that it was pointless to continue his denials.

This admission was noted by Sergeant Smith, however, they decided that they would take him there just to confirm his story. Sure enough, on arrival at the shop the members of staff unhesitatingly identified him as the person that purchased the items on the Saturday.

The suspect then made another admission. He admitted that the topcoat, collar and other items found at the scene of the break in were also his. He took them back to the shop in Hamilton and showed the officers how he had broken into the premises. Whilst there, a member of the public approached the officers and told them that just before midnight he had seen the suspect drink from the public water tap near to the shop.

Details of the crime were circulated to neighbouring forces and very quickly Dunbartonshire Constabulary contacted Hamilton Burgh Police. A very slow process but it was all that was available at that time and very often had good results.

It transpired that they had a housebreaking in their area on Friday the 26th of February. Entry had been gained via a skylight and dropping into

104

the shop by use of a rope. An unsuccessful attempt had been made to open the safe by drilling holes and inserting blasting powder.

The thieves had stolen a small amount of money and some pocketknives. Two officers from Dumbarton Burgh and Dunbartonshire County attended at Hamilton later that day. They examined the items seized by the Hamilton officers and thought the pocketknife found at the scene of the crime matched the description of ones stolen from the shop in their area. They took the pocketknife with them for identification purposes.

They later contacted the Hamilton Burgh Police confirming that the knife was one stolen from the premises in their area. There were now further questions for the suspect to answer.

In relation to the Hamilton case, Wilson was remanded in custody appearing at Hamilton Sheriff Court, where he pled guilty. He received a lengthy custodial sentence. He later appeared at Dumbarton Sheriff Court with a similar result.

Presenting Sergeant Smith with his certificate and money, Provost Keith said that he was very pleased to present a member of the force with such an award. The circumstances reflected great credit on the Sergeant and his meritorious conduct.

On presenting the certificate and one Guinea award, the Provost said that the actions of Sergeant Smith were entirely worthy of Sherlock Holmes himself.

Sergeant Smith showed great determination in pursuing this investigation and a great deal of time too. He must have been quite proud and satisfied at the eventual outcome and of course his reward.

Chapter 27:

THE EXTENDED ARM OF THE LAW

Criminals have always travelled from area to area to commit their crimes. The most common reason was that they would probably not be recognised in these other areas. Unlike today, the use of motor vehicles was not an option, therefore public transport was the chosen mode of travel and most commonly the train.

Police officers around the country were well aware that criminals travelled extensively and knew to keep a watch on train and bus stations for unusual characters and strangers to their towns and cities.

On Tuesday the 9th of August 1904, DCs Campbell & Robertson of Dundee City Police, were on duty in the city. They were out and about, in the course of their daily duties, looking for known criminals, when their attention was drawn to four young men, hanging around the Tay Bridge Railway Station.

The men's appearances and the way they were acting looked suspicious to the Detectives who approached the group and identified themselves as police officers. They then asked the young men who they were and where they were from.

The men identified themselves as

- *John McMillan (18) of 75 High Riggs,*
- *James McMillan (17) of 19 Leven Street,*
- *William Mullarkey (16) of 35E Fountainbridge and*
- *Simon Reid Milne (16) of 6 Downfield Place, all in Edinburgh.*

They said that they had only just arrived in Dundee that day from Edinburgh. Three of them said that they were employed by the St. Cuthbert's Co-Operative Society. They had a few days holiday and intended to return to Edinburgh on the following Thursday morning.

Being naturally suspicious, the Detectives weren't convinced by their responses. They asked where they were living and returned with them to their lodgings nearby. The housekeeper said that all four were staying in the one room and had arrived on the Saturday morning, the 6th of August, contradicting the young men's account of having arrived in the city that day.

The Detectives instructed the Housekeeper to make sure the room remained locked until their return. All four young men were then taken to the Central Police Office in Dundee where they were locked up. Of course, this could not happen today due to the extensive consideration of people's rights etc. However, in those days the police had much more discretion.

When searched the officer found the following items in their possession:

- *£1 15 shillings in silver coins*
- *A rusty table knife with no handle*
- *Mufflers*

The Detectives then returned to the lodgings where the Housekeeper opened the room for them. A search revealed three keys and a chisel under one of the bed covers, and in another bed the officers found a jimmy underneath a pillow.

The items were seized, and enquiries then made with Detectives in Edinburgh, to find out if they were aware of these youths and if they had any outstanding housebreakings, as there were none in Dundee. This was a sensible course of action to take and is still a common practice today.

Detectives Knox and Rothney, of the Edinburgh City Police, were aware of these youths and surprised to learn that another associate, Thomas Johnston, wasn't with them. They decided to find Johnston and question him about his friends and why they were in Dundee.

Johnston was traced at his home address at Downfield Place by the Detectives. He was extremely talkative and admitted that all five had been involved in a Housebreaking at a shop in Airdrie the previous Friday night. Thomson was duly arrested and taken to the police office.

It is always amazing how talkative some people can be, with very little persuasion, whilst others will tell you nothing. There is no rhyme or reason to it. On many occasions criminals will attempt to strike a deal by telling the police everything, however, the police do not have the power to make such promises. That is in the domain of the Procurator Fiscal.

The Edinburgh Detectives contacted Airdrie Burgh Police and explained the full circumstances. Sergeant Brodie informed them that they were investigating a Housebreaking at Mrs Cameron's shop on Alexander Street, Airdrie between Friday the 5th and Saturday the 6th of August 1904, when £11 1s and 8d was stolen.

When this was put to Johnston, he confirmed the location of the shop and the amount stolen.

CC Burt of Airdrie Burgh Police was made aware of the information received from Edinburgh and he personally communicated with the Dundee & Edinburgh City forces, requesting that the five be detained pending uplift by Burgh officers. In those days communication was very basic but co-operation between police forces was very good. The four were presented to the court and it was explained that they were wanted in the Airdrie area. The court agreed to their detention until the appropriate authorities could attend and remove them to their area.

Sergeants Kellock and White were sent to Dundee to arrest the four young men detained there and Sergeant Brodie to Edinburgh to arrest Johnston.

All were returned to Airdrie and admitted the housebreaking.

CC Burt and Sergeant Kellock attended at Mrs Cameron's shop on Alexander Street, with the jemmy recovered from the accused's bedroom. This was placed against the marks at the point of entry to the premises and the marks on the till, where it was forced.

They matched perfectly. *How times have changed in the science of crime scene examination!*

On Thursday the 11th of August all five appeared at Airdrie Sheriff Court when they were remanded in custody. On Monday the 29th of August, all five appeared from custody at Glasgow Sheriff Court, with Sheriff Scott Moncrieff presiding. They all pled guilty to the charge of housebreaking and were sentenced to four months hard labour.

Why they were in Airdrie at all is not known! As to why they also went to Dundee, we will never know.

Chapter 28:

THE KELVINSIDE SENSATION

In the early 20th century notable cases were reported quite graphically in the newspapers of the day. It was the only way to make the public aware of these cases and generally the reporters were very descriptive with their headlines, to grab attention.

One of these events took place on Tuesday the 17th of March 1908, an extraordinary event took place at Kelvinside House, Beaconsfield Road, Glasgow.

Kelvinside House was an impressive building, sitting in its own private grounds on Beaconsfield Road. The house belonged to the Fleming family (who owned plantations in Clarendon, Jamaica, and, in 1839, purchased and developed the Kelvinside Estate as a residential suburb.) The house was originally known as Beaconsfield House on Balgray Hill, then renamed Kelvinside House. After the Second World War, Kelvinside House was taken over to be used as 'The Westbourne School for Girls.' In 1991 the school merged with Glasgow Academy and the house sold. Nowadays, it stands as luxury flats, and the extensive grounds have been replaced by blocks of modern flats.

James Brown Montgomerie-Fleming Snr. was a senior partner at Messrs Montgomerie and Flemings Solicitors in Glasgow. After Fleming senior died, his son James carried on the family tradition by studying law.

James Jnr. was born on 8 March 1884 at Musselburgh, East Lothian, the only son of James Brown Montgomerie-Fleming, and Jane Montgomerie-Fleming (nee Prichard), of Kelvinside House, Kelvinside, Glasgow. He grew up in Kelvinside House with his two sisters.

After studying at Kelvinside Academy, he attended Glasgow University to study Scots Law in the 1909/10 session, aged twenty-five, and was apprenticed by Messrs A.J. and A. Graham at 198 West George Street, Glasgow.

James enlisted shortly after the outbreak of the 1914-1918 War, joining the Sportsman's Battalion in September 1914 as a Private. In December of that year, he became a Lieutenant in the East Yorkshire Regiment, and took part in the Battle of Gallipoli from July to December 1915. Evacuated from Suvla Bay, he was invalided to Cephalos suffering from appendicitis. After recovering he was transferred to France and was promoted to Captain, fighting at the Somme, where he earned promotion to Major, for conspicuous service in the fields.

The 6th Battalion of the East Yorkshire Regiment fought in the Battle of Langemarck in August 1917, part of the larger Third Battle of Ypres.

Major James Brown Montgomerie-Fleming died of wounds on 18 August 1917, aged thirty- three, likely sustained in this attack, and is buried in Dozinghem Military Cemetery. His obituary records that he was a keen sportsman and a student of nature.

In 1908, however, the twenty-three-year-old became embroiled in what newspapers of the time called 'one of the most sensational and dramatic incidents in the criminal history of Glasgow.'

At about 1:20 a.m. on Tuesday the 17th of March 1908, the occupants of the house, including the servants, had all gone to bed with the exception of James. He was studying for his law exams and was reading in the smoking-room. He decided to go to bed, walking through the dining room on his way to his room. As he did so he thought he heard a noise, though he wasn't sure if it was in or outside the house.

James made his way to the morning room on the first floor to investigate. The room was dark and he walked to the window and looked through the blinds. He was sure he could see a man concealed in the ivy below the window.

He then headed to his bedroom where he armed himself with his loaded revolver. He then telephoned the Maryhill Police Station, explaining what he had seen and asked the police to attend.

After he called for assistance, he returned to the morning room. He could feel cold air blow in the room and sensed that someone was inside. He switched on the electric light and saw a male standing in the middle of the room who James later described as 'a big burly chap, a strong looking fellow of the Bill Sykes type.'

James immediately pulled out his revolver, showing it to this man, saying that he had called the police and said it would be best for him that he come downstairs and await their arrival.

110

James was taken aback by what happened next. The man, without warning, pulled a revolver from his pocket, pointed it at James and fired. The bullet narrowly missed the head of James and embedded itself in the wall behind him.

Keeping his presence of mind James fired three shots, one of which struck the male on the chest. The man dropped fatally to the floor but before doing so he fired a second shot, later recovered from woodwork.

Almost immediately after this, Inspector Cowan and Sergeant Godfrey arrived on the scene, observing the body on the floor and James Brown Montgomerie Fleming standing with revolver in hand.

Two Doctors also arrived at the scene. Dr Wilson, who was called by James following the shooting and Dr McCall the Maryhill Division Casualty Surgeon. Life was pronounced extinct.

The police officers searched the body of the male and found on his possession one mask, one 15-inch sheathed knife, an electric lamp, thirty-two cartridges, a pair of pliers, two screwdrivers and a half penny. The revolver, with two cartridges still in the chamber, was lying by his side.

The body was removed to the Police Mortuary and later that day formally identified as being John McLeod of Coatbridge. He was initially identified through his fingerprints. His father travelled from Coatbridge to make the identification.

A Fatal Accident Inquiry was held on Wednesday the 25th of March 1908 at Glasgow Sheriff Court, Sheriff Scott-Moncrieff presided. The jury heard all relevant witnesses and were shown the various productions.

Constable John McLean, of the Maryhill Police, gave evidence that he had seen a man walking in the Kelvinside area just before midnight on the 16th of March. He later identified this man as John McLeod.

Detective Trench (of the Oscar Slater case fame), of the Central Division of the City of Glasgow Police, gave evidence of McLeod's previous convictions and that he was a known expert housebreaker with three previous convictions.

James Brown Montgomerie-Fleming gave evidence of his finding McLeod in the house, calling the police and the discharge of firearms.

Sheriff Scott-Moncrieff addressed the jury saying:

'As this case has attracted a good deal of attention, it was proper that it was disposed of in this way. Mr Fleming has given his evidence in a clear and satisfactory manner. It is clearly the case that he acted in defence of his own life. The law on the subject is quite clear and even though the deceased had not fired first, if a revolver had been presented at him, he was quite justified in defending himself from a man who had entered the house with felonious intent. I suggest that you agree to a verdict in the following terms 'That John McLeod on the 17th of March at about 1:30 a.m. was shot dead within Kelvinside House by James Brown Montgomerie-Fleming, who resides in that house. Deceased had entered the house with felonious intent to steal therefrom and was discovered by Mr Fleming in one of the rooms.

On approaching him he showed him a revolver and warned him that he had communicated with the police and asked him to follow him downstairs. Deceased responded by pulling a revolver from his trouser pocket and fired two shots at Mr Fleming, who in turn fired three shots at McLeod, one of which penetrated McLeod's heart and he died almost immediately.'

The Sheriff added that the jury might exercise the power that the act gave them to add to their verdict that they considered that Mr Fleming was entirely justified in acting as he did, in defence of his life.

The jury deliberated for a minute and announced through their foreman, that they were in accord with his Lordships suggestion and returned a verdict accordingly.

Justice was done.

But just who was John McLeod?

John McLeod was also known as Charles Webster or John Gibson. He was born in Auchencairn, Kirkcudbrightshire. His family moved to Airdrie when he was a young boy, attending Victoria School and later training as a Mason. In 1900 he joined the Royal Scots, however, he deserted shortly after.

As noted by the officers during the discussed trial, John was a prolific housebreaker. One of his convictions followed him being found loitering behind a pub in Coatbridge in possession of housebreaker's tools for which he received fourteen days.

In 1901 he was arrested in Airdrie by Inspector Jackson having broken into a Pawn Brokers in Buchanan Street, Airdrie. He was arrested along with two others after the Inspector chased them across rooftops. He was also found to have broken into a workshop in Rochsolloch Road, Airdrie where he stole the tools found in his possession. Rochsolloch Road was near to his own home at Dalhousie Terrace, Deedes Street, Airdrie. He received two months imprisonment for these crimes.

112

After his release, in 1903, he was arrested again following a housebreaking at Cairnhill House in Airdrie, the home of Provost McCosh, stealing £800 worth of jewellery. He had been caught pawning the jewellery. He was also convicted of breaking into a jeweller's shop and was sentenced to three years imprisonment at the High Court in Glasgow.

His last conviction was at the Sheriff & Jury Court in Edinburgh in July 1905. He received eighteen month's imprisonment for breaking into two mansion houses. He was also ordered to complete his previous sentence.

McLeod died in March 1908 and was buried at New Monkland Cemetery on Friday the 20th of March. The service was held in his father's house in Hospital Street, Coatbridge.

Chapter 29:

CATCHING THE 'KISSING CAT-BURGLAR'

Alexander Scott Nicoll, the son of a Crofter, was born on the 8th of November 1885 at Southfield, Monikie in Fife. He grew up in the local area, working on farms when he left school.

On the 19th of January 1909, Alexander travelled south and joined Airdrie Burgh Police and allocated the Collar No. 17. A year and a half later, on the 19th of August 1910, he married Mary Brown, a widow, who had four young children. The family settled at 22 Milton Street in Airdrie.

Alexander was a steady and reliable officer and worked on Beat duties throughout the Burgh for nineteen years. At the beginning of January 1928, he was appointed the works Constable at the 'Imperial Tube Works,' Victoria Place, Airdrie. Due to this move, the family moved to a new house to 43 Kennedy Drive.

Employing police officers on works premises was a usual occurrence, with large works paying for the services of a Constable to deal with issues within the confines and boundaries of their works. Their duties also included patrolling the perimeter of the premises.

On Friday the 13th of January 1928, Alexander was on late shift duty, at the Tube Work. Other officers were also on duty in and around the Cairnhill and Bellsdyke areas of the town, for a specific reason.

There had been several good quality housebreakings and the houses were mostly owned by the better off residents of the town. The locality had also seen a whole new housing estate constructed and many of the local constabulary had been provided with houses, so, there was perhaps some personal interest in catching the culprits.

At about 7.10 p.m. Constables Bannerman and McCaskill were patrolling on Victoria Place when they saw a young man walking toward them from the direction of Cairnhill Road. He stopped near to the entrance of the house named 'Heathpark.' The light from a nearby streetlight allowed them to see his face but they did not recognise him. They walked past him to get a closer look, but still, they did not recognise him as a local.

They decided to turn back to speak to him, however, he had walked off onto Woodburn Avenue. The road curves to the right and they lost sight of him momentarily. They hurried forward and saw him standing at the junction of Woodburn Avenue and Bellsdyke Road.

Due to the recent housebreakings the officers were naturally suspicious. They took cover in the gate of the house called 'Ashfield', some 30 yards away from this junction.

They waited only a few minutes when they saw two known local youths, named McLuskie and Docherty, walk past the gate they were standing inside. The youths obviously did not see the officers. They walked to the junction where the other person was standing and the three began to talk to each other for about three minutes.

They stopped talking and McLuskie and Docherty walked off down Woodburn Avenue toward Victoria Place. The officers let them go, as they were more interested in the stranger. However, when they looked back toward the junction, he had gone!

The officers continued their patrol, scouring the streets looking for this youth. They were unsuccessful and returned to the police office at 10 p.m. They were no doubt disappointed that they had failed to find their prey.

Unknown to them, the youth had walked down Bellsdyke Road and onto Faskine Avenue, the new housing estate, part of which bordered on to the Imperial Tube Works. On the way he had entered the grounds of a several houses.

At about 9 p.m. Constable Nicoll was checking the perimeter of the works. Being aware of housebreakings in the area he also decided to have a walk around the new houses in Cairnhill.

As he was walking on Firhill Avenue, he saw a youth leave the driveway of the house at No. 25 and then move quickly into the driveway of No. 27. He was obviously suspicious of the youth and made his way to investigate. He walked to the rear of the house and found the youth trying to open one of the ground floor windows. Constable Nicoll moved forward, grabbed him by the collar and arrested him. To say the young man was startled does not perhaps describe his reaction at that time! Constable Nicoll checked the house at No. 25 which appeared to be in order. He made the occupants of both houses aware of what had happened and then walked his prey to Airdrie Police office.

When Constables Bannerman and McCaskill arrived back at the office they were made aware of Constable Nicoll's arrest. They went to look at the prisoner and immediately identified him as the youth they had seen on Victoria Place.

This youth identified himself as William Lennie, originally from Aberdeen. Immediately the officers recognised his name from intelligence bulletins as being wanted by several police forces in England. He also admitted to committing six housebreakings in Airdrie, in addition to the one he was arrested for.

It was established that most of the stolen property had been sold, however, some items of jewellery were recovered from females that Lennie had met at the local 'Hippodrome.' It was later learned that he was a popular figure at that location, especially with the ladies, as he was obviously generous with his ill-gotten gains!

Both McLuckie and Docherty were arrested and charged with 'being known or reputed thieves, found in Woodburn Avenue, Airdrie, with intent to commit crime.' Contrary to Section 409 of the Burgh Police (Scotland) Act 1892. An excellent and very well used piece of legislation.

They both pled guilty and were sentenced to sixty days imprisonment.

Lennie was another matter. He was remanded in custody. He pled guilty on Monday the 30th of January at Glasgow Sheriff Court, to seven charges of Housebreaking and Attempted Housebreaking.

Sheriff Blair heard that Lennie had been involved in crime since the age of eight, in 1915, when he was convicted on two charges of theft of money. In 1917 he received 10 strokes of the birch following a conviction on a charge of housebreaking. In 1926 he was convicted of housebreaking in Edinburgh and sentenced to three years in Borstal. He had escaped from Borstal in November 1927 and fled to England, where he had committed numerous crimes. Sheriff Blair sentenced him to eighteen months hard labour and ordered that he be sent to England to face his charges there.

Officers from Liverpool arrested him in Glasgow and returned with him. He faced forty- eight charges of Burglary and one of Assault in Manchester and Liverpool. He was known as the 'Kissing Cat-Burglar.' He would climb the down pipe of houses and break into the upper levels late at night or early in the morning. If females were asleep alone, he would kiss them after he had gathered his stolen property. Unfortunately, one of the women had woken as he was doing so and he struck her on the head with a torch, causing serious injuries. An unusual change to his behaviour.

He pled guilty to all the charges at Manchester Assizes.

Passing sentence, Justice Wright said, 'You are just under twenty-one but you have already had a long career of crime and you have shown the enterprise and the intelligence of a hardened criminal.

'It is difficult to know what to do with a case like yours. You have pleaded guilty to three acts of burglary and asked for forty-five other cases to be taken into consideration and one case of a violent attack on a young girl. You have also made away with property valued at £400.

'I have to impose a custodial sentence of seven years imprisonment to run consecutively with the Scottish conviction.'

The result was the clearance and conviction on a total of fifty-six charges between Airdrie, Liverpool and Manchester, all down to the alertness of Constable Nicoll. The Judge highly commended him for his alertness in arresting Lennie. Constable Nicoll and his tenacity is rightly commended. He could have just returned to his normal duties and none of these crimes would have been detected.

Alexander remained at the Imperial Tube Works until his retirement on the 11th of February 1939. He was immediately employed by Stewarts & Lloyds Work as their works security officer, where he remained for fifteen years. In his spare time, he was a keen golfer and member of Easter Moffat Golf Club.

Alexander died on the 30th of July 1958 at Hairmyres Hospital, East Kilbride, at seventy-two years of age, following a period of illness.

Chapter 30:

KNICKER KNOCKER KNICKED

The police do not always handle serious and frightful cases. Oftentimes they are asked to attend and deal with unusual and sometimes funny incidents instead. People will commit crimes which sometimes baffle the officers dealing with them and along with that comes the excuses provided for committing these crimes.

At about 7:30 p.m. on Monday the 20th of January 1913, Constable Keith Meston had just left Coatbridge Police Station on Muiryhall Street and was walking to his beat on Main Street.

As he walked down Dunbeth Road toward Main Street, his attention was caught by a man hurrying along the street, who appeared to have something bulky under his jacket. He decided to follow the man.

After a short distance, the man became aware of the presence of Constable Meston and quickened his pace, the officer did likewise. This continued for a few seconds until the man burst into a full run. The chase was on.

Constable Meston chased the man along Main Street, past the Theatre Royal, left onto Jackson Street, then right onto Coats Street. The chase ended halfway along Coats Street when Constable Meston caught up with his prey. A quick search under the man's jacket revealed three pairs of brand-new blue ladies' flannel knickers! *Probably not what Constable Meston thought he would find and I would have loved to see his face when he held these up!*

Constable Meston asked the man where they had come from, and he replied that he had bought them from a man on Main Street. Unsurprisingly, Constable Meston arrested him and walked him the short distance to the police station.

The accused was presented to Inspector Scott, the officer on duty. The circumstances were explained, and the accused gave his name as Peter

Crelly, a tube worker, residing at Coats Street, Coatbridge.

As he was being placed through the prisoners book, a young female, Mary MacFarlane, a shop assistant working at Lavelle's Clothes Shop, Main Street, Coatbridge, came to the front bar to report the theft of three pairs of lady's flannel knickers. As she looked through to the charge-bar she saw the accused Crelly. She immediately pointed to him and said, 'He stole them.' A second shop assistant who came into the police station just behind Miss MacFarlane also confirmed the identity of the thief. Their timing was impeccable.

Both girls were then shown the knickers which they positively identified as those stolen from the shop. They did so by identifying the manufacturers labels and price labels that were attached to them. The accused stood, head bowed and said nothing.

The girls described how they had been working in the shop, just before 7:30 p.m. when they saw Crelly standing in the doorway. Several items were hanging on display and when the accused walked away, they noticed that three pairs of ladies' underwear were missing.

Miss MacFarlane had checked the various closes on Main Street but there was no trace of the accused. That is when she decided to attend the police station.

The accused Crelly was charged with the theft and replied, 'I have had a drop of drink and regret what I have done.' *The demon drink once again being used as an excuse for committing crime, which is still being used today!*

Crelly appeared from custody on Wednesday the 22nd of January at Coatbridge Police Court. He pled guilty to the charge. The CC, William McDonald, prosecuting the case, presented the facts.

Bailie Kirk commented, 'Taking a drop of drink is no excuse for taking property that did not belong to him.' He fined Crelly £1 or ten-days imprisonment. The fine was paid.

People do some strange things! The culprit gave the excuse that he had been drinking, but why steal knickers? Were they for his wife, girlfriend? Who knows? Certainly, Constable Meston wasn't just going to let this man go.

This story also shows the intuition of police officers who know their beat and know when someone is acting suspiciously or is up to no good. This comes with experience and watching the behaviour of people. If a police officer worked a specific area for some time, they would get to know all of the habits and peculiarities of the area and instinctively know when something wasn't right.

Seeing a regular police officer in an area gives the general public a feeling of reassurance and protection; they can approach the officer, speak in confidence and be listened too.

We have mentioned previously that the police need the public on their side to be able to function. The role of the old beat officer was perfect for this, being visible and approachable.

Shopkeepers always liked to see a police officer pop into their premises for a chat and usually a cup of tea or coffee. A good beat officer could always detect when a kettle was on the boil!

Chapter 31:

NEIGHBOURHOOD WATCH

A community spirit is a great thing, with people looking out for each other. This has been the case for many, many years and as a consequence a lot of crimes have been detected.

Wednesday the 1st of July 1914 was a public holiday in Strathaven. The Hamilton family, who lived in 'Shalimar' Villa, Crosshill Street, decided to go away for the day. Henry Hind Hamilton was a local merchant and was fortunate to have his own motor vehicle. The family left in the early morning to enjoy their break.

In the early afternoon, a woman who lived on Bowling Green Road, near to the Hamilton's, was looking out of her upstairs window when she saw two men at the rear of 'Shalimar'. She saw them enter the house through the rear door. She knew the Hamilton's were away for the day and was immediately suspicious.

The neighbor ran downstairs and into the street, where a group of children were playing. She gathered them together and, along with another female neighbour, they all headed for 'Shalimar' Villa. As they walked into the driveway, they heard noises from upstairs in the house. The women walked toward the back door.

As they reached the corner of the house, they saw two men run out of the back door, running across the croquet green and jumping a fence into a park. They were then seen running toward Townhead Street. One of the men was carrying an overcoat and the other, an umbrella.

The women sent one boy to fetch the police, whilst a group of the others gave chase to the men through the park.

The ladies went into the house to see if anyone else was still there. Once inside, they could see the back door lock had been forced and the inside of the house ransacked. The front door had a chair wedged against the door handle to prevent it from being opened from the outside.

The two upstairs front bedrooms were in the worse state, with drawers and contents strewn across the floor. The wardrobes were lying open and clothes thrown across the floor.

Meanwhile, the children had followed the men along Townhead Street. They met two police officers on bicycles, Constables John Pirie and Alexander Clark. The boys told the police officers what had happened at 'Shalimar' and that the men were last seen on Townhead Street. The children gave them descriptions as best they could.

The police officers rode off in different directions to try and find the men. The officers met up at Southend near to Station Road, a short distance from the Railway Station. They met two joiners, who were working at a nearby house. The officers asked if they had seen two men in the past few minutes. The joiners said that they had seen two men run into a field at the far side of Southend.

The officers headed into the field and began to make a search. They quickly spotted movement in an adjacent hay field and saw two men walking quickly toward the Railway Station. The officers returned to their bicycles and sped toward the Station, where they caught the men crossing the tracks near to one of the goods sheds. The men were stopped and identified themselves as:

- *James Wallace, 13 Govan Street, Glasgow*
- *John Small, 219 Commercial Road, Glasgow*

Both denied any knowledge of the housebreaking and were arrested and taken to the police station. In their possession were return train tickets for Glasgow.

The police officers searched in the area that they had seen the two men and found an umbrella lying in the field.

The ladies and the children were brought to the police station, where they positively identified the two men.

When Mr Hamilton and his family returned from their day away, he contacted the police office, having been made aware by Mrs Coats of the incident earlier.

Constables Pirie and Alexander attended and obtained details of the break-in. Mr Hamilton reported that a silver card case, a silver bangle with nine silver coins attached, an umbrella, an overcoat and 2s and 6d had been stolen. Mr Hamilton identified the overcoat and umbrella, recovered from the accused and the field, as being his property.

The men were charged with the housebreaking and held in custody pending their appearance at Hamilton Sheriff Court.

A search the following morning, once again involving the local children, recovered the other outstanding card case and bangle discarded on the route taken by the two men.

The two accused appeared at Hamilton Sheriff Court on Thursday the 2nd of July. Both plead 'Not Guilty'. They were remanded for further enquiries.

They made a second appearance on Thursday the 6th of August 1914, at a pleading diet at Hamilton Sheriff Court. They pled 'Not Guilty' and were remanded for a Jury trial on the 25th of August.

On Tuesday the 25th of August, the pair appeared from custody. The jury were empaneled with Sheriff Stodart presiding. The prosecution case was led by the Procurator Fiscal Mr William Thomson. The relevant witnesses were called and provided their evidence. Mr Thomson in summing up said that the accused clearly knew it was a holiday in Strathaven and decided to travel from Glasgow to commit opportunist crimes.

Mr McLaughlin, appearing for the defence, called no witnesses and the accused did not give evidence. In summing up he said that it was a case of mistaken identity, his clients only being in Strathaven for a quiet day away from the city.

The trial lasted for three hours. Sheriff Stodart addressed the jury and sent them away to deliberate. They were gone less than ten minutes, when they returned with a unanimous guilty verdict.

The Procurator Fiscal presented a previous conviction for both accused, for Theft by Housebreaking. Mr McLaughlin urged the Sheriff for a lenient sentence as he said that he was convinced that it was the firm intention of both to join the colours at this time of national crisis.

Sheriff Stodart was unconvinced, stating that in all the circumstances he could not impose a sentence of any less than nine months imprisonment.

The accused were taken from the Court to Barlinnie Prison in a prison van. As it stopped at the gates of Barlinnie and the prisoners were taken out, Wallace slipped his handcuffs and ran from his escort in an attempt to escape.

He managed to get approximately 100 yards when one of the police officers chasing him, felled him with a precision blow between his shoulder blades. He was then taken inside to serve his sentence.

This is yet another case committed in a small rural community by travelling criminals taking the opportunity of a holiday period to commit their crimes.

Like many of these stories, it emphasises the importance of local community relations and co-operation. The neighbour could have ignored what she had seen, however, she knew the family and knew that they were away. She immediately alerted neighbours and gathered all the children to investigate what was happening. If she hadn't done this, it is likely that these criminals would have escaped capture.

The children would have seen this as a great adventure, chasing the bad men and alerting the police to what was happening. Furthermore, the local officers used excellent local knowledge to ensure that the culprits were captured and brought to book. There was no technology involved, just pure and simple good policing.

I am afraid that today we have lost that local policing experience and knowledge as officers cover such vast areas and have little connection with local communities. Some areas very rarely see a police officer. In the past, a police officer would be living and working in that community.

Chapter 32:

SHEEP RAIDERS

I am sure that at some time during our service we have all been in some unusual searches and operations! However, how many had the CC leading the way?

On Saturday the 16th of October 1926, the muster room at Lanark Police Station presented a sight more akin to a Butchers Shop or a restaurant kitchen!

The centre of the room was lined with a number of items such as kitchen utensils of all descriptions, a clothes basket, a delft basin, several sacks and pots and pans galore. All the containers were filled with mutton or mutton fat, the sacks had sheep shanks protruding from them whilst quarters of mutton lay stacked in the baskets. Some had been neatly cut and other parts were quite ragged, some cooked and others not!

They were there due to recent complaints of sheep stealing in the Lesmahagow area. This had started following the Parish Council Relief being stopped some three weeks earlier.

Only days earlier, skins, legs, heads and other rejected portions of sheep had been found in the River Nethan, as if in open challenge to the local police. The sheep had been cornered in a field, killed and slaughtered all under the cover of darkness. Enquiries revealed the location of the incident as 'Hill Farm,' about 1.5 miles outside Lesmahagow on the Coalburn and Lesmahagow Road.

Constable Trussler, from Lesmahagow, made enquiries into the incident.

The decision was soon made, at the very top, to deal with the issue. CC Andrew Keith and Lanark senior officer, Superintendent Pennie prepared a raid on the local community. Even back then, senior officers working on significant cases were closely involved, but not too many at the rank of CC or Superintendent led operations from the front!

Search warrants were craved and granted, and a motor bus hired. In the very early hours of the Saturday morning, when it was still dark, the bus set off from Lanark with thirty of Lanarkshire's finest, led by Inspector Jordan, on board. They met the local Lesmahagow officers, Sergeant Hendry and Constable Trussler, at the outskirts of the town.

Silently they made their way to the area known as Turfholm where cordons of officers were drawn around several houses. Armed with their warrants the officers entered several houses and a large amount of mutton was recovered in every space available, such as the chimney, roof rafters, below beds, under floorboards and all places conceivable. Mutton bones were even found burning on fires being used as fuel. To the officers' amazement, one man, found in bed unwell, with mutton under the covers stated he was suffering from having eaten too much mutton. He was swiftly arrested.

Eleven arrests were made, and they appeared at Lanark Sheriff Court on the Saturday morning. Four pled guilty and the rest pled not guilty, bail was set at £5 each and the case continued until the 20th of October.

The trial was called at Lanark Sheriff Court on the 20th of October. By then, one additional accused pled guilty. Evidence was then led for both prosecution and defence. Having heard the witnesses the Procurator Fiscal dropped charges against six of the accused as he could not reasonably expect a conviction on either theft or reset, which was accepted by the Sheriff. This left five accused that had pled guilty, to be sentenced.

Strong arguments were placed before the Sheriff from both sides and in summing up Sheriff Harvey said, 'This is not a case that usually came before the court. The accused in this case are not criminals or at least not like the usual criminals. I have some admiration for them on coming forward and pleading guilty. I accept that you are Martyrs, but Martyrs have to pay a Martyrs' price. I am here to administer the law and the law must be maintained.

This was an open and flagrant breach of the law and I am not prepared to admire a Martyr who refused to pay the price.'

He sentenced the five accused to three months hard labour. Although we look at this in a light-hearted manner today, we must remember that 1926 was a period of great hardship for people with the General Strike and other industrial issues. The accused in this case had committed the crime to feed their families. They did not try to sell the mutton to make money or for any other reason.

Chapter 33:

THE BIG BANG

Criminals of today do not use explosives to commit their crimes very often. However, in the late 19th and early 20th centuries, their use of these was very common and the explosives very easy to acquire, due to the number of mines and other works using them. One of the uppermost considerations of using explosives in the commission of crime is how to actually use them! If you don't, there could be serious consequences.

In March 1932 at Glasgow Sheriff Court, three men appeared on charges of housebreaking using explosives.

During the late evening of Thursday the 18th of February 1932, the three men, all from Glasgow, forced entry to the offices at William Baird & Co, Castle Colliery, Bothwell. The colliery was bounded by Station Road, Uddingston Road and Elmwood Manor (now the Fairways Housing Estate.) It wasn't too far from the Police Station either! Either they didn't know that the police station was so close or they were very bold criminals indeed.

Once within the office, they used explosives to force entry to the safe where they thought the wages were being kept, as Thursdays were the usual delivery day.

Unfortunately for them, one of the local Constables was investigating an accident at the Colliery, when he heard a loud explosion and observed the door of the safe smash through the colliery office window at considerable speed and land a few feet away from him.

He ran to the Colliery office where he could hear movements within. He took cover and watched as the three left the office. He rushed at them, causing them considerable surprise and pushed them toward a small nearby office, once inside he locked the door, trapping them inside. He did not have to wait too long as other officers, having heard the explosion, arrived on the scene to find their colleague, baton in hand, standing by the door.

The three were arrested and searched. They were found to have housebreaking implements, such as crowbars, hammers and chisels, plus two and a half sticks of gelignite, 6ft of fuse and a detonator. The three were detained in custody. An examination of the office indicated that perhaps they used too much gelignite to blow open the safe.

On their appearance for trial, all three pled guilty as charged. Two of the accused, with previous convictions, received eighteen months hard labour and the third received six months hard labour. A fourth male, acting as look-out was later arrested and sentenced to nine months hard labour.

Even more unfortunate for them was the fact that the safe they blew open was actually empty, there were three safes in the office and they picked the wrong one!

Chapter 34:

A SOLDIER OF NO CONSEQUENCE

Police officers very often, whilst investigating one crime, have the uncanny knack of catching criminals for other crimes. This story explains one such case.

On the 27th of July 1948, George Walker, a twenty-year-old serving with the Cameron Highlanders, appeared at Airdrie Sheriff Court. He was charged with housebreaking at 49 North Road, Bellshill on the 20th of July 1948.

The circumstances being that Watson and another man, George Paterson Mills Fleming McCarroll, were travelling in a taxi stopped by police at Mount Vernon. The officers had been looking for a stolen car, similar to the taxi.

The taxi driver was asked to provide the registration number and jokingly replied, '999.' McCarroll and Walker, seated in the rear of the taxi, began to laugh. The officers looked into the rear of the vehicle and instantly recognised Walker as one of their regular customers.

They also noticed that there were two suitcases beside them.

The officers asked the taxi driver where he had picked them up and he replied that he had picked them up on North Road, Bellshill and had been asked to take them to Tollcross.

Closer examination of the suitcases showed that they bore a label with the name 'William Murray'. They asked Walker's companion his name and he replied 'George McCarroll'. Not the most astute criminal to be stopped by the police. At that point the officers arrested the two men and instructed the taxi driver to take them all to Baillieston Police Station.

Enquiries were made with the Police at Bellshill and a voters roll check revealed that the William Murray resided at 49 North Road. This was the address where the taxi had uplifted the pair.

Police officers attended the address and discovered that it had been broken into. The occupants, Mr and Mrs Murray were away on holiday, returning the following day. A check of the contents revealed a number of electrical items, tablecloths and some jewellery. One of the items had a wedding card within relating to the Murray's.

Further enquiries revealed that McCarroll was also responsible for another housebreaking at Uddingston on the 19th of June 1948. He was identified by fingerprints and at a subsequent identification parade.

The accused appeared from custody at Airdrie Sheriff Court, on the 27th of July. Walker pled 'Guilty,' saying nothing in his defence, and was sentenced to three months imprisonment at Barlinnie Prison.

Notably, matters did not end there. On Saturday the 25th of September 1948, Walker was released from Barlinnie Prison, having completed his sentence for the Bellshill housebreaking.

As he left the prison, he was met by a welcoming party from Lanarkshire Constabulary who informed him that he was being arrested on a charge of Theft by Housebreaking at Baillieston, on the 24th of December 1947. The police used this method to arrest wanted criminals frequently. Checking with the prison authorities for dates of release and attending to greet their 'customers' as they left.

The premises of Buchanan & Co (Wagons) Ltd of Easterhouse, had been broken into on Christmas Eve. Four cases of rum and two cases of Gin had been stolen. Mr Buchanan had bought these to distribute as presents to customers and staff at a total cost of £82 (£3049.00 today). None of the property was recovered.

Walker had been identified by fingerprint, having left his impressions on a bottle of varnish within the Managing Directors office of the premises.

He appeared at Airdrie Sheriff Court on Monday the 19th of October 1948 and tendered a plea of guilty and once again said nothing in his defence.

The Procurator Fiscal, Mr Nixon, said that technically Walker was still attached to the army. He then went on to read a letter from his commanding officer, it was short and to the point, "Private Walker is still technically attached to the Cameron Highlanders, in that he had joined on the 9th of July and absented himself four days later. He has never been a soldier of any consequence and it is unlikely that he ever will be."

Sheriff Stevenson said that there was very little he could say and was disappointed in Walker's behaviour, conduct and failure to serve his country. He then sentenced Walker to six months imprisonment.

Contrastingly to Walker, McCarroll pled 'Not Guilty' and was remanded in custody pending his trial.

On Friday the 3rd of September 1948, McCarroll appeared for trial at Airdrie Sheriff & Jury Court. Sheriff Stevenson presided and empaneled a jury of eight men and seven women.

The trial was heard and all prosecution witnesses provided their evidence. McCarroll gave evidence, claiming an alibi that he was in Coatbridge visiting the home of his mother on the 19th of June and that he knew nothing of the Bellshill housebreaking, which was the responsibility of George Walker.

McCarroll's defence agent called his wife as a witness. She stood in the witness box, remaining silent and refused to answer any questions. Three other defence witnesses failed to appear!

Sheriff Stevenson then charged the jury following the closing speeches. The jury retired for fifteen minutes and returned with a majority verdict of guilty.

Sheriff Stevenson thanked the jury for their time and prompt decision. Two previous convictions, for housebreaking, were presented by the Procurator Fiscal, Mr Nixon. The Sheriff commented that the accused had wasted the court and witnesses' time by maintaining his innocence when it was clear that he was responsible for the crimes. He sentenced McCarroll to sixteen months imprisonment to start from that day.

A very 'switched on' Sheriff who could clearly see through McCarroll and his solicitor.

Chapter 35:

PAYROLL ROBBERY

Greed is a terrible thing and consumes so many people, whether for monetary or other advantage. It is generally uncontrolled and people will not let anything get in the way of their desire. There are many examples of which this is only one.

At about 1 p.m. on Tuesday the 1st of December 1949, two employees of Colville's Dalzell Works in Motherwell, Mr Richardson, the accountant, and Stewart Young, the works security man, entered the Commercial Bank, Airbles Road, Motherwell and withdrew £17,493 in cash. Once they had collected the money it was placed into a leather bag. The money was to pay the workforce.

As they walked outside to a waiting taxi, they were attacked by a male brandishing a pistol. Mr Richardson was struck on the hand with the pistol and he released his grip on the bag. The assailant grabbed the bag and ran off to a nearby vehicle. The vehicle had clearly been waiting for him as it drove off immediately. It travelled a short distance and stopped, picking up another male before speeding off again. This male had obviously been acting as a look- out.

The scene was witnessed by several people who had been around the bank at the time. One of them, a female passenger in a car, had noted the numberplate of the car and passed it onto her husband. He then ran into the bank and gave staff the number and told them to call the police.

The works security officer, Mr Young, entered the taxi and explained to the driver what had happened. The driver offered to pursue the vehicle that had made off, however, Young told him not to, as they had a gun. Instead, he instructed the driver to drive to the police station, which he did.

On arrival at the High Road police station, Young informed the police of the robbery. They were already aware due to a call from the bank.

DI Ebenezer Cowie of the Motherwell & Wishaw Burgh Police led the investigation. All of the witnesses present at the time were interviewed and statements obtained. One interesting aspect of these statements was that the security man, Stewart Young, made no attempt to prevent the robbery taking place.

They established the exact amount stolen and circulated details of the vehicle. It was quickly established that the number plates displayed on the vehicle were false. However, the car was found a short time after the robbery, abandoned in Motherwell. It transpired that the car was hired on the day of the robbery in Ayr. Enquiries established that a false name had been used to hire the vehicle. However, the staff at the hire company knew the man as a local driver named Thomas McCloy Shearer of 143 George Street, Ayr. A rather stupid mistake to make in such circumstances or did he think because the crime was committed outside the local area that he would never be traced?

DI Cowie and DS Ludovic McPherson, together with Detectives from Ayrshire, visited Shearer and interviewed him regarding the robbery. He very quickly admitted his involvement and that he was only the getaway driver. He named his accomplices as James Harkness Moffat from Maybole, Robert Richmond of Ayr and Thomas Hawthorn Robertson of Prestwick Road in Ayr.

He further added that he only received £15 for his part in the robbery and only knew of the amount stolen after it had been reported in the newspapers. He did not receive anything from the crime. He also described a 'dummy run' that they had made in November. They had picked up someone he did not know in Hamilton and drove to the bank. The unknown person described the bank and how the money was withdrawn.

He also told the officers that at the time of the robbery he did not see any of it due to the way the vehicle was parked. He added that on the day of the robbery he hired the car and drove Robertson, Moffat and Richmond to Motherwell. Richmond was dropped off a distance from the bank as a lookout. He then drove to the bank where Moffat got out of the car. He said that he was only gone a few minutes and returned with a leather bag. He drove off, picking up Richmond and then dumped the car in Motherwell. They then walked to the bus station and travelled back to Ayrshire by bus.

The police then called on Robertson who lived at lodgings in

133

Prestwick Road. A search of the house and grounds recovered £9,800 buried underneath a hen house. Robertson was arrested and denied any involvement in the robbery. He said he knew nothing of the money recovered. It is common for criminals to deny everything up until they have no alternative!

His landlady was interviewed and stated that he had lived with her for six years and regularly had friends at her house. She knew two of them as Robert Richmond who lived locally and Stewart Young from Hamilton. She went on to tell the officers that she had visited Young's house in Hamilton with Thomas Robertson a few weeks earlier.

When Robertson was searched, he was found to have two letters sent by Stewart Young. Both related to the robbery and sent after the event, telling him to keep quiet as the police were asking too many questions.

Moffat and Richmond were also arrested and £3,000 cash recovered. Both were a bit more talkative. Moffat informed the officers that he was the one that snatched the bag and admitted to having a gun, but it could not fire. He also confessed to throwing the gun away after the robbery.

They also described a 'dummy run' in November, when along with Robertson and Shearer, they travelled to Young's house in Hamilton. They then all drove to the bank where Young explained the procedure for withdrawing the money.

They corroborated Shearer's version of events adding their own involvement.

Moffat explained how he saw Young and the other man exit the bank as planned and he ran toward them. He produced the gun and struck the other man on the hand with it and snatched the bag. He then ran to the car and Shearer drove off as described.

The Detectives then returned to Hamilton and arrested Stewart Young at his home in Miller Street. Young was a former Hamilton Burgh Police officer, having served for twenty-five- and-a-half-years and was employed by Colville's on retiring from the police. He denied all knowledge of the robbery and no money was found at his home.

All five were later charged with the robbery, however, Shearer was eventually used as a Crown witness.

The connection between them was Robertson and Young, who had been friends for some time having met in Hamilton whilst Young was still a serving police officer. The four – Young, Robertson, Moffat and Richmond – had met several times at a pub in Ayr to discuss their plan, which was devised by Young.

On Tuesday the 10th of January 1950, Richmond and Moffat appeared at the High Court in Edinburgh, pleading guilty to the charge. They both received four years penal servitude.

Young and Robertson were committed for trial which took place on the 27th and 28th of February 1950 at the High Court in Glasgow. They were both unanimously found guilty with their co-accused and Shearer giving evidence against them.

They were sentenced to six years penal servitude. £6,593 of the stolen money remained outstanding. Neither had any previous convictions.

Thomas Hawthorn Robertson was a former Scottish Professional Football Player making 182 senior appearances for Ayr United, Dundee & Clyde. He scored sixty-six goals. He died in 1962 in Ayr aged fifty-three.

Stewart Young initially appealed his conviction but withdrew it shortly after. He lost his reputation and police pension because of his actions. He had been described as a good police officer and good employee by Colville's management. His greed for money obviously overtook him!

He died in 1991 aged eighty-nine.

It is difficult to understand why a former police officer would resort to such violent criminal activity. Did he think that because he had been a police officer that he could commit the perfect crime or was it simply just greed that drove him to crime?

Chapter 36:

THE CASE OF THE BIG TOE

There has been significant advances in forensics including Fingerprints and DNA which have changed and improved the investigation process. However, the thorough investigation skills of forward-thinking police officers, reviewing the limited evidence before them, have led to incredible detections and cases which have changed the legal landscape. One such officer was DS Peter Scott who received a Parchment Certificate (citing the case as the most outstanding detection of the year) by the FBI for his work on an unusual case, which highlighted the significance of other identifying marks other than fingerprints.

On Wednesday the 20th of December 1950 a Lanarkshire man, William Gourlay, was convicted at the Sheriff Court in Hamilton on two charges. The first was Theft by Housebreaking at Mossband Mine, Newarthill on the 22nd of October 1950 and stealing 5lb of Gelignite and 28 Detonators and the second was Housebreaking and Opening a Lockfast Place with Intent to steal, namely a safe, by use of explosives, at the Odeon Cinema, Motherwell on the 23rd of October 1950.

William was not a stranger to this method of housebreaking, he had regularly stolen explosives for use in his housebreaking activities.

On the 23rd of October 1950, Gourlay and an unidentified accomplice, were disturbed by Motherwell & Wishaw Burgh Police officers making a check of their property on the second half of their nightshift. The two made off over the roof of the building and headed out of Motherwell toward Bellshill. The police gave chase, later accompanied by their Lanarkshire Constabulary colleagues.

Gourlay was captured, in significant pain, close to the Burgh and County boundary on Motherwell Road, Bellshill. It transpired that he had broken his leg jumping from the roof of a building they had run across to evade the police. For his efforts, Gourlay was convicted and sentenced to two years imprisonment.

However, this period of incarceration did not appear to put Gourlay off his criminal enterprise! Shortly after his release from prison he was at it again.

During the early hours of the morning, on Saturday the 28th of June 1952, a housebreaking took place at the Bellshill and Mossend Co-operative Bakery in Bellshill where a safe had been blown open and the contents stolen. When the housebreaking was discovered, the police were called and a scene of crime carried out.

DS Peter Scott, of the Bellshill C.I.D. attended the scene. He quickly detected the strong smell of explosives and examined the premises for fingerprints and any other evidence which might identify the culprit. To his disappointment, there were no fingerprints at the point of entry or on the safe, indicating that the housebreaker had worn gloves.

However, another piece of unique evidence proved interesting and helpful, after all fingerprints were not the only source of identification. DS Scott found footprints on the side of the safe. It appeared that the culprit took off his shoes and socks and walked barefoot around the premises, picking up flour from the floor onto the soles of his feet. Photographs of the footprints were taken and investigations commenced.

One of the first things to do was check the method used by the housebreaker, namely the use of explosives whilst opening safes. A check of the intelligence system revealed that there were seven people listed as having safe-blowing convictions in the local area and it was decided that if and when they were brought into custody, their footprints would be taken. It is amazing the ingenuity of the officers at the time to consider taking these marks for identification purposes.

It didn't take long for the detectives to arrive at William Gourlay. Not only had there not been any recent safe-blowing crimes in the area but Gourlay had only recently been liberated from prison and he lived in the local area.

By chance, on the 22nd of July 1952, Gourlay was brought into Bellshill Police Station for questioning by British Transport Commission Police C.I.D. officers on a charge of having been found in a railway goods yard in Holytown. Whilst in the police office DS Scott decided that he should be not only fingerprinted but also footprinted!

Gourlay was astonished when the police took the impressions from his feet and asked why they were doing so. He was asked if he had committed the crime and if he had ever been in the bakery, he denied both. The prints were sent away and lo and behold, the toe prints matched those left at the crime scene. Gourlay was arrested and charged with the housebreaking.

He appeared for trial at the High Court in Glasgow on the 4th of November 1952, pleading not guilty with the only real evidence against him being his toe prints. Two Glasgow Detectives, Superintendent George McLean and DI William Cannon of the City of Glasgow Police Fingerprint Department gave evidence of the identification of Gourlay's left toeprint. The officers were challenged by the defence as there had never been such an identification and no person in the country had sufficient knowledge of foot or toe prints to make such claims. The officers refuted this and pointed out that there were twenty- two similarities in the marks left at the scene and the print of Gourlay's left toe.

At the conclusion of the case, the Judge, Lord Birnam, addressed the jury. He made specific reference to the toe print evidence and informed them that they may be making history in this case as to his knowledge, there had never been a conviction sought by the Crown on the evidence of a toe print alone, in the United Kingdom.

The jury retired and took only fifteen minutes to return with a unanimous guilty verdict. Lord Birnam thanked them for their time and turned to Gourlay sentencing him to three years in prison.

The jury did in fact make history as this was the first toe print conviction in the United Kingdom and perhaps beyond. Nor was it the last toe print conviction as only a few months later James Walker Adams broke into a warehouse wearing socks with holes in them, leaving behind sole prints. Adams was defended by the same lawyer that represented Gourlay and ended up with the same result, he too was imprisoned for his crimes.

It appears that the perfect crime involves gloves and undamaged socks as they leave no prints or any identifying evidence (unless you steal them from a murdered homeless man like George Francis Shaw did).

It may be worth highlighting the fact that the general public are of the opinion that once fingerprints, footprints, DNA etc have been identified then that is the end of the matter and the case has been proved and the suspect can be convicted. This could not be further from the truth. These marks are merely intelligence at that point, indicating that the possible suspect may have been at that location at some time.

Police officers have to gather evidence which, when presented in court, shows that beyond all reasonable doubt, these marks were left by the suspect at the time the crime was committed. If this cannot be done the case will very likely fail. Therefore, getting an identification is the start of the investigative journey and a lot of hard work is involved to prove that the person committed the crime.

Chapter 37:

EXPLODING MINCE

For many years police officers walked their beats and became familiar with every person of note, street, building and premises in their area. Their local knowledge was incredible and they could generally solve crimes very quickly due to their in depth understanding of the people and area. On the nightshift police officers would check the property in their area which included shops, banks, business premises and anywhere that held something of value which may be of interest to those with criminal tendencies. This process was known as 'Pullin Padlocks'. Unfortunately, this has long gone and in my opinion is a great disadvantage to police officers' understanding of their local area.

Sometimes crimes are detected by pure chance and perhaps due to a police officer just being in the right place at the right time.

At about 2:30 a.m. on Saturday the 12th of August 1961, Constable William Watson was on night shift in Cleland. It was a quiet night and he was in the process of checking the property on Main Street.

Everything appeared to be in order until he reached the Co-operative building at 25 Main Street (close to where the current Scotmid is located). He thought he could hear a scraping noise coming from inside the premises. The exterior at the front to the shop appeared to be okay, so he headed to the rear yard.

He shone his torch at the rear of the building and could immediately see that one of the doors had been forced open. He shone his light on the doorway and walked toward it. As he was about to go into the shop he was startled as three men ran out of the door, almost knocking him over.

Constable Watson had to make a decision: which one to chase? Two headed to the front of the building and the third vaulted the wall at the rear. He decided to follow him. The officer also leapt over the wall and continued to chase his suspect into an adjacent field.

A severe struggle then took place between Constable Watson and the suspect resulting in quite a bit of shouting. The officer also drew his baton and landed several blows on the suspect. This noise was heard by a local resident, who went to investigate. On looking into the field, he could see the two men struggling and then recognised Constable Watson. He immediately went to his assistance and both managed to subdue the suspect. Thankfully there are members of the public that will happily provide assistance to the police when required.

Together they removed him to the nearby Cleland Police station, where he was locked up.

Constable Watson had a significant injury to his face, including cuts and bruises. The suspect had also tried to gouge his eye, causing considerable pain and inflammation. The officer had to attend hospital on an ongoing basis for treatment, for a considerable time. This was once of the hazards of the job and something that is not highlighted enough. Police officers put their lives and safety on the line on a daily basis with very little recognition!

Assistance arrived at the police office and the Co-op was checked. Constable Watson had disturbed the men as they were dragging the safe, containing a considerable amount of money, to the middle of the floor. The lock of the safe had been packed with explosives wrapped in mince, ready to be detonated. Constable Watson's intervention had prevented the safe being accessed.

A search of the area for the other suspects proved negative.

The suspect in custody was Robert Wilson, thirty-two years of age from Glasgow. He was charged with the Housebreaking at the Co-op and assaulting Constable Watson. He pled guilty to the charges at Hamilton Sheriff Court and was remitted to the High Court for sentencing, due to his seven previous convictions for similar crimes.

On Friday the 1st of September 1961 Wilson appeared at the High Court in Edinburgh in front of Lord Mackintosh. His Lordship highly commended Constable Watson for his bravery and tenacity in tackling the accused and despite serious injuries, subduing the accused and taking him into custody. His Lordship clearly understood the bravery of Constable Watson and wanted to make a public comment on this.

His defence asked for leniency as the accused had a young family and he was the sole bread winner for the family.

Turning to the accused, Lord Mackintosh told him to stand and described him as a dangerous and despicable character. He said that his criminal history spoke for itself, and he should have thought about what consequences his actions would have on his family, prior to embarking on his criminal adventure. His Lordship said that he had no option other than to sentence him to four years imprisonment, a significant and appropriate sentence in the circumstances.

Chapter 38:

STOP THAT BUS

The theft of vehicles was and still is one of the most popular crimes. Ever since the introduction of mechanically propelled vehicles, there has been an insatiable desire on the part of criminals to steal them. It is not only high specification motor cars that attract the thief and anything on wheels is fair game!

In the early hours of Sunday the 2nd of August 1969, Constables Delmer Bowman and David Meikle of Lanarkshire Constabulary, were on patrol in their police minivan. Constable Bowman was driving.

Whilst driving near to Craigneuk the officers saw an Eastern Scottish bus travelling toward Wishaw Town Centre. The bus did not have its interior lights on, which was unusual as they were required to have them on during the hours of darkness. The other strange thing was that the destination on the front of the bus was Airdrie Cross, which is not exactly in the vicinity of Wishaw.

The officers followed the bus through the town onto Stewarton Street, near to the police office. The bus had come to a stop at traffic lights and when these changed to green, Constable Bowman overtook it with the blue roof light on the police vehicle flashing.

Constable Meikle also waved his torch at the driver indicating for him to stop.

The driver did stop and Constable Bowman stopped his vehicle. The officers got out and walked toward the bus, however, the driver decided that he was not hanging about. He put the bus in gear and drove past the officers, turning into McAlpine Street, which unfortunately for him was a cul-de-sac.

The officers ran back to their van and followed the bus. On turning into McAlpine Street they could see that it was stopped on some waste ground. Constable Bowman stopped the van close to the kerb at the side entrance to Stewarton House.

Constable Bowman ran to the driver's cab and tried to pull the driver from his seat, however, he had other ideas and began to drive the bus once again. Constables Bowman and Meikle ran to the front of the bus and shone their torches at the driver to try and get him to stop but he continued toward them. Both had to jump out of the way to avoid being struck.

It was clear that the vehicle was now out of control and it careered on toward the side entrance of Stewarton House. Unfortunately for Constables Bowman and Meikle their police van was in its path and was basically wiped out by the bus, which finally came to a halt, pushing the police van through a wall. No doubt the first thing that went through the officers' thoughts was the amount of paperwork that this would now involve!

Constables Bowman and Meikle rushed to the driver's cab and wrestled the driver to the ground, securing their arrest. He was taken to Wishaw police station where he identified himself as Jeramiah Ferguson Jnr. from Airdrie.

Enquiries later revealed that Ferguson was formerly employed by Western SMT as a mechanic at their Stewarton Street depot in Wishaw. He admitted stealing the bus from the Connor Street depot in Airdrie with the intention of taking it to the Stewarton Street depot.

He said that he knew he was caught when he saw the police van with its flashing light and thought it safer to stop on McAlpine Street rather than stop on Stewarton Street. A rather fanciful tale I suspect!

Ferguson was charged with the theft of the bus, other Road Traffic offences and Assault to the endangerment of life, an Attempted Murder charge having been dropped at an earlier date.

He appeared from custody at Hamilton Sheriff & Jury Court on Wednesday the 5th of November, maintaining a 'Not Guilty' plea. The trial took place with all the police and other witnesses. The accused maintained his original story.

The jury retired for fifty minutes, returning with a guilty verdict on the Theft of the Bus and Road Traffic charges and 'Not Proven' on the assault to endangerment of life charge. That, unfortunately, is the difficulty with jury trials.

Sheriff Nigel Thomson was clearly siding with the prosecution evidence. He sentenced Ferguson to eighteen months imprisonment and banned him from driving for life.

Constables Bowman and Meikle were also left with a considerable amount of paperwork regarding their unfortunate police van!

Ferguson was well known to the police in Airdrie. He was brought up in the Gartlea area and had a liking for vehicles, generally someone else's! He was later heavily involved in Frauds and eventually moved from the area to West Lothian, living in Bathgate. He died in 2020 at the age of seventy.

PART FIVE:

BREACH OF THE PEACE

Another common crime for the police to investigate is Breach of the Peace, where people conduct themselves in a disorderly manner, generally involving shouting and swearing. On most occasions a Breach of the Peace is the result of the consumption of too much alcohol.

However, a Breach of the Peace can really cover any eventuality.

Chapter 39:

THE RETURN OF MARJORIE

Some people find themselves on the wrong side of the law on a regular basis. The majority of these people are generally involved in very minor crime however they do clog up the court system and take precious time away from the more serious business of the courts. However, some of these individuals and cases can be quite amusing and lighthearted.

On Monday the 4th of March 1907, at Wishaw Burgh Police Court, Marjorie Stewart or Craig, of Carfin Road, Craigneuk, made her usual appearance in front of the bench. Marjorie was a regular who generally brought a bit of colour to the proceedings, always pleading guilty to her Drunk & Incapable or Breach of the Peace charge.

Her charge this time was that having been drunk, behaved in a riotous and disorderly manner and committed a Breach of the Peace. This was her fortieth appearance!

You can imagine the surprise when she was called before the bench and asked how she wished to plead. The Judge, expecting the usually witty and light-hearted response from Marjorie, was stunned when he heard the words 'Not Guilty,' escape from her lips!

The court went into an uproar and as word spread, it began to fill with spectators eager to hear Marjorie's case.

The witnesses were made aware and told to be prepared to give their evidence. There were five witnesses, Sergeant Ross, Constables Watson and Arthur and Marjorie's husband and daughter.

The body of the court was bulging with expectation!

Sergeant Ross was called and entered the witness box. Marjorie could be seen smacking her lips as she eyed the Sergeant from head to foot.

When Sergeant Ross was asked if he knew the accused, he replied 'Oh yes, I know her very well'. He then went on to explain the circumstances. Between ten and eleven o'clock on Saturday the 2nd of March, he saw a disturbance on Carfin Road caused by Marjorie. She went inside her house and could be heard shouting and screaming. The next thing, everyone in the house was thrown out, including her husband, who appeared to be the subject of her abuse. She then barred the door preventing anyone returning. It would appear that the disturbance was regarding a shilling that her husband had alleged she stole from him.

Marjorie jumped to her feet, interrupting the Sergeant trying to tell her side of the story. The audience were loving it as a ripple of laughter spread through the court. She went at it 'hammer and tongs,' shouting that she wanted 'justice and fair play,' crying out that she was the real victim of a conspiracy between the police, her husband and daughter.

She again belted out, 'Where did I break three panes of glass?' This puzzled the court as no- one had mentioned glass being broken. The Sergeant interrupted her, stating, 'Perhaps you are thinking of the windows you broke in the house last year?' A further bout of laughter broke out.

Baillie Nimmo warned the audience to maintain order and Marjorie to stop interrupting. Sergeant Ross finished his evidence and left the box, the glare of Marjorie following him all the way out of the courtroom, which then turned to Constable Watson as he entered the witness box.

She shouted, 'Oh, he's a bonnie man,' as he prepared to take the oath. This caused tremendous hilarity and some embarrassment to Constable Watson, causing him to blush and laugh, with Marjorie continuing by saying, 'Don't blush, you are bonnie.'

Constable Watson corroborated Sergeant Ross adding that when he got into the house, he found Marjorie hiding under the bed. She shouted, 'And did you see him?' she indicated towards her husband, and continued, 'Kick me when I came out from the bed?'. Constable Watson stated that he did not see this happen and she again shouted, 'Ye know yer lying.'

The clerk of the court, Mr Jack, called to Marjorie, 'wheesht, wheesht,' and to stop her evil tongue, as she called out some profanities.

The witnesses changed over with Constable Arthur following Constable Watson, dealing with the same interruptions and colourful language from Marjorie during his time on the stand.

With the police evidence over, the Fiscal called Marjorie's husband, William Craig. She shouted, 'Aye, that's just the man to call.'

Her husband entered to the court with evil stares from Marjorie as she called out, 'Did ye get yer shillin', did ye?'

'No,' he replied, as Marjorie once again set off on a bout of anger and swearing – that she had done nothing wrong and that she was a good wife. How could he stand there accusing her when she once saved him from falling into the fire when drunk?

'You should be ashamed of yourself,' she cried, calling him some very choice names. Baillie Nimmo once again had to intervene to bring peace to the court. Mr Craig was told to leave the witness box having given little evidence. As he walked past the dock, Marjorie spat at him, having to be restrained by the court officer.

The next witness was her seventeen-year-old daughter, Jeanie. She was a pitiful character, dressed in rags. Her appearance enraged Marjorie as she leapt from the dock, striking out at her with her fists, landing several blows. Once again, the weary court officer had to drag her back into the dock.

Jeanie stuck her tongue out at her mother which sent her off once again. The sight of all of this in the court room must have caused great amusement for the onlookers with laughter rippling around the room.

The Judge called for calm as the court erupted, bringing a halt to proceedings for several minutes.

Jeanie then began to give her evidence. She had hardly uttered a word when Marjorie called out at the top of her voice, 'She is nothing but her father's fancy wife.' As you can imagine this brought gasps from the members of the public who had rarely heard such accusations or language in a courtroom.

The Fiscal warned Marjorie that she was heading for the jail if she continued like this. Marjorie's reply was not of the nature that could be repeated.

The trial now finished, thankfully, Baillie Nimmo turned to Marjorie, shaking his head, telling her that he had never experienced anything like it in all his years on the bench. He passed sentence of thirty days imprisonment.

Marjorie burst out laughing, saying, 'Whit, why dae ye no gie me sixty, I can get half a crown when I get oot.' By this she referred to the fact that prisoners were allowed half a penny for every day they were in prison, payable on their release.

The court officer and a colleague carried her from the dock, like a woman possessed, and escorted her to the cells to start her sentence. It must have been like a scene from a comedy show.

Peace and quiet once more descended on the court. Until of course, her next appearance, of which there were many. In one year alone she spent one-hundred-and-eleven days in prison.

Her appearances did slow down as she got older; however, she did add colour to the court up until the mid-1920's.

In July 1933, Marjorie fell, under the influence of alcohol, from the upper storey window of her house in East Hamilton Street, Wishaw. She was taken to Glasgow Royal Infirmary, where she sadly died from her injuries a few days later. She was seventy-one-years-old.

I have no doubt that Marjorie's death would have been received with some sadness, as police officers and those that work in the courts do strike up a strange sort of relationship during their years of interaction. Her demise was indeed sad and is a common tale of a wasted life.

Chapter 40:

UNRULY SALVATIONISTS

Public protest and demonstrations have been a significant problem for the police for many years and indeed continue to be so. The police have to be seen to police these situations fairly and impartially. In Lanarkshire, religion is one of the most common sources of protest and demonstration, however the following story is quite an unusual and controversial one.

One of the most regrettable incidents in the history of Motherwell was the passing in 1907 of a byelaw prohibiting public meetings in the streets, owing to a complaint from some of the residents at the Cross.

On a Sunday afternoon in the autumn of 1907, an army marched on the home of Motherwell's provost. Looking out of the window, Provost William Purdie and his wife Agnes would have seen a crowd with a mix of uniformed officers and evangelicals, many with the letter 'S' pinned to their chests. They were angry, and they wanted action.

However, this was not an uprising. These were the members of the Salvation Army. They had come to seek Purdie's help in freeing some of their members from jail. It was a scene from a troubled autumn that divided the feelings of the public and a tale of religious fever, institutional conflict, and central to it all, municipal traffic congestion.

During this time, Motherwell Cross was a popular location for religious meetings on Sundays. Outdoor preaching had been a part of the evangelical revivals in Scotland for centuries and had been occurring in Motherwell since at least the 1890s.

The main intersection, with its central location and heavy foot traffic, offered an ideal spot for such meetings and several churches and religious organisations met there on the weekends. This included the Salvation Army, which at the time of the controversy, had been preaching there for almost a decade.

By 1907, the Cross was becoming crowded. On Sundays, the collected congregations could number as many as five-hundred people and these crowds completely blocked the pavements and the roads. Vehicles would have to be guided slowly through the mass of people if they could get through at all. Along with this, meetings, debates, prayers, sermons, and religious music could go on from 2 p.m. to 11 p.m. The noise bothered many of the residents of the Cross, for whom Sunday was their only day at home. After receiving several complaints, the local police turned to the town magistrates for assistance. They issued a decree that no more meetings could be held on main streets starting on the 1st of July 1907. At first, this seemed to be the end of it.

The other congregations moved to smaller streets or indoor venues and the Salvation Army branches of Motherwell and Glasgow agreed to move as well. But the London head office of the Salvation Army was incensed. Salvationist preaching had received push-back in other parts of the country, and so they told the Motherwell branch to stand its ground as a matter of principle. Ironically, in 1906, less than a year before these events, General Booth, the founder of the Salvation Army, was welcomed in the town by the local council and wished every success in his work.

So, as July 1st came and went, the Sunday crowds at the cross remained. When police tried to intervene, they were pelted with stones and pennies (meant for the collection basket.) The police took several names and at a trial held later in the Lesser Town Hall, which lasted from 10 a.m. till 10 p.m. twelve were convicted and sentenced to three days' imprisonment or a fine of 7s 6d.

The following Sunday the crowd was even greater, and the same procedure was adopted by the authorities, with thirteen persons being arrested and sentenced to seven days' imprisonment or a fine of 10s. The fines were paid.

On the 21st of July 1907, Motherwell locals and Salvation Army officers, Maggie Bell, Flora Harrison, and George Martin were charged with defying the order of the magistrates. They were ordered to appear in court that Friday, the 26th, and found guilty by Bailie William MacNeill. They were given a choice: to pay a fine of 2 shillings sixpence or face twenty-four hours of jail time. They chose the latter and were sent to Glasgow that evening for their imprisonment. In the end, however, they did not have to serve a full twenty-four hours and were released at eight o'clock the following morning.

Although this incarceration was short, the Salvation Army played it to full effect. When the three detainees arrived back in Motherwell, they were driven from the train station into town accompanied by a large crowd and two brass bands. They were dressed in imitation prison uniforms and waved from under a banner which read, 'Released from Prison after imprisonment for preaching the Gospel at Motherwell.'

Evidently, they were not welcomed by everyone. At the meeting that evening, as Colonel Byers recounted their twenty-four-hour ordeal, the voice of at least one annoyed local could be heard yelling over the cheers, 'Not long enough!'

Instead of calming down, things were escalating with the situation continuing throughout August and up to November. On one occasion police officers were chased along the street for about five-hundred-yards pinning them against railings and some public-spirited individuals assisted them to fight off the crowd. One young lad giving a Detective a stick, which was used to good effect. However, the young man was then chased home and besieged by a mob of angry Salvationists, and he too had to be rescued.

Ultimately, after months of seemingly never-ending protests and disruption, the order was withdrawn, and meetings could be held, subject to the jurisdiction of the police and limits on the numbers preaching and attending.

Overall, the public were divided on the issue of the Salvationists and debates raged in the local newspapers. Some disagreed with the Salvation Army's approaches. They felt that the gatherings were too boisterous, too disruptive, and too antagonistic. Meanwhile, others felt that these congregations in the street were a good thing for the town. The messages against smoking, drinking, and gambling were wholesome, and the meetings were considered preferable to young people causing trouble elsewhere in town.

Thankfully, by December, the controversy over the meetings at the Cross began to ease which was partly due to the inclement winter weather, increasingly moving the faithful indoors. The Town Council also began to arrange with religious bodies to allow for shorter meetings that would not take up the entire weekend. Though there would be occasional flare ups over the coming years, the drama had largely run its course. Yet, it was not forgotten by the locals.

For at least three decades afterward, 1907 was referenced in the newspapers simply as the 'troubled period.'

Lanarkshire has historically been a melting pot of religious unrest; however, it is usually between Catholics and Protestants. It was surprising to learn that the Salvation Army was involved in situations such as this, although those involved were sticking to the principle of free speech and the right to gather for religious purposes and were prepared to put their liberty on the line to do so.

I am sure the local police would have been quite happy to see those particular protests disappear!

Chapter 41:

TRAGEDY AT THE OLD CROSS

James and Agnes Mallin were a married couple who lived in the Thrashbush Poor House, also known as the New Monkland Poor House, located at Commonhead in Airdrie.

The poorhouse was a place for the desperate, providing free medical and other care for the very poor who couldn't support themselves. The conditions were harsh and when inmates were admitted they had to have a bath, (for some, probably the first bath they had ever experienced) all of their clothing was removed from them, and they were issued with a uniform. Husbands, wives and children were separated and could be punished for talking to one another. Inmates followed a prescribed daily routine with the able bodied put to work, although not compulsory, with women doing domestic jobs, such as cleaning, working in the kitchen or laundry, while men were allocated more physical jobs.

Both were local to the area. James was born around 1871 at Arden in Plains. His family were of Irish descent and his father worked in the local coal mines. At the age of eight, James was also working in the mines where he had an unfortunate accident when he was about nine-years-old, resulting in the loss of one of his legs, which meant he was only able to walk with the aid of a crutch.

However, James continued to work in the coal mines until the introduction of the Workmen's Compensation Act of 1906 which placed stringent restrictions on employers. From then he obtained casual work above the mines and at local Tube Works, continuing to live with his parents at Arden until they passed.

Just prior to the accident he had been caught by the local police, together with a group of other boys, breaking into the offices of the 'Barblues' Coal Pit and damaging a bell. They were found guilty at the Airdrie Police Court and sentenced to '8 stripes of the birch rod'. Birching was a form of corporal punishment with a birch rod, typically applied to the recipient's bare buttocks, although occasionally to the back and/or shoulders.

After the death of his parents, James fell on challenging times and had to depend on lodgings at the New Monkland Poor House in Airdrie for accommodation. Whilst there, James met Agnes Torley, also a native of Airdrie. Agnes was a regular at the Poor House, having been admitted there on numerous occasions. The two struck up a relationship and on the 5th of March 1918, they married at St. Lukes Church in Glasgow.

Both remained at the Poor House and unfortunately Agnes had a bit of a drink problem. She was a regular in the Burgh Police cells for being Drunk and Incapable and committing Breaches of the Peace. Notably, James was also partial to a drink but not to the extent of Agnes which obviously created problems in the relationship and regular arguments, however, James remained faithful to her. In fact, both were well known to the local police for drinking and causing disturbances; however, it would appear that Agnes was the most prolific of the pair. No doubt they would have been on first name terms with quite a few of the officers, as is normally the case.

Over time, James had managed to find employment as a watchman/timekeeper at the local Tube Works, but the wages were not sufficient to maintain a rent on property or adequately support both. Fortunately, in August 1923, Agnes got some good news from her sister in Glasgow. There was the possibility of work for both and her sister agreed that they could stay with her until they found somewhere to live together. It was agreed that they would go to Glasgow and hopefully their luck would change.

On the morning of Saturday the 4th of August 1923, Agnes decided to go to the local pawn shop in Airdrie to recover some clothing that she had earlier pawned while James said that he would collect 7 shillings and 6d from the Insurance offices in Coatbridge. They arranged to meet at Coatbridge fountain in the late morning and both went their separate ways. Just before 11 a.m. James walked to the 'Whitelaw Fountain' at the junction of Main Street and Sunnyside Road. As he approached, he saw Agnes, in quite a drunken state and as he got closer, she began to shout and swear at him, causing quite a scene with passers-by.

To avoid any further embarrassment, James walked away from her onto Bank Street and toward Langloan. He walked for a couple of hours and eventually decided to return to Airdrie. He jumped onto a Tramcar which then travelled toward Coatbridge town centre. As the tram was passing the 'Whitelaw Fountain,' he saw that Agnes was still there, in an even worse state than earlier. Clearly the pawn money had been well and truly spent! He decided to keep out of her way, and she would go to her sister's in Glasgow.

At about eight o'clock that evening, James was standing with some other men at the Old Town Cross at High Street in Airdrie. His heart sank when he saw Agnes walking toward him, shouting and swearing at him, causing him great embarrassment. Once again, he walked away to avoid any further abuse. He returned to the Old Cross at about 10 p.m. where the Salvation Army Band regularly played at their meeting. To his dismay, Agnes was still there and creating quite a scene. When she saw James, she immediately turned her attention to him, giving him quite a tongue lashing.

Having been subjected to the abuse at various times of the day, James's temper gave way. He walked over to Agnes and punched her face, knocking her backward with some force. Such was the blow that she fell immediately to the ground, striking her head on the pavement.

Death was instantaneous as a blood vessel burst and caused severe compression on her brain.

People in the crowd ran to her and gathered around her lifeless body. Exclamations were made that she was dead. When James heard this, he became extremely distressed and began wailing and pushing through the people to see Agnes. He had to be held back by several members of the crowd.

The Burgh Police officers, who were nearby attended to Agnes and called the ambulance wagon. A local Doctor pronounced her dead shortly after.

James was arrested and taken to the Anderson Street Police Station where he was charged with the murder of Agnes.

Following local court appearances, James was remanded in custody and on Saturday the 8th of September 1923, he appeared at a pleading diet at the High Court in Glasgow. He immediately tendered a plea of guilty to a charge of Culpable Homicide, via his solicitor, Mr David Linning. The Advocate Depute explained the background to the case and the tragic history of the accused and his wife, stating that James Mallin had nine previous convictions for Breach of the Peace.

The circumstances were endorsed by Mr Linning who further explained the distress of his client and great regret at what he had done as could be seen by his appearance, the circumstances had an impact on his health. Linning also noted that Mrs Mallin had eighteen previous convictions for Breach of the Peace and Drunk & Incapable.

His Lordship listened to both and agreed that these were indeed tragic circumstances, nonetheless, a death had occurred and the only option available was a custodial sentence. He imposed twelve months imprisonment on Mallin. The judge showed great care in his decision, realising the unfortunate background to the case, which was not very common in those days.

James Mallin served his sentence and returned to Plains where he eventually settled at Jarvie Avenue. He worked latterly as a watchman at roadworks in the area until he died at home on the 2nd of May 1937 at the age of sixty-four. He never re-married.

Accidents, similar to the one that befell James, were commonplace in that era. Too often people just gave up and fell into alcoholism or criminality. James was of a stronger disposition, trying to maintain his self-respect and look after himself as best he could.

Chapter 42:

IF IN DOUBT...

As we previously mentioned, a Breach of the Peace charge can and did cover most eventualities. The old saying was, 'If in doubt, charge them with a Breach...'. It can involve some strange behaviour and indeed, on occasions there may not be anything said at all and merely the behaviour of an individual is sufficient to cause fear and alarm.

Early on the morning of Thursday the 7th of March 1940, Isabella Bow was working in the back store of her confectioner shop in Main Street, Kilsyth. She heard the shop doorbell ring and went out to the counter to see who was there.

On entering the front shop, she saw a man standing, just inside the entrance door. No-one else was in the shop. He stood there, just staring at her in total silence. He stood for about thirty seconds, turned and left the shop. She recognised him as a local man called George Shaw.

Thinking no more of it, she went back to where she had been working in the back store.

About ten minutes later, the shop doorbell rang again. Isabella went out to the counter and there, standing just inside the door, in total silence, was George Shaw. She asked what he wanted. He stared straight ahead and not a word was said. After a few seconds, he again turned and walked out.

Isabella stood, shaking her head and then returned to her work.

Another twenty minutes or so passed and the again doorbell rang. Out she went to the front shop and there, once again was George Shaw. Standing rigidly still, straight faced and in total silence. Isabella asked what he wanted and why he kept coming into the shop to which he gave no response, instead turning, walking out the front door.

The exact same thing happened a further three times in the space of the following two hours. George Shaw entering the shop, standing in complete silence for a short period of time before leaving the shop.

Isabella was becoming quite concerned by this behaviour and was quite upset. She called the police and an officer attended, noting her statement. It was clear that she was upset and she closed the shop for the day. *Why did she take so long to report this? Was it because she knew him and didn't want him to get into trouble?*

The officers, having been given the name of George Shaw, quickly traced him to his home address at Courthill Crescent, Kilsyth. He was arrested and taken to the police station. The interviewing officers experienced the same behaviour, he sat staring ahead, only to answer questions about his personal particulars, stating that he was thirty-one years of age and employed as a labourer. This is not an uncommon occurrence in interviews, although nowadays it is usually after they have consulted a lawyer!

The officers charged him with a Breach of the Peace by standing in the shop, without speaking to the alarm and annoyance of Ms. Bow.

He was kept in custody, as it was feared he would continue this behaviour, if released.

He appeared from custody on Monday the 18th of March 1940 at Kilsyth Police Court. He stood in the dock, in silence, only nodding in response to questions about his name and address. He admitted the charge by once again nodding his head.

The Judge asked if he would promise to refrain from this behaviour to which he agreed, of course, by nodding his head.

His sentence was then deferred for six months, and he was liberated.

Fortunately, his behaviour ceased, and he does not appear to have come to the attention of the police after this event.

Why did he behave like this? It was never explained, however, Isabella Bow was described in the newspapers as 'The pretty, blue eyed, blonde shopkeeper.' Perhaps he was infatuated by her, having seen her previously in the shop and surrounding area?

It may be purely coincidence, however, several indecent assaults on females were reported in the month of April 1940, in and around the Donaldson Avenue area of Barrwood in Kilsyth, during Black-out hours. George Shaw lived in Courthill Crescent, also in Barwood and only a short distance from these attacks.

No one was ever arrested for the attacks!

Chapter 43:

NEVER 'TIP' THE WAITRESS

Alcohol, crime and Breach of the Peace, go hand in hand. Disorderly and violent behaviour, fueled by alcohol is probably one of the most common situations that a police officer will encounter.

Saturday the 3rd of September 1955 was a busy night in 'Picozzi's' Fish Restaurant at 118- 120 Bank Street, Coatbridge, with customers enjoying their early evening supper.

Isabella and Michael Picozzi were working away behind the counter and their waitress was busy serving the meals.

One lady, Mrs Owens, on finishing her meal, spoke politely to the waitress as she collected the dishes. Mrs Owens then handed her some coins as a tip for her good service. At this, one of the customers sitting opposite Mrs Owens, called Edward Gallacher, commented out of the blue, saying, 'You shouldn't have done that, it's a stupid thing to do.'

Mrs Owens tried to ignore him as she got up from her seat and started to put her coat on. Gallacher also stood up and walked the few paces over to her. He repeated what he had said and for no reason grabbed Mrs Owens around the throat with both his hands and began to shake her violently.

Mrs Owens began to scream, clearly in a very distressed state, as she tried to release Gallacher's grip. Mrs Picozzi ran from behind the serving counter, shouting at Gallacher to leave the lady alone. This had no impact whatsoever.

Mrs Picozzi then pulled at Gallacher's arms to release his grip on Mrs Owens. This resulted in him releasing Mrs Owens, who fell to the floor, crying. Gallacher then grabbed a metal fork, holding it in his hand like a dagger and lashed out at Mrs Picozzi, striking her on the arm, causing a three-inch laceration, which bled heavily.

On seeing this, Michael Picozzi telephoned the police. The call was relayed to the police box at Coatbridge Fountain, which was answered by Constables Bob Clare and Alex Watchman.

Michael also tried to help Mrs Picozzi and he, too, earned a punch in the face for his efforts.

At this point several male customers, incensed by what they were seeing, decided to intervene and made for Gallacher, who tried to make a run for the door. He was stopped and pulled back inside, where the other customers began to administer some summary justice. No doubt these people were regular customers in the café and had some form of loyalty to the owners and didn't like their supper being interrupted in this way.

Fortunately for Gallacher, Constables Clare and Watchman, were on the scene very quickly. As they entered the shop, they could see Gallacher struggling on the floor under a group of men. The officers pulled the good citizens away from Gallacher and placed him under arrest. By this time, he was bleeding from his nose and mouth. Gallacher continued to struggle with the officers as he was removed from the shop.

Gallacher was described as going 'berserk' by this point and began kicking out at both officers, striking them on the legs. They succeeded in eventually getting him into a police van and off to Coatbridge Police Station, where he was placed into the cells.

Gallacher's doctor had to be called to administer some medical treatment to his nose and ribs. He was eventually charged with:

- *Assaulting Isabella Owens by seizing her by the throat and shaking her violently*

- *Assaulting the proprietress, Isabella Picozzi, by striking her on the arm with a fork*

- *Assaulting Michael Picozzi by striking him on the face with his fist*

- *Assaulting Constables Clare and Watchman by kicking them on the legs*

- *Maliciously breaking three plates and a saucer*

- *Conducting himself in a disorderly manner, shouting, swearing and using obscene language thereby committing a Breach of the Peace*

Mrs Picozzi required stitches in her arm, however, Mrs Owens and Michael Picozzi did not require any treatment.

On Monday the 5th of September, Gallacher appeared from custody at

Airdrie Sheriff Court, pleading guilty to all the charges.

Mr James Farrell, the Procurator Fiscal, explained the circumstances in graphic detail. He informed the Court that Gallacher had thirteen previous convictions for violence and Breach of the Peace.

Gallacher's solicitor did not have much to say other than, 'My client has rather an indistinct recollection of the events which took place on Saturday, as he had been drinking all day.

Apparently, he loses control of himself when he is in that condition.' Gallacher was sentenced to three months imprisonment.

Although this sentence was appropriate, it was not always the case. When comparing similar cases, it is clear that there was and still is no consistency with regard to sentencing, which does not send a very good message to those involved in this sort of behaviour.

With regard to Edward Gallacher, I wonder if he was ever welcome at the restaurant again?

PART SIX:

ASSAULT

One of the aspects that is totally missed by politicians, courts and the general public, is that a police officer leaves home not knowing what the day will entail or what dangers they may encounter. In contrast, the armed forces know that if deployed to danger or war zones then they will likely be involved in some sort of conflict. A police officer never knows what is ahead of them as they leave home and their loved ones. Every day, every call, every situation, every corner turned is different and has all sorts of dangers possibly lying in wait.

Chapter 44:

DANGERS OF THE JOB

To the general public, police officers must remain outwardly cool and calm whilst inside their stomach is churning as they try to think of their best course of action, making split second decisions, that will be poured over and scrutinised by senior officers or perhaps lawyers at a later court case.

Over 100 years ago things were no different, in fact police officers then did not have the technology and equipment, such as radios and officer safety equipment, available to their current counterparts.

In the early hours of Thursday the 18th of July 1895, Constable George Donald was on the beat on Main Street, Coatbridge. It was a quiet summer's evening and the streets were clear.

There had been a recent General Election which had caused quite a stir between the Unionists and the Irish community in Coatbridge, resulting in quite a few arrests following disturbances in the town and the police not the most popular people with some of the locals.

Constable Donald was checking the property on his beat and had just finished checking the Theatre Royal on Main Street. He travelled toward Jackson Street to check a Public House on the junction of Main Street and Jackson Street. As mentioned earlier, police officers had to check the property on their beat and would generally do that on their own, in the cold and dark of winter. Quite an adrenaline filled experience when you hear an unexpected noise, voices or indeed rats running over your boots in a darkened alley or close. He walked to the rear of the premises to make sure all was in order and having done so, walked to the junction, where he stood for a few minutes.

As he was looking around the buildings and works around him, he heard a scuffling noise from behind. Curious, he turned to see what was causing the noise when pain throbbed in the left side of his chest. He was swarmed by a group of men, kicking and punching. Constable Donald was violently forced to the ground, constantly beaten. Unable to call for assistance or fight back, he succumbed to the beating rather than taking drastic actions.

The men only ran off when Constable Donald lost consciousness, leaving him lying on the ground bloody and bruised.

It was some twenty minutes later when another officer on patrol nearby, found Constable Donald still on the ground unconscious. He ran to his colleague and noticed that the left side of his tunic was wet. He put his hand onto the tunic and on pulling it away could see that there was blood on his hand.

He opened Donald's tunic, revealing a gushing stab wound, and immediately called assistance by blasting on his police whistle. Other officers quickly arrived and the ambulance wagon was called. Constable Donald had to be rushed to the Glasgow Royal Infirmary.

He spent several days in hospital. He had a significant stab wound to the left of his chest, hidden behind old and fresh blood, which concerned the Doctors. However, once they managed to clean the wound, they were able to ascertain its depth and stitch it. Meanwhile the police made enquiries in the local area and very quickly three names were provided to them. All three lived locally and were known to the police as all had been arrested during the recent disturbances. The three were traced and arrested.

On Wednesday the 24th of July, the three made an appearance at Airdrie Sheriff Court. They pled 'Not Guilty' and were remanded in custody. They were Hugh Cook of Jackson Street, Hugh Mulraney of Jackson Street and John McAuley of Coats Street.

Unfortunately, Constable Donald was unable to identify his attackers, due to the suddenness of the attack. However, when interviewed later, one of the men, Hugh Cook, admitted to stabbing the officer because he had wrongly thought that Constable Donald was responsible for arresting him during the recent disturbances and he wanted to seek revenge. Hugh realised he had got the wrong man when he saw the officer's name in the local papers.

Mulraney and McAuley were released from custody with Cook remaining on remand.

Hugh Cook appeared at the High Court in Glasgow on Thursday the 29th of August 1895 on a charge of Attempted Murder and gave his occupation as an Iron Worker. He pled guilty and was sentenced to six months imprisonment.

As we have seen so often, the punishment for the attempt on the life of a police officer is given little recognition by the courts. Six months for such a savage attack and leaving the officer unconscious on the ground is quite ridiculous.

The day-to-day activities of a police officer can be very dangerous indeed and as mentioned, not everyone fully appreciates just how often they encounter danger of all sorts. If lawyers, judges and others walked in the footsteps of police officers, only for a short time, they may just appreciate the abuse and violence that is directed toward them, rather than looking back from the comfort of an office or court room on a situation that they cannot fully comprehend.

Chapter 45:

A SHOCKING ATTACK

There are many cases where a broken relationship has been the cause of criminal behaviour with jealousy being a driving force. Sometimes this leads to 'stalking' on the part of one of the parties and sometimes it has serious consequences.

On Monday the 22nd of March 1937, Thomas Henderson, an eighteen-year-old warehouse porter of 'Nairoo', 78 Alexander Street, Airdrie, appeared at Airdrie Sheriff Court on a charge of assault to permanent disfigurement. The circumstances of the case and the method of assault were quite shocking.

The victim in the case was Robina Boyd, a seventeen-year-old Surgery Assistant from 5 Woodhall Avenue, Calderbank. She had previously lived at Wattston, near Greengairs, with her mother.

Henderson first met Robina on the 8th of November 1935, they struck up a friendship and began seeing each other on a regular basis, going for walks and to the cinema. They had only been going out on a few occasions when Robina had cause to have words with Henderson regarding his behaviour. It would appear that he made advances toward her which were not reciprocated, and they had an argument. That evening they went their separate ways.

The couple did not have any contact for over a week until they met on South Bridge Street, Airdrie. Henderson apologised for his conduct the previous week and the two made up their differences. They began to see each other again and met regularly on Saturdays and Sundays with the occasional meeting during the week.

It wasn't a perfect relationship, with repeated quarrels and arguments, mostly regarding his behaviour, getting to the point where Robina couldn't take it anymore and broke off their relationship.

They did see each other occasionally, however, it was quite

uncomfortable when they did.

At the beginning of September 1937, Robina had been out in Airdrie and missed the last bus back to Wattston. She met another young man that she knew from the village and the two began walking back to Wattston together.

As they walked, near to Dalmacoulter Farm, Riggend, they met Henderson who was out on his bicycle. Henderson stopped and approached the pair. It was clear that he wasn't happy, shouting and becoming quite violent. He ran toward the young man and punched him in the face.

Robina ran off and Henderson pursued her on his bicycle.

He caught up with her and began to pull at her on the roadside. Fortunately, she was outside one of the few houses in the area and the occupants came out when they heard the shouting. Henderson made off on his cycle and Robina was taken into the house and attended to until she was fit to return home.

The incident was reported to the police and Henderson charged with assault. He was later found guilty at court, however, was admonished by the Justice on the bench.

Over the following months the couple did meet occasionally, however, it always resulted in arguments and eventually, in January 1937, Robina, now living in Calderbank, informed Henderson that she did not wish to see him again. This did not go down too well with him.

Unknown to Robina, Thomas Henderson continued to follow her and watch her from a distance. He was clearly jealous and maybe suspected that she was seeing someone else. Today this would be seen as a serious case of 'stalking,' a term unheard of in those times.

On the 25th of January 1938, she was out in Airdrie with a young man. They were heading toward The Rialto cinema at the bottom of South Bridge Street. Out of nowhere appeared Henderson, he grabbed Robina by the arm, saying, 'Come on, you're going to the pictures with me.' He looked at the other young man, 'You better keep back, or I'll smash you.'

Robina was furious and told Henderson that she was going to report him to the police, which she did. She walked to the Burgh police station on Anderson Street and reported the incident to a police officer.

The Constable walked with Robina to Bank Street where they saw Henderson standing. She pointed him out to the officer, who approached him and warned him that if he did not cease annoying Robina, he would find himself in serious trouble. Henderson was then sent on his way.

The Constable walked with Robina to the Cinema Picture House on Broomknoll Street, where she went in by herself. At the end of the film, she caught the bus for Calderbank at 10 p.m. *No doubt Robina thought that she would be safe now that the police officer had warned Henderson off.*

The bus dropped her at Woodhall Avenue, Calderbank. On getting off, she was surprised to see Henderson standing waiting for her. He walked over and started talking to her, saying that he wanted to start seeing her again and that he was sorry for his behaviour.

Robina tried to make it clear that she wanted nothing more to do with him and it was over. As she began to walk home, he walked with her, making her feel uncomfortable and frightened. She stopped a passer-by, whom she recognised and asked if he would walk with her to the police office as she was afraid of the man following her. The passer-by did not think this appeared to be serious and refused to get involved. She walked on, meeting another two men and again appealed to them to help her. They too, declined to get involved. Notably, the reluctance of people to become involved is not an uncommon occurrence in these situations.

The first man, however, had followed the couple at a distance, to see what was happening, perhaps realising that all was not well?

Robina then quickened her step to get away from Henderson, however, he followed and refused to go away. As she reached the entrance gate to the police station on Main Street, Henderson caught up with her and pulled her by the left shoulder so that she was facing him. Robina caught sight of something in shining his hand, which she thought was a knife. She said something like, 'Don't stab me.' *She possibly realised the seriousness of the situation due to Henderson's persistent behaviour. She also probably and correctly, knew that he could be carrying a weapon.*

Henderson replied, 'Do you think I am going to murder you?' He then made a swift move with his hand and she immediately felt a burning sensation on her face, mouth and chin. She screamed quite loudly and attracted the attention of Constable Corbett inside the police station, who ran outside to ascertain the cause of the screams. He met Robina, who was holding her face, and the passer-by, who explained that he was sure Henderson had assaulted the girl.

Constable Corbett took Robina into the police office and prised her hands from her face. He could see that the skin on her face had been burned by some corrosive substance. Dr Kinstrie, a local doctor, attended

174

to her and she was later taken to Glasgow Royal Infirmary for treatment.

A search of the area was made for Henderson, but he could not be found at that time. At about 12:40 a.m. he was traced to his home address in Airdrie and arrested by Inspector McKenzie and Constable Corbett. He was cautioned and replied, 'I have nothing to say.'

Robina was treated at Glasgow Royal Infirmary by Dr Greer, who found that she had extensive third degree burns to her face, mouth, neck and chin. He stated that although not life threatening, she would be permanently disfigured and require surgery.

Police enquiries revealed that Henderson had been a former pupil of Airdrie Academy. He was interested in the sciences and the teachers at the school took an interest in former pupils and would help them when they could. On the 18th of January, Henderson had attended the school and spoke to the Science Master. He asked if he could be given some acid as he wished to etch some copper. Henderson was given twenty-five cubic centimeters of concentrated nitric acid in a test tube. This is what was thrown into Robina's face.

Henderson appeared at Airdrie Sheriff Court in front of Sheriff D.A. Guild. On receiving the plea of guilty and hearing the prosecution and defence presentations, Guild made the following comment, 'You have pled guilty to one of the most serious forms of assault known in law. I am informed, and it has not been disputed, that you are a person thoroughly familiar, from your chemical knowledge, of the effects upon the human frame, of the implement you employed, namely nitric acid.

For an action of this kind there can be no excuse. Had it not been for the skilled medical attention that this unfortunate girl received, the consequences might have been more infinitely serious. Even as it is, it would appear that they are irreparable, and you are responsible for that.

Had you been a person of more mature years, I would have seriously considered remitting you to the High Court, which could impose a significantly more severe sentence. However, keeping in view what has been said about your youth, I have decided not to take that course, and again keeping in view your youth I will impose a lighter sentence than I would have done if you had been older. I sentence you to twelve months imprisonment.'

I am sure many of you will agree, that an attack of this nature is one of the worst imaginable. The sentence of twelve months was totally inadequate, and, in my opinion, Henderson should have been remitted to

175

the High Court for sentencing.

Very little was said about Robina and the impact on the remainder of her life, in the comments delivered by the Sheriff, which once again emphasises the lack of understanding or appreciation of the impact on ordinary law-abiding people's lives.

Sadly, this continues today.

Chapter 46:

A TERRIFYING FAMILY

Violence is an everyday aspect of life and some people live their lives in a way that violence is at the very core of their being. The violence usually escalates in a manner that brings pain and suffering to innocent people and on many occasions the criminal justice system does not reflect the impact that violent crime has on the community.

Just after 5 p.m. on the evening of Friday the 13th of June 1958, the police emergency telephone system was ringing off the hook.

The residents of Craigneuk in Wishaw were witnessing a full-scale battle on the 'The Green' on Hillcrest Avenue. The area was a large expanse of open ground and was filled with at least a dozen men battling.

This was no skirmish or half-hearted effort, they were in possession of scythe blades, knives, iron bars, large bolts, hammers and other weapons. The blood was flowing and a few of the participants appeared to be suffering serious injuries.

When the police arrived, the battle was still in full swing. Batons drawn they waded in making several arrests, several other participants ran off on seeing the police.

Four men were taken to Law Hospital near Carluke, all four were well known to the local police:

- *William 'Fargo' Walsh of Wingate St.*
- *Joseph King of Stonecraig Street*
- *Robert McLaughlan Jnr. of Laurel Drive*
- *Marcus McLaughlan of Laurel Drive*

Arrested and placed in the cells was Robert McLaughlan Snr.

Of the four taken to Law Hospital, 'Fargo' Walsh was the most serious. He had numerous head wounds and was soon transferred to the Edinburgh Royal Infirmary, where he died on Monday the 16th of June. His cause of death was a fracture to the base of the skull and a brain injury due to intracranial infections. This was now a murder investigation.

Early police enquiries had established that on the evening prior to the fight, a group of men had arrived at the house of the McLaughlans, on Laurel Drive, challenging them to fight. It was said that the background to the incident was religion, Catholic and Protestants, but the actual reason was unknown. The group had been quite drunk and this incident had been purely verbal with considerable shouting and swearing.

On Monday the 16th of June, Robert McLaughlan Snr. and his son Marcus McLaughlan appeared at Hamilton Sheriff Court on a charge of Mobbing & Rioting. They were liberated on a £10 bail undertaking. Quite surprising considering the result of the incident!

On Tuesday the 17th of June four additional accused appeared at Hamilton Sheriff Court:

- *Robert McLaughlan Jnr.*
- *Joseph King*
- *Samuel Walsh*
- *James Gerald Smith*

They too were liberated on a £10 bail undertaking.

Police enquiries took them to South Wales where they traced Thornton McLaughlan who was on National Service with the Royal Artillery. He had fled back to camp following the incident however, several witnesses had named him as being involved. He appeared on Friday the 20th of June and was again liberated on the same undertaking.

The final and eighth accused was eventually arrested and placed before the court on the 28th of June. He was Thomas McLaughlan, again liberated on the same undertaking.

The police investigation failed to identify who struck the fatal blows to 'Fargo' Walsh. As a result, the Procurator Fiscal libelled charges of Culpable Homicide as well as Mobbing and Rioting against the eight accused.

The trial took place at Hamilton Sheriff & Jury Court in January 1959. Once again, it is surprising that the case was not heard in the High Court. The circumstances as described by witnesses, the injuries sustained, weapons used and the fact that a life was lost because of the fight, should surely have seen the case taken to the highest court?

The trial finished on Thursday the 8th of January with the jury retiring for an hour and forty minutes. On their return they delivered the following verdicts:

On both charges:

- *Thomas McLaughlan – a unanimous verdict of guilty*
- *Marcus McLaughlan – a unanimous verdict of guilty*
- *Robert McLaughlan Snr. – a majority verdict of guilty*
- *Robert McLaughlan Jnr. – a majority verdict of guilty*
- *Thornton McLaughlan – a majority verdict of guilty*

Samuel Walsh, Joseph King and James Smith were found 'Not Proven' on all charges.

The five guilty men were remanded in custody and remitted to the High Court for sentencing.

On appearing at the High Court for sentencing the Mr R. King Murray, Advocate Depute, informed the court that all five had extensive previous convictions, numbering more than thirty between them.

He outlined the circumstances of the case to his Lordship who retired to consider the sentences.

When he returned his Lordship sentenced the men as follows:

- *Robert McLaughlan Snr. – three years imprisonment;*
- *Thomas McLaughlan – four years imprisonment;*
- *Marcus McLaughlan – four years imprisonment;*
- *Robert McLaughlan Jnr. – four years imprisonment;*
- *Thornton McLaughlan – two years imprisonment.*

Robert Jnr. was already serving a two-month prison sentence imposed on the 5th of January for another crime. He was informed that his four-year sentence would commence on the expiry of his two-months.

Did this four-year sentence deter the McLaughlan's from further criminal activity? For one of them it most certainly didn't.

On Thursday the 4th of July 1963, Marcus MacLaughlan and William McIlwain, of Alexander Street in Wishaw, were convicted for the vicious attack on a sixty-four-year-old widow on Union Street in Carluke.

She had been visiting friends and was on her way home when she encountered McLaughlan, McIlwain and a third man, James Edment from Carluke. As she crossed the road, she was attacked by the three men. She was punched in the face, kicked on the legs and fell to the ground. One of the men dragged her, face down, across the rough surface of the pavement, causing serious facial injuries. However, she held on tightly to the shopping bag that she was carrying as they tried to force it from her. It contained some shopping and her purse.

So violent they were, that the handles of the shopping bag broke and it was wrenched from her grasp. The three men ran off laughing at the lady still lying, bleeding, on the ground.

They passed a woman out walking her dog, who recognised Edment from the local area. She could also see a man, later identified as Marcus McLaughlan, carrying a bag, later identified as the shopping bag.

What was the total of their haul from this violent assault and robbery? It was £9 8s and 6d plus a pension book. They threw away her messages and the shopping bag.

The police and an Ambulance were called by residents and the lady was taken to Law Hospital. She had serious facial injuries and bruises to her body. She had to be kept in hospital for two weeks as she initially lost her sight, and it was thought that an infection she caught would penetrate her eyes and permanently blind her. Fortunately, this was not the case.

Police enquiries traced Edment who very quickly supplied the names of his accomplices. All were arrested and an identification parade held.

The lady and the woman walking her dog, identified the three accused and they were charged with Assault and Robbery.

Following the trial, at Lanark Sheriff Court, where the lady was once again put through her horrific ordeal, all three were found guilty.

McLaughlan and McIlwain each received fifteen months imprisonment and an additional nine months, to run consecutively, for a separate charge of reset. A very lenient sentence considering the evidence and previous convictions.

Edment, who had no previous convictions, had his sentence deferred for background reports. On the 12th of July he re-appeared at Lanark Sheriff Court, where he was sentenced to three months imprisonment, no doubt his early co-operation with the police went in his favour.

Over a year later, on the 4th of November 1964, Glasgow Rangers played Red Star Belgrade in a preliminary round of the European Champions Clubs Cup at Highbury Park in London.

Some of the travelling support included Marcus McLaughlan, Thornton McLaughlan, Hugh McLaughlan, Robert Marshall, William Wright and William McIlwain all from Wishaw.

They were staying with their relative John McLaughlan in Ealing.

Surprisingly, they did not have tickets and never saw the game. However, that did not stop them celebrating a victory in the pubs around the West End, Highbury and Ealing.

They decided to visit two girls they knew from Wishaw, who were living in the Ealing area at Colebrook Street. They arrived at No. 37 and a party got under way. Several people, living in separate flats in the building all came to the party in the rooms of an Irishman, Michael McLoughlin.

Late into the evening the topic of conversation arrived at religion. Michael McLoughlin, being a Catholic, mentioned something about Rangers result which didn't quite agree with the lads from Wishaw. A large-scale fight then broke out in the flat.

Women ran onto the street, shouting a screaming, whilst the fight raged on. Another local resident called the police and, on their arrival, they were met with carnage, with blood covering the walls and carpet.

Michael McLoughlin was lying in a pool of blood in the flat and had to be removed to Ealing Hospital. He had serious head injuries and nine stab wounds to his body. He was in a terrible state and close to death.

The seven Scotsmen were taken into custody and remitted to the Old Bailey for trial. However, the police investigations could only identify William McIlwain as being responsible for the attack on McLoughlin and none of the witnesses would speak up against the others. McIlwain received a sentence of three and a half years for causing grievous bodily harm. The McLaughlan's and others walked free.

It isn't unusual for people to be 'forgetful' or to look the other way when crimes are being committed. Unfortunately, this leads to guilty people walking free from their charges.

Two days prior to the brawl, on the 2nd of November 1964, a robbery took place at a shop in Leith. The female shop assistant was attacked by two men, one of them placing his hand over her mouth and she was forced to the floor where both assaulted her by punching and kicking her. They robbed her of £41 in cash.

The men were seen to run from the shop by passers-by and jump into a taxi. The men were not arrested immediately and made off from the scene.

Police enquiries traced the taxi journey to an address in Blackburn in West Lothian and there the residents named two men, Marcus McLaughlan and William McIlwain, from Wishaw as being the person who visited them. They occupants knew nothing of the robbery and knew the two men from previous prison sentences.

Enquiries in Wishaw revealed that McLaughlan and McIlwain had travelled to London for the Glasgow Rangers v Red Star Belgrade football match. Clearly, they had decided to get away from the area as they knew the police would be after them!

Fortunately for the Edinburgh Police, their suspects were now in custody in London, following the fight in Ealing.

Officers travelled to London where both were interviewed. Surprisingly, they denied the allegations, admitting they had been in Edinburgh on a day out and had travelled to Blackburn to meet with an old friend.

Unfortunately for them, the girl in the shop, passers-by and the taxi driver had all identified them as being the persons that had come from the shop in Leith at the time of the robbery.

Both were charged and on Monday the 16th of July 1965 appeared at the High Court in Edinburgh for trial. They pled 'Not Guilty,' and all witnesses were duly called to give their evidence, positively identifying both.

The jury retired for a matter of minutes and returned with a unanimous verdict of guilty. The Advocate Depute informed his Lordship that McLaughlan had sixteen previous convictions and McIlwain had twelve, and that he was serving the recent sentence in England.

Lord Cameron made the following remarks, 'You have been convicted on the clearest possible evidence of a brutal assault. You are incorrigible ruffians and I cannot expect that any sentence I pass will have the slightest effect. All I can do is put you out of circulation for a considerable time. I sentence each of you to six years imprisonment.' At least this was a substantial sentence for a vicious and violent attack on a young lady.

The McLaughlan family appear to have been quite a considerable thorn in the side of the authorities and continued to be so for some time.

PART SEVEN:

MURDER

Murder has many aspects and is not just as simple as one person killing another. It can involve things such as jealousy, rage, revenge, pre-meditated, spur of the moment action and religion. Each has to be painstakingly investigated to establish a motive (which is not always present) or background to the murder, any witnesses, the details of the victim, cause of death and other forensic evidence.

A murder investigation takes time, resources and attention to detail. It is also a skill to be able to investigate such crimes taking in to account the legal aspects of an investigation and balancing the rights of the accused and the wider public, which can cause anger in the wider community.

It is desirable to detect these serious crimes quickly and efficiently to build public confidence and on occasions put public fear at rest and allay the possibility of a serial killer being at large, as the media can sometimes sensationalise these cases.

Due to the danger involved in policing, sometimes the victims of murder are police officers themselves, as we will highlight in the following pages.

Chapter 47:

DEADLY MEAL

Although female criminality is relatively common, their involvement in serious crime and as a consequence execution, in the days it was legal, was not.

Between 1800 and 1868, two-hundred-and-seventy-three people were publicly hanged in Scotland, comprising two-hundred-and-fifty-nine men and fourteen women and by comparison between 1869 and 1899, sixteen men and one woman were hanged.

This was mirrored in the 20th century where thirty-four people were hanged, again, only one being a woman. She was from Coatbridge, in Lanarkshire.

The case we describe in this instance is Elizabeth Jeffrey, who was the first woman, in Scotland, to be hanged in the reign of Queen Victoria.

Elizabeth Nicholson or Shafto or Jeffrey stood trial at the High Court in Glasgow on Thursday the 10th of May 1838, on two charges of murder:

- *You the said Elizabeth Nicklson or Shafto or Jeffrey, lately residing at Carluke, are charged with administering on the 4th of October, last, to Ann Newall or Carl residing in Carluke, a quantity of arsenic, which you mixed up with meal and water and whiskey, and which you pretended was a medicine for her benefit and the said Ann Newall or Carl having drank thereof, became violently ill, and died next day in consequence of having swallowed the said mixture.*

- *You are also charged with having on the 28th of October last, administered to Hugh Munro, then labourer or miner at Carluke, and lodging with you, a quantity of arsenic which you had mixed up with porridge and the said Hugh Munro having partaken of the porridge became ill and, continued so the two following days. You are likewise accused of having on the 30th,*

October last, administered to the said Hugh Monro a quantity of arsenic which you had mixed up with rhubarb and the said Hugh Munro died in consequence of having partaken of the same.

Ann Newall or Carl was an elderly lady who did not keep very good health. She lived next door to Jeffrey. Elizabeth Jeffrey had been 'looking after' her and providing her with food and refreshment, at a financial and subsequently greater cost.

On the 4th of October 1837 Jeffrey made Ann Carl something to eat. It was a basic meal of water and some whisky. She helped Ann to eat. Shortly after this meal Ann Carl died. No suspicion fell upon Jeffrey at this time as the deceased was elderly and of poor health.

Hugh Munro was Jeffrey's lodger and a worker who was making good money at the time. Indeed, Jeffrey had borrowed £5 from him which was a considerable sum for that era. There was a problem, however, Jeffrey was unable to pay this money back!

Mr Munro was a highlander, from Skye. He came home on Saturday the 28th of October in good health and good spirits. He was looking forward to a meeting he was to have with his friends in Skye. When he arrived home, he was given some porridge made by Jeffrey.

Very soon afterwards he was seized with dreadful thirst and pain. This continued for two days when on the 30th of October she gave him a mixture of rhubarb. His condition worsened significantly, and he died the following day in extreme agony.

Initially, no-one had been suspicious when Ann Carl had died, however when Hugh Munro died in excruciating agony about four weeks later and was buried by request of Jeffrey (as indeed Carl was also) in a great, hurry, suspicion and local gossip soon began to gather.

The Procurator Fiscal was made aware and enquiries began. Firstly, both bodies were exhumed from their graves, and certain portions of the stomachs extracted for medical examination. A shocking revelation was to be made. The evidence of the two surgeon's at Carluke, as well as from that of two highly experienced chemists in Edinburgh, to whom portions of the matter found in the stomach's has been sent, stated that minute quantities of arsenic, but quite sufficient to cause death, had been discovered in each of the stomachs.

The papers do not give an exact date of Jeffrey's arrest, but it appears to have been several days after the Munro's death, showing that the police handled her case quickly and efficiently.

It was also established that the prisoner had purchased arsenic at two different times by the hands of another person, for the purpose, it was alleged, of killing rats. She had said that her house was infested, although no witnesses could support that claim. None of the neighbours had ever seen a rat about the premises.

These purchases were made immediately preceding the death of Carl and Munro. Add to this that it was proven that the prisoner mixed up the dose for the sick woman Carl herself and the porridge she gave to Mr Munro.

Notably, Jeffrey had been making it known in the town that she had repaid Mr Munro the money she borrowed which came to the police's attention and so they decided to investigate. The motive became clear when Mr Munro's belongings were checked and there was no money to be found. It is not uncommon for people to commit crime, including murder, to avoid repayment of debts, in fact, nowadays such crimes occur to avoid repaying drug debts, etc.

With regard, to the murder of the old woman Carl, the Advocate Deputes theory was, that Jeffrey had tried her hand on her, to discover how much poison it would take to kill the young man. It was also known that houses were very scarce at Carluke, and that Jeffrey wished to make room for a more productive lodger.

The trial ran for a total of 18 hours and the jury ultimately found Jeffrey guilty of both murders. They could not explain why but asked for mercy to be shown. Notably, it was a totally different era and would have created significant coverage which may have earned her some public sympathy. However, I think her preparation for the crime in testing it on the other lady makes it quite clear it was deliberate and not a random act.

His Lordship sentenced her to be executed.

Jeffrey thought she had a reprieve until Thursday the 17th of May, when an answer to an application to the Home Secretary, Lord John Russell, from a group of Quakers and other 'eccentric' individuals in Glasgow, was refused.

Lord Russell commented, 'These characters say it was a mighty piece of unheard-of cruelty to execute BURKE! But we have no patience with them, their mawkish ravings are an outrage on nature and common sense, how humane, and kind, and charitable they are to the cold-blooded murderer while not a sigh is given for the innocent butchered victims!'

When the Jeffrey realised there was no hope, she took to continuous prayer.

At about 8 a.m. on Monday the 21st of May 1838 the scaffold was prepared at Jocelyn Square (Jail Square), outside the County Hall in the Saltmarket, Glasgow. The crowd, around the scaffold was particularly large. She was taken to the scaffold, accompanied by a Clergyman, in earnest prayer.

The papers reported that 'she gave the signal, when the drop fell, and in a minute, she ceased to exist. The crowd then left the ground in good order.'

We have to ask ourselves an important question: when people decide to commit crimes such as murder, do they think of consequences? Clearly, such crime committed in the heat of the moment do not allow for careful thinking or reasoning, however, cases such as the one of Elizabeth Jeffrey are a different matter. She thought about the crime and how to commit and it is accepted that she tried out her dreadful plan, on an elderly lady to see what would happen. She knowingly purchased poison and applied it to the food of Hugh Munro and basically watched him as he died. She must have considered the consequences or like many, did she think that she had committed the perfect crime?

Chapter 48:

MOTHERWELL MURDER & SUICIDE

There is no such a thing as a routine or straightforward case, especially when murder is involved. Many murders are committed in the heat of the moment without a thought for the outcome or those that are left behind. There are many unusual and distressing cases and this is just one of them.

At about 6.30 p.m. on Wednesday the 24th of February 1904, the manager of Love's Market at 111 Brandon Street, Motherwell, was working in the premises on his own, clearing up after the day's business.

As he was working away, he heard two loud noises which sounded like gunshots. He made his way outside but could not see any commotion in the street. He then noticed that the blinds were drawn at the premises next door, Clunes Jewellers, 109 Brandon Street. This was unusual as the blinds usually remained open until the owners secured the shop.

He tried the door handle, but the door was locked. At this point Mrs Clunes, the owner of the shop made an appearance from across the street. She had been heading to the shop to meet her son, a watchmaker. The shop manager told Mrs Clunes what he had heard and she immediately became agitated.

Both made their way to the rear of the shop, again this door was locked. The shop manager said that he would go and fetch Dr McDonald, who lived nearby at Hawthorn Cottage and was well acquainted with the Clunes family.

On the arrival of the Doctor, it was decided to force entry. They found a wheelbarrow in the yard next to the Jewellers. Using this as a battering ram, they forced the door open. The lights were on and all three walked inside.

They were shocked as they walked past the partition separating the rear of the shop from the public area. Behind the partition lay George Clunes with an injury to his chest. Lying across the serving counter was

Brownlow North Laing with a severe injury to the rear of his head. Dr McDonald was no doubt used to seeing sights such as this but the other man must have found it deeply distressing.

Mrs Clunes collapsed and was taken to the rear of the shop and placed on a seat. Dr McDonald examined the bodies and observed that Clunes had a gunshot wound to his chest and Laing a gunshot wound to the rear of his head. Both were dead.

Everyone then left the shop and the shop manager from Love's ran to the High Road Police Station. He informed officers of their discovery. Several officers, led by Superintendent Alexander Moir, attended at the shop.

By this time, a large crowd of curious on-lookers had gathered to watch the events unfold.

Superintendent Moir established that other than the door being forced open with the wheelbarrow, no-one had disturbed anything within the premises. He also established that all points of entry and exit had been secure when the witnesses tried to enter the shop.

He then examined the front and rear doors. Both had been bolted from the inside. Lying next to Clunes was a six-chamber revolver with two empty chambers. These discoveries indicated that whatever had happened had only involved the two dead men within the shop.

The first man was George Clunes, the son of the owner. He was twenty-five years of age, born in Airdrie and worked as a watchmaker on the premises. He trained as a watchmaker in Greenock, returning home after his father died. He lived in Orchard Street, Motherwell.

The second was Brownlow North Laing aged thirty-two-years, an employee of Mrs Clunes, also a watchmaker. He originally came from Forres and at the time of his death, boarded at 37 Melville Drive, Motherwell.

A further examination revealed some personal correspondence on the counter beside Laing. One of the letters was to his brother, alluding to the fact that Mrs Clunes was to retire and pass the business to her son, George. Laing mentioned in the letter that he was not too happy with the situation or indeed working for George Clunes. He wrote that he intended opening his own business as tensions had risen between him and George Clunes since he had made this known.

Superintendent Moir investigated the content of the letter and did establish that Laing intended to set up his own business. Mrs Clunes confirmed that there had been several heated arguments between the two regarding this.

With all the evidence before him, Superintendent Moir concluded that George Clunes had become so incensed that he had become unstable, resulting in him murdering Laing by shooting him through the back of the head and then turning the revolver on himself, shooting through his heart. This shows just how unstable people can become in certain circumstances and can see no way out of such situations other than resorting to such terrible deeds.

The family of Barlow Laing erected a memorial to him, which stands at his grave in Cluny Hill Cemetery in Forres. It was erected on the 11th of April 1905.

A truly tragic set of circumstances that could and should have been settled by other means.

Chapter 49:

THE MURDOSTOUN MURDER

Lanarkshire has been the home to a number of psychiatric hospitals over recent centuries. These were used to treat people with a multitude of quite serious and some perceived mental illnesses. Some patients, with serious conditions, were confined in the establishments whilst others were allowed a certain amount of freedom within the grounds and in the local communities. This gave great concern for a large number of members of the public for a variety of reasons including the safety of their families and loved ones.

Sixty years ago, at 1:25pm on Sunday the 22nd of October 1961, a young man was walking his dog along Foulburn Road, Cleland, which lines the large, wooded area on the Murdostoun Estate, in Lanarkshire. This was known locally as 'The Big Wood'. The Murdostoun Estate, at that time, was owned by Captain John Christie Stewart, CBE, Lord Lieutenant of Lanarkshire.

The dog ran from the road into the woods and the young man followed the dog for about 60 yards. The dog had stopped, sniffing at something lying on the grass. As the man moved closer, he could see the body of a man lying on the grass, face down. On closer inspection, he could see that there was an injury to the back of the head, which was covered in blood. Quite a scary and awful discovery for him.

He placed his dog onto its lead and ran from the woods onto the lane. A car was travelling toward him and he waved his arms frantically to attract the drivers' attention to stop. The car stopped and he tried to explain what he had seen however, it was clear that he wasn't making much sense.

A tractor then drove toward them and the young man flagged the driver to stop, which the driver did. He began pointing into the woods and asked the two drivers to follow him. All three, and the dog, walked to where the body was lying.

The tractor driver left the other two, telling them to stay where they were whilst he went to telephone for the police. He returned to his farm and reported what he had seen.

The local police officers attended at the designated location and were shown to the body. The circumstances were clearly suspicious, and the immediate area cordoned off.

The officers were also aware that they had an ongoing missing person from the nearby Hartwood Psychiatric Hospital, who closely resembled the body. The name of the missing person was Alexander Allardice.

The CID were contacted and investigations commenced, led by Detective Chief Superintendent William Muncie. Closer examination of the scene identified a large blood- stained stone lying close to the body. The area was photographed and the stone seized as a production for forensic examination.

The trunk of a tree, next to the body, was examined and approximately eight feet up the trunk was blood, and brain matter. This was clearly a violent attack.

Detectives contacted staff at Hartwood Hospital and made them aware of the discovery. Several of the patients were allowed daily parole to leave the grounds in their own clothes. Many of them walked to the nearby villages, using the roads and lanes around the estate.

Mr Muncie requested that this parole be temporarily stopped and no clothing cleaned until enquiries were conducted. Staff agreed to do so, and all patients were accounted for. A police car also attended at the hospital and picked up a male nurse, who knew Allardice, and took him to the scene.

On arrival, the nurse was shown the body, which he positively identified as Allardice.

When the body was turned over, the officers noticed that the right hand was in a cadaveric spasm with twigs and pine needles clutched in the palm and fingers.

Subsequent post-mortem examination, conducted by Drs Edgar Rintoul and J.A. Imrie, confirmed that the death was caused by several violent blows to the back of the skull, causing a compound fracture and laceration of the brain. The weapon used was the large rock found beside the body. It was found to have blood and brain matter from the deceased on its surface. Death was estimated at being sometime between the 17th and 19th of October.

Allardice had been in psychiatric institutions from the age of nine and in 1940, at the age of twenty-three, he was placed into Hartwood Hospital, having displayed signs of abnormal behaviour.

He had been missing from the hospital since Tuesday the 17th of October. Staff were asked to prepare lists of those allowed out on parole between the 17th and 19th of October and that their clothing be seized for examination.

Detectives were deployed to the hospital to begin a visual examination of the clothing, of which there were more than forty items. Special lighting was provided to assist the officers.

Shortly after the work commenced, two members of staff made the officers aware of a specific patient, James Barr, who had returned to the Hospital on the afternoon of the 17th of October. He had blood staining on his jacket. He had accounted for this by telling staff that he had a nosebleed and used his jacket to stem the flow of blood.

In addition, Barr had been found walking over five miles from the hospital by an off-duty member of staff, who had returned him to the hospital in his own vehicle. Barr had only been entitled to parole within the grounds of the hospital.

His clothes were put aside and examined by forensic members of staff. They noticed that his clothes had dark marks, like blood stains, and that there were pine needles in the cloth.

The remainder of the other patients clothing were examined however, none showed any sign of blood staining or anything else which might connect them to the incident.

Barr's background was examined, and it was ascertained that he had been admitted to the hospital some nine months earlier, in February 1961. He had been placed there following an appearance at Glasgow Sheriff Court on charges of theft of a motor car. He was only twenty- one-years-old, from Devol Crescent, Pollok, had no previous history of violence, nor had he displayed any signs of violence during his time at the hospital.

Meanwhile, enquiries were ongoing in the local area. Two farm workers were interviewed who provided evidence that on the 17th of October they had seen Allardice, who was known to them from walking in the area. They also knew that he was a patient at the hospital. He had stopped and spoken to them for a few minutes and gave both a penny caramel. He then walked off.

About fifteen minutes later, a second, younger man, had walked past them. They did not recognise him and he walked off in the same direction as Allardice. From their position they saw the two meet a couple of hundred yards away. The two walked off into the woods out of sight. They didn't see them again. They identified this younger man as James Barr.

Detectives detained Barr at the hospital. He was cautioned and replied, 'He wanted to take a liberty with me, so I clubbed him on the head with a stone.'

Barr was arrested and charged with murder. He appeared at Hamilton Sheriff Court on Tuesday the 24th of October and was remanded in custody. Psychiatric reports were ordered by the sheriff.

On Monday the 29th of January 1962, Barr appeared at the High Court in Glasgow, with Lord Sorn presiding. Nicholas Fairbairn QC, appeared for the defence, presenting a plea in bar of trial based on insanity.

Two doctors were called to provide psychiatric evidence of their examination of Barr. Dr Angus McNiven, of Gartnavel Hospital, said that when he examined Barr, he found him to be showing typical signs of schizophrenia in its most severe form and 'very, very grossly insane.' This was supported by the second doctor.

Lord Sorn accepted the plea and ordered that Barr be detained at Her Majesty's Pleasure, at The State Hospital, Carstairs.

At 5pm on Thursday the 24th of February 1965, Barr was having dinner within the State Hospital. Part of his dinner was a hard-boiled egg. As he sat at the table, he began to choke. Staff rushed to him as he fell to the floor, however, despite their efforts, he choked to death with the egg lodged in his throat.

This case makes consideration of open prisons and institutions controversial since provision of basic freedoms to inmates can sometimes create an environment conducive for crime and strengthen stereotypes associated with incarcerated people.

Unfortunately, we cannot access any records to establish the full background of the victim and accused.

From the information available, the accused, whose psychiatric evaluation confirms significant psychiatric problems, did not have any history of violence.

There was a suggestion in the local community of a sexual angle in the case: it was alleged that Allardice had initiated unwanted advances at Barr. It is, however, not possible to confirm such speculative diagnoses.

Chapter 50:

MURDER IN BISHOPBRIGGS

Gerard and Angela McCabe were a young married couple living in their privately owned home at 20 Norfolk Crescent in Bishopbriggs. The couple married in Glasgow in 1966, Gerard was twenty-nine years of age and Angela only twenty-one-years-old. At the beginning of May 1967, they were blessed with the birth of a daughter, Margaret Maria McCabe.

Angela celebrated her 22nd birthday on the 7th of May 1967. Gerard was the manager of his mother's public house in Glasgow and as such the couple were relatively comfortable, in financial terms.

On the evening of Friday the 26th of May 1967, Gerard had been working in his pub. His wife and baby were visiting friends in Glasgow and he had arranged to pick them up and take them home. It was just after 10.30 p.m. when he collected them and dropped them off at home at about 10.50 p.m. However, Gerard had to leave them as he was also catering for a function in Glasgow and had to return to clear things away and pay his staff.

It was about 3.25 a.m. when he eventually returned home. As he drove into the driveway, he was surprised to see a light still burning in the living room. He thought that perhaps Angela was up with the baby. He parked his car and opened the front door of the house, walked inside and shouted that he was home. He did not receive any reply.

He walked into the living room to a horrific sight.

Angela was lying on the floor of the living room, dead. Her jersey had been pulled up to her neck, her skirt and clothes were ripped aside, and the baby's cardigan was found covering her face.

There were some bloodstains on the wall and fireplace in the living room and a smear of what appeared to be blood on the back of the living room door. Other than this, the house was described as 'in an orderly condition.'

Distraught, Gerard then immediately thought of his child, and ran upstairs to her bedroom, where he thankfully found her sound asleep. Gathering himself he called the police to report the tragedy.

Uniformed officers attended and confirmed the report, thereafter the CID and senior officers attended at the house, which was secured.

Detective Chief Superintendent Muncie attended early in the morning, taking charge of the enquiry. By this time news was spreading through the area causing a considerable amount of panic especially amongst females, no doubt scared that a serial killer was on the loose.

A pathologist had examined Angela in the house and stated that in his opinion the weapon used was a single edged knife, just over an inch wide. A post-mortem later established that she had been stabbed through the front of the chest. The wound involved her aorta and pulmonary artery. She bled to death because of the wound. There was no evidence of a sexual assault having taken place. There is no indication that this was a violent attack, rather the circumstances indicated that perhaps Angela knew her murderer.

A check of the contents of the house revealed that a pair of scissors, a plastic holder, driving licence, photographs, miscellaneous papers and a purse containing £15 had been stolen.

The murder investigation was going at a strong pace with additional resources drafted in, including dogs to search the nearby woods and banks of the canal and an underwater unit to search the Glasgow Branch of the Forth & Clyde canal and Bishopbriggs burn.

Dogs followed a positive track from the house east across a field toward Balmuildy Road, where a bridge crossed the canal about a quarter of a mile away from the house. One of the dogs had found a plastic driving licence holder and photographs, at a hedge bordering the road just before the bridge. The holder contained the licence of Angela McCabe. This was normally kept in her purse, which was missing from the house.

A second dog took up a track from a field opposite the McCabe's house. It followed a track into the rear garden of the house bordering the field. The officer with the dog could see clear footprints in the soil. The footprints appeared to be identical to ones found in a garden to the rear of the McCabe's home. Casts were taken of both sets of footprints.

The investigating officers also centred their attention on a wooded area to the north of the house, which was in clear sight. There was a 'Tinkers' encampment there.

A DI and three Detectives were instructed to attend the encampment and interview the occupants. Before they left, they were shown the footprints and told to look for footwear with a similar pattern.

There was only one family there with a series of tents and temporary structures. The detectives spoke to all present, who denied any knowledge of what had taken place. They spoke to a seventeen-year-old boy, Alexander Lewis Hutchison Reid. Outside his tent were a pair of boots which appeared to have a similar pattern to that left in the soil. He was asked to accompany the officers, which he did.

The boots were compared to the footprints and initially there was some excitement. However, one of the Identification Branch pointed out that although the sole matched, the heels of the boots did not match the prints in the soil.

Reid, however, unaware of this conversation relating to the boots, appeared very keen to distance himself from the boots. He admitted ownership of the boots and said that when he went to bed, they were inside his tent but when he woke up, they were outside. Why did he say that? Was he trying to say that someone else had worn his boots during the night?

The DI and additional officers were sent back to the encampment to search it in detail.

Wrapped in the canvas of one of the tents was an archers bow. Found in an extinguished campfire, some distance from the tents, was a burned purse. This appeared to be identical to the purse belonging to Angela McCabe. It was later shown to Brian McCabe and he formally identified the purse as belonging to his wife.

At the same time, door to door enquiry was ongoing in the local area. One man interviewed recalled that the previous evening he was in a Bishopbriggs public house when he heard a man talk about his toolbox being broken into at his workplace and a knife stolen. The witness could only provide a surname and could not say where the man lived.

The voters roll for the area was checked and a list drawn up of people with the surname. By pure luck, the officers struck gold on a visit to only the third name on the list.

The man confirmed he was in the pub and on the 26th of May, his toolbox was broken into at the Alexandra Transport Company Limited at Wilderness Sand Quarry, Balmuildy Road, Bishopbriggs. This was near to the encampment. He described the item stolen as being made from a large hacksaw blade, he had sharpened the cutting part of the blade and made it the end into a point. He then told the officers that another item stolen was an Archers Bow.

A full statement was obtained, and the contents related to Mr Muncie.

Reid was still assisting the police with their enquiries at Bishopbriggs Police office. The investigating officers cautioned him and asked him about the Archers Bow they had found at the encampment.

The officers could not believe their ears. Reid immediately admitted that he had killed Angela McCabe. He also admitted stealing the blade and Archers Bow. He told the officers that he had buried the blade, which he used to stab Angela McCabe and would show them where it was.

He returned with the officers to Norfolk Crescent. They entered the rear garden of the next- door neighbour's garden, pointing to a vegetable patch stating that he had buried it there.

An officer dug the patch and after a few turns of the soil he found the blade, exactly as described by its owner.

Reid was interviewed on return to the police office. He stated that he had been in the McCabe's house during the day on Friday the 26th of May. He had been going around doors offering to sharpen tools. Angela McCabe had asked him to sharpen some knives and she had given him a cup of tea after he had done the job.

He said that she had invited him back later that evening. That would be highly improbable as she knew that she was visiting friends that evening. He continued, stating that when he returned to her home, she had invited him in and when she took his jacket off, he threatened her with a knife. For no apparent reason he struck out at her with the blade, striking her on the chest. He was no doubt trying to make things look better for himself by saying that he had been invited in when there is very little chance Angela would have done so, had she even been there, as we know she was not at home until later.

Reid also admitted a housebreaking in Firhill Street and an assault on a six-year-old boy in Maryhill Road, Glasgow. Further enquiries with the City of Glasgow Police identified both crimes.

Reid was then formally cautioned and charged as follows:
- *on 9th January 1967, break into the premises occupied by Bashir Ahmed at 127 Firhill Street, Glasgow, and there steal 6,000 cigarettes, a quantity of confectionery and £20 of money.*
- *on 6th March 1967, in the common court at 616 Maryhill*

Road, Glasgow, assault Frank Ward, aged six years, 604 Maryhill Road aforesaid, and did seize him by the neck, compress his throat, strike his head against a wall and strike him on the face and head with your fists to his injury.

• *on 26th or 27th May 1967, in the premises occupied by Alexandra Transport Company Limited at Wilderness Sand Quarry, Balmuildy Road, Bishopbriggs, Lanarkshire, force open a lockfast cabinet and steal therefrom a low-bow and a knife.*

• *on 26th or 27th May 1967, in the house occupied by Gerald Brian McCabe at 20 Norfolk Crescent, Bishopbriggs aforesaid, (a) assault Angela Maria Pisacane or McCabe, residing there, and did stab her with a knife and kill her; and (b) steal a pair of scissors, a holder, driving licence, photographs, miscellaneous papers and a purse containing £15 of money.*

He replied, 'I did not mean to do any harm. She fell. I went home. I thought she had fainted. I saw a purse lying on top of the dresser. I lifted it.'

At the time of the offence, Reid was seventeen years old. The Procurator Fiscal instructed that psychiatric assessments be made.

In 1967 psychiatric assessments, including IQ tests, concluded that Reid was suffering from a mental disorder within the meaning of the 1960 Mental Health Act, namely mental deficiency. Based on these reports, the Crown decided not to libel murder, but one of Culpable Homicide, based on diminished responsibility. Unfortunately, this is a common situation in such circumstances as the Crown know that there will be no chance of a murder conviction with such psychiatric evidence available.

On the 8th of September 1967, Reid, having been advised by his lawyers, pled guilty to that charge before Lord Walker in the High Court in Glasgow. Surprisingly, pleas of 'Not Guilty' were accepted for charges one to three, including the violent assault on a six-year old.

The judge then heard oral evidence from two psychiatrists (Dr Macpherson and Dr Campbell) to the effect that Reid was suffering from a mental disorder.

Because of that evidence, the judge imposed a hospital order in terms of Section 55 of the Mental Health (Scotland) 1960, detaining Reid in the state hospital at Carstairs, a high security psychiatric hospital. He also made a restriction order in terms of Section 60, restricting the appellant's discharge without limit of time. So, his incarceration began.

However, in August 1986, after being moved to a more open regime at Sunnyside Hospital, Montrose, Reid attempted to abduct a child aged eight from a caravan park. The girl was on holiday with her parents, having travelled from France. He was subsequently convicted of assault and attempted abduction and sentenced to three months imprisonment. Another disappointing sentence. He was returned to Carstairs.

There was no right of appeal, on his original conviction, until the introduction of the Criminal Justice (Scotland) Act 1980, based on fresh evidence being presented. In the years following 1967, the appellant's psychiatrists came to the view that he was not in fact suffering from a mental disorder, but rather from an untreatable dissocial personality disorder.

Over the years, Reid made many applications to be released into the community. In 1994 he applied to the sheriff at Lanark. His application was refused. Then in 1996 he sought judicial review of the sheriff's decision. This was ultimately rejected in the House of Lords and he remained in Carstairs.

The Mental Health Public Safety and Appeals (Scotland) Act 1999 was enacted to prevent any further review in civil proceedings of cases such as Reid's, where the patient is regarded as a danger to the public. He challenged the legality of this Act and ultimately appealed to the Privy Council.

On 15 October 2001, the Privy Council dismissed his appeal. He then took his case to the European Court of Human Rights. The court concluded that his detention was justified, although he was awarded damages in respect of certain procedural breaches.

In 2005 he commenced a late criminal appeal in terms of Section 60 of the Criminal Procedure (Scotland) Act 1995. Fresh evidence was not the focus of that appeal. Rather the focus was an attack upon the 1967 psychiatric reports as being inadequate to support a finding of mental deficiency, and a submission that he had never suffered from mental deficiency.

The appeal was heard in 2007. Evidence was led from four psychiatrists. The court held that no miscarriage of justice had been made and refused the appeal.

On 13 February 2009, he applied to the Scottish Criminal Cases Review Commission. On the 10th of June 2010, the Commission referred the case to the High Court on the basis that there was fresh evidence indicating that the appellant did not have a mental disorder and might therefore have suffered a miscarriage of justice.

The case came before Lords Reed, Bonomy and Drummond Young, hearing verbal evidence from four psychiatrists. There was also available to the court a report dated 9 November 2010 by Dr Chiswick, Consultant Forensic Psychiatrist.

The opinion of the court was as follows:

'The four consultant forensic psychiatrists who gave evidence were agreed that were the appellant to be sentenced today for the offence of culpable homicide to which he pled guilty; they would have no psychiatric recommendation to make. They would equally have no hospital recommendation to make on the ground of his dissocial personality disorder, since none considered him treatable. We note also that the three consultant psychiatrists who examined the appellant at the time of his re-offending in 1985 made no psychiatric recommendation. All were also agreed that intelligence is, in general terms, innate, but the various tools that measure intelligence can produce varying results depending on factors such as education. All were also agreed that since admission to the State Hospital, the appellant's diagnosis has consistently been that of dissocial personality disorder. We note also that the appellant was not hospitalised when the mental assessments were made and that these were simply carried out while he was on remand at Barlinnie. He was not subject to any formal psychometric testing.'

Each psychiatrist who gave evidence was of opinion that a reliable diagnosis of mental deficiency could not be made and that the original diagnosis in 1967 was incorrect.

Having heard evidence and submissions, the court issued their judgment on 3 February 2012. The court was satisfied that there was a reasonable explanation why the evidence relied upon had not been heard in 1967; that the evidence was credible and reliable; and that the evidence was cogent, important evidence of a kind and quality which would have been of material assistance to the sentencing judge in 1967. The court also concluded that, in face of a finding as a matter of fact that the appellant's IQ was seventy or more, it would not have been objectively correct for a forensic psychiatrist to diagnose the appellant in 1967 as suffering from mental deficiency. That approach being perceived to be inconsistent with the earlier appeal court's decision (2008 SLT 293) the case was remitted to a larger bench.

Deciding on the appeal the court stated that the crime committed by the Reid in 1967 was a horrific and appalling one. Bearing in mind the requirements of punishment, deterrence and protection of the public, the only appropriate sentence for this crime was, in their view, a life sentence.

Accordingly, they decreed that the hospital order and restriction order should be quashed, and a discretionary life sentence substituted. The court still considered Reid as having 'a persistent and permanent psychopathic/ anti-social personality disorder, manifested by abnormally aggressive and seriously irresponsible behaviour.' They cited the 1986 case as an example stating that it raised grave doubts concerning the safety to other people of allowing him to be released from institutional care.

The court also took into consideration the Crown submission that, had Reid been sentenced to life imprisonment, in 1967, for either murder or culpable homicide, he would by now have made several unsuccessful applications to the Parole Board, and would still be serving his life sentence in prison. They said that in the future, The Parole Board would exercise extreme caution when dealing with any application made by the Reid.

They believed the decision they made was substituting one system of confinement for life for another system of confinement for life, subject always to the Parole Board's discretion exercised with the protection of the public as the overriding factor in their considerations.

It is hoped that with Reid suffering from an untreatable dissocial psychopathic personality disorder, which had already manifested itself in a horrific and unprovoked killing, should never be released.

So, where is he now?

It is believed that Reid is still incarcerated somewhere in the prison system, however the Scottish Prison Service will neither confirm nor deny this, and will only release the information, if the prisoner agrees to do so.

Chapter 51:

BURIED ALIVE

There are many crimes and famous cases which have shocked people on a worldwide basis. Cases such as the serial killers Peter Manuel in Lanarkshire, Peter Tobin in England and Scotland or further afield, mass murderers such as Charles Manson in the United States, all have books, movies, documentaries covering the gruesome details.

It always comes as a shock to communities when it happens on their own doorsteps, however, nowhere is immune to such terrible and horrific crimes.

On Saturday the 2nd of March 1968, an eighteen-year-old Motherwell girl, named June Roy, was reported missing from her home at 78 Clapperhowe Road, Motherwell. She lived with her parents, John and Elizabeth. John worked in the nearby Steel Works.

On the following Tuesday, the 5th of March, a suitcase containing female clothing was found in woodland near to the banks of the River Clyde, alongside the main road from Motherwell to Hamilton. The clothing was positively identified as the property of the missing girl.

An intensive search was made of the area and a bucket bag containing personal items was found; these were also identified as her property.

Unfortunately, the River Clyde was in spate at that time and if she had decided to commit suicide by drowning, a search of the river at that stage would have been impossible.

The question remained as to why she had taken her clothing from home – obviously in anticipation of leaving for some reason, which meanwhile was unknown, and then suddenly abandoned the case and contents.

Furthermore, her personal effects, including cosmetics, were found nearby. The circumstances were such that the CID became involved at an early stage and DI Ian Alexander was appointed the Senior Investigating Officer (SIO).

It was known that June Roy was employed in a local engineering works in the personnel department and that she had been friendly with a fellow employee named Michael Finnigan, who worked in the engineering shop. Finnegan lived with his parents at Hunter Road, Whitehill in Hamilton.

The enquiry team learned, from the missing girl's parents, that Finnigan had called at their home on the Saturday evening, inquiring for June and had in fact, along with her sister, made a search of cafes she was in the habit of frequenting. Finnegan returned on the Sunday around lunch time and had two meals with the other members of the household. He outwardly showed anxiety that his girlfriend was 'still missing.'

On Wednesday the 6th of March, along with DS McKillop, DI Alexander decided to make some inquiry at the works where both were employed to establish any reason for the disappearance of this eighteen-year-old, good-looking girl.

A number of her work mates were interviewed and from one of them it was learned that about 4.15 p.m. on the Saturday, while as a passenger on a bus, he had seen Finnigan walking on the bridge over the River Clyde on the main Motherwell to Hamilton Road towards Hamilton.

DI Alexander saw Finnigan for the first time that night at 7 p.m. at the police office in Motherwell, where he arrived accompanied by his father. Prior to their first meeting, it had been established that, because of the inquiry made at the factory, Finnigan was known to engage regularly in river fishing. It happened that that part of the River Clyde was a favourite spot for anglers as the River Avon, a tributary of the Clyde, joins the main stream near to the location mentioned above.

Finnegan went into detail, giving an account of his fishing expedition on March the 2nd, with his cousin, Neil Coyle, from the banks of the River Avon near to where it joins the River Clyde, and admitted having been seen by a work mate walking on the bridge over the river at about 4.15 p.m. that day.

On Thursday the 7th of March, the next line of inquiry took the police to Neil Coyle's home, which strangely enough was sited directly beneath that of Finnigan. He had obviously been primed by Finnigan in what he had to say to the police should he be interviewed, as his account corroborated exactly with what Finnigan had said previously. Except that Coyle insisted that at no time during that day did Finnigan leave him, that the area where they had been fishing was confined to the River Avon near to where it joins the Clyde and at no time did Finnigan go across the bridge on to the other bank.

DI Alexander believed, from Coyle's general attitude and what they had already learned from inquiries, that he was lying, and this was made known to him. DI Alexander's opinion was borne out at lunch time the following day when Coyle walked into Motherwell police office and informed DS McKillop that the statement, he had made the previous evening, was not true and that Finnigan had left him on two occasions when they were fishing on March the 2nd. He added that Finnegan had told him he was going to meet June Roy.

People retracting their statements happens often, mostly when they realise the magnitude of what they have done and the weight of evidence against them. Sometimes it is simply just remorse at what they have done.

Coyle also intimated that Finnigan had dug a trench in the woods on the banks of the River Clyde for worms to be used as bait and had told him later that day that he was going to kill June Roy; he had decided to dig a grave rather than a trench and that he was going to bury her there. This grave was dug by Finnigan with a spade he had brought from his own home that same morning.

About 11 o'clock that Saturday morning Finnigan left Coyle for the first time as he had made a prior arrangement to meet June Roy at 11.30 a.m. outside the public library at Motherwell, about three-quarters of a mile away.

For some reason Finnigan asked Coyle to exchange jackets and Coyle agreed, although no reason was given for this request, possibly it may have been to mislead others later in identification. On the other hand, it may have been further premeditation on the part of Finnigan. A jacket identical to that which he borrowed from Coyle was found in Finnigan's house when it was searched for clothing.

If this jacket had been subjected to scientific examination, and it readily could have been, then the result would have been negative. It was thought that this was the more likely reason, which demonstrates further Finnigan's callous, cold-blooded planning.

Finnigan returned to a pre-arranged meeting point on the banks of the River Avon and informed Coyle that he had seen June, but owing to her being out on an errand her time was limited and he had made a further arrangement to see her at 2.30 p.m. that day, again outside the library.

He left Coyle around 2 p.m. to keep this engagement, still wearing Coyle's jacket. He returned to the area where they had been fishing just after 4 p.m. and there they met again.

Coyle saw that Finnigan's hands were streaked with what appeared to be blood; he later said that he thought Finnigan was kidding when he said to him, 'I've done it, I have killed her.' Finnigan handed Coyle the jacket he had borrowed from him, pointing out a blood stain on the sleeve, which they decided to burn off.

Finnigan then washed the blood from his hands at the river side and they finished the contents of two bottles of beer they had brought with them.

Finished recounting that fateful day, Coyle then volunteered to show the police the area where he saw Finnigan digging a trench for bait and this was the spot where Coyle later assumed, he had dug a grave.

These comments show how easily people can return to a normal life, having committed the most horrendous crimes. Why? Possibly because they think they will never be caught!

When the ground was probed with a spade, a lady's brown shoe on a left foot and the lower part of a leg covered with mauve coloured trousers appeared. The missing person 'inquiry' was now a murder.

Unfortunately, June's body was not the first nor the last victim to be found in or under the river as the length of the River Clyde, from rural Lanarkshire into Glasgow City Centre, has and still is the location of dozens of murders. This is presumably because murderers hope that the evidence would wash away with the tide, though that is only my opinion.

At 1.30 p.m. that day (7th March), DI Alexander and his DS saw Finnigan at the works where he was employed and conveyed him to the police office at Motherwell.

At 2. 55 p.m. on returning from the locus after the body had been uncovered and it had been established that it was the body of June Roy, they spoke to Finnigan in a room at Motherwell police office where DI Alexander cautioned him and told him that he was making inquiry into the death of June Roy.

Finnegan replied, 'I hit her with the shovel.' He was then charged with her murder.

Finnegan then said that he wanted to make a voluntary statement in which he exonerated his cousin Neil Coyle and gave a detailed account to the senior officer who interviewed him on what he did with June Roy.

The subsequent post-mortem revealed that she had died as the result of having her throat compressed and while still alive having been buried in earth, this being borne out by soil found well down her gullet. There was also a large open wound on her chin had been the result of the blow he struck with the spade.

Finnegan had admitted that he had done this when he saw her moving.

It was determined that June was eight months pregnant and the pathologist reckoned that had she remained alive the child would have been naturally born. It was also made known, from the examination, that the accused had sexual intercourse with her before he murdered her.

Could this have been why he committed the crime? In any case, the brutality and violence he used cannot be condoned in any way and makes the circumstances even more shocking.

The indictment against Finnigan was drafted and read as follows:

'You did on the 2nd of March 1968, in woodland on the East bank of the River Clyde, about 200 yards south of the Motherwell to Hamilton Road, Motherwell, assault June Roy of 78 Clapperhowe Road, Motherwell, and did compress her throat, bury her while she was alive and cover her with earth, strike her with a spade and did murder her.'

Finnigan pled guilty at the High Court in Edinburgh on Thursday the 11th of April 1968.

The sentence passed on Finnigan was that he should be detained during Her Majesty's pleasure.

The killing of June Roy was one of the most callous murders in the criminal annals of Scotland. Even at a time when the public was becoming used to horrific violent crimes this despicable act shocked and sickened everyone. The murders attributed to the alleged 'Bible John', highlight this.

I have said alleged 'Bible John' as it has never been sufficiently proven that he existed. When I worked at Partick Police office, I reviewed those cases regularly when letters or telephone calls were received with 'new information'. Each of these murders was horrific in its own right and were correctly given due attention in the media. However, I never found any evidence that the victims were murdered by one person.

The brutality of the murder of June Roy shows a coldness which is rarely seen but June's murder never hit the headlines like 'Bible John' or 'Manuel' and has been more or less forgotten, despite the fact that hundreds of people pass near to where she was buried, on a daily basis.

PART EIGHT:

SCOTTISH POLICEWOMEN

Chapter 52:

SCOTTISH POLICEWOMEN

The history of women in policing dates back to the late nineteenth century when the wives of policemen, in county areas and small towns, were responsible for looking after male and female prisoners and the cleaning and maintenance of police stations, free of charge. It was seen as their responsibility as the wives of a police officer.

In cities, women were employed as turnkeys and matrons to look after female prisoners and feed them whilst in police custody. One of the most famous is 'Big Rachel' Hamilton, previously a forewoman navvy, who was sworn in as a Special Constable during the Partick Riots of 1875.

In Scotland, and throughout the British Isles, there was an active 'voluntary patrol' of women acting as 'Auxiliaries' or 'Special Constables' during the First World War. Their main duties were similar to social workers, concentrating on the prevention of prostitution, helping and advising young women and children whom they encountered whilst on patrol. Furthermore, HM Gretna Munitions Factory employed in a policing role between 1916 and 1918, searching women workers as they entered and left the site and making sure that they behaved.

However, it was in September 1915, that Emily Miller was appointed as the first female investigation officer (lady assistant) by the City of Glasgow Police. She was appointed to the Criminal Investigation Department (CID) with limited responsibility. She could only take statements from women and children in cases of sexual assault and abuse, becoming highly specialised in this area of police work.

However, it was not until 1919 that she was officially appointed as a 'policewoman' rather than 'lady assistant'. Another officer was appointed at the same time, Georgina W. McLeod. Emily was eventually given the power to arrest people in 1924.

Dundee, Glasgow and Aberdeen local authorities agreed, in 1918, that women should be admitted to their local police forces in small numbers as they had performed a valuable role during the war. Scotland's first paid, uniformed, policewoman was Jean Thomson (nee Wright), who was appointed in Dundee in 1918 and served for three years until 1921.

The number of policewomen in Scotland remained minimal. By 1928 there were sixteen policewomen in Scotland: eleven in Glasgow, two in Edinburgh, two in Ayr and one in Aberdeen.

By 1939 the City of Glasgow had created a Policewomen's Department which numbered fifteen officers, however, their role was still defined as a CID role relating to statement taking and the investigation of offences against women and children.

During the Second World War women, across Scotland, were recruited into policing as Women Police Auxiliaries once again. In Glasgow two-hundred-and-twenty women were employed in this capacity, led by Dr Violet Roberton, magistrate and member of the police committee, as Commandant of the Women's Auxiliary Police Corps (WAPC). After the war, the WAPC was stood down and many women joined the police forces as full-time officers.

Women have been involved in Scottish policing for over 100 years. However, it was only in the early part of the 20th century that women were allowed to play an active role in this previously male dominated environment. This was no doubt due, in some way, to the Suffragette movement.

Even though women did begin to work as police officers, there were very few and their role extended mostly to missing persons and crimes involving children. Added to their limited duties, women were required to resign from the police force if they married.

Even as late as 1970 the Scottish police forces only had 382 women in their establishment. It was The Sex Discrimination Act of 1975 that finally allowed women to be recruited on the same terms and conditions as men. This resulted in policewomen being given the same operational status as their male counterparts, being on patrol and undertaking duties in all aspects of policing.

The following stories show that early pioneers of women's policing forged the way ahead for the women of the future, making a significant impact and creating better conditions for current officers.

Chapter 53:

ALICE ELIZABETH CAMBRIDGE

MOTHERWELL & WISHAW BURGH POLICE – 1934 to 1944

In 1934, Motherwell & Wishaw Burgh Police appointed their first policewoman. Who was she?

Alice Elizabeth Cambridge was born in September 1906 at Batheaston, Bath in Somerset. When Alice was still young, before she started school, the family moved to Motherwell, where her father had obtained employment in the local steelworks as a boiler feeder. The family eventually settled at Hillhead Avenue in Motherwell.

The family grew to six children, with the addition of four sisters and one brother for Alice, between 1909 and 1925. Sadly, one of her sisters died shortly after birth in 1917.

Alice attended Dalziel High School in Motherwell and was involved with her local church, Holy Trinity, as a Sunday School teacher. She taught the bible and arranged many performances by the children at Sunday School. Alice was also a member of the Girl Guides and went on to become Captain of the 1st Motherwell Division.

On leaving school, Alice worked in clerical jobs in Motherwell. She gained qualifications in shorthand, typing and accounting, winning prizes for her aptitude and skills.

Motherwell & Wishaw Burgh Police was formed in May 1930. Notably, there were no female police officers at that time, however, in 1934 the CC, George Lamont, applied to the Town Council to fill a vacancy with a policewoman.

The police recognised the need for women in the Force due to the increasing police-work that involved women and children. It was considered best at that time to have women dealing with such incidents. The adverts of the time stated that they wanted 'single or widowed women' to apply. You can imagine such an advert now! This practice of policewomen dealing primarily with children and domestic abuse remained until the mid-1970s and by then, many forces had Policewomen departments.

In 1934, the Motherwell & Wishaw Burgh council agreed to employ a policewoman, subject to the approval of the Secretary of State for Scotland.

The duties were to include:

- *Searching*
- *Feeding prisoners*
- *Shorthand writing*
- *Typing*

The appointment was to be made in terms of the Police (Women) (Scotland) Regulations 1932 as amended by the Police Regulations 1933. The wages on appointment were to be 53s per week with an economy deduction of ten percent, with plain clothes allowance. It would appear the officer was not to have a uniform!

In addition, one Constable was to be transferred to the Detective Department with an additional expenditure of £32 10s per annum. The introduction of a female officer allowed the force to transfer an officer to supplement the Criminal Investigation Department.

Evidently, the Secretary of State for Scotland approved the request and so the process began with adverts placed in the local newspapers.

One of the applicants was Alice Cambridge. She was selected for interview and impressed the panel with her skills, knowledge and enthusiasm for the role. Her qualifications were far more impressive than the other candidates and she was offered the job.

Alice started in her new role on Monday the 10th of July 1934, working from the police office in the High Road. She was thrown in at the deep end on her first day, attending juvenile court. The magistrate looked toward her as she sat near the bench and asked, 'Are you this child's mother?' The clerk had to explain to the magistrate that Alice was the new and first policewoman in the Burgh force and that she would be regularly attending the sittings.

Later that year, she had a particularly harrowing case to deal with. On the 5th of October 1934, Alice was working within Motherwell Police Office when a young woman was brought to the public office by a member of the public.

The woman was particularly distressed and was handed into the care of Alice. It transpired that the woman had been at Hamilton Sheriff Court appealing to be placed on the Poor Roll in order that she could look after her illegitimate three-month-old child. Her mother was also in attendance, and they had an argument regarding the father of the child.

The woman left the court in tears with her young baby. She walked to the Clyde Bridge, between Hamilton and Motherwell, where she stopped at one of the parapets. Passers-by didn't see exactly what had happened, however, they saw her with the baby, then heard a splash and the baby was gone. It had fallen into the river. A passing driver took her to the police office. The baby was never found.

Alice interviewed the woman, who was continually in tears, claiming she didn't know what had happened and everything had 'gone black.'

The woman was eventually charged with Culpable Homicide, the trial taking place on Monday the 17th of December 1934. Alice was called to give her evidence and was praised by his Lordship. Following all the evidence, much of which was medical, the jury found the woman 'Not Guilty' of the charge and released.

Throughout her career, Alice was heavily involved with community work and provided talks and lectures to many groups in the local area about the work of the police and policewomen in particular. She was a perfect advocate for the police service and the comments in the local newspapers were very positive about her presentations.

Due to Alice's success in her role, her duties increased significantly and in November 1938, the Burgh appointed a second policewoman, Marion Kerr of Calder Street.

Marion remained with the force until early 1941, when she married local policeman, John Carmichael. As was the case in those days, Marion resigned from the police. A replacement was sought and another officer appointed, namely Janet Weir of Merry Street. There were not many women in the police, and the turnover was very high. As previously mentioned, this was due to the fact that women could not remain in the police if they were married.

World War II increased the workload even further and the Women Auxiliary Police Corp augmented the numbers of the force. As a result of increased work and numbers of policewomen, Alice was promoted to Temporary Sergeant in charge of all policewomen. A role which she thoroughly enjoyed, eventually becoming DS.

However, love blossomed for Alice, and she decided to marry. Her husband-to-be was DI James Harris of the Motherwell & Wishaw Burgh police. James was a widower, his wife had been tragically killed in a road accident in Cathcart in 1931, leaving him to bring up their daughter. Alice resigned from the police shortly before her marriage.

Alice and James married on the 7th of June 1944 at the Holy Trinity Church in Motherwell. They set up home at James's house at 13 Muir Street in Motherwell. At the time of the marriage, Alice was thirty-seven-years-old and James was fifty-four.

In October 1947, Alice gave birth to their only child, David.

In September 1949, James retired from the police after thirty years' police service. The family remained in Motherwell, raising David in the town.

James died in February 1978 at the age of eighty-eight. Sadly, Alice died shortly after, on the 21st of July 1978 at the age of seventy-one. They had been married for thirty-three years.

David remained in Motherwell after his parents' death and died in 2000 at the young age of fifty-seven years.

Alice paved the way for many future female police officers, and it must have been quite challenging in those early days, with responsibilities and opportunities for advancement severely limited. In addition, female supervisors had no authority over their male colleagues, even those of junior rank. However, the determination and success of women in the police at that time has forged the way for the women of today, who now enjoy full equality with their male colleagues.

Having said that, it would appear that policewomen in Motherwell & Wishaw were very much accepted by their colleagues, as many of them married each other!

Chapter 54:

ISABELLE RANKIN

LANARKSHIRE CONSTABULARY

Since Alice's days, women have taken a much more prominent role in policing, reaching the highest ranks in the service. The following story is of one such woman, Isabella Rankine, who was not only a competent police officer but a very brave one too.

On the 3rd of June 1955, two young Glasgow neds escaped from a Borstal in the East Lothian area. John Robinson (18) and Gilbert McCawley (17) headed back to their roots in the Gorbals area of Glasgow. On June 10th they were seen on Rutherglen Road

Policewoman Rankine.
—B.E.M. for chasing armed youth.

by Constable Alexander Davidson of the City of Glasgow Police. He approached both, who were known to him, and apprehended them. McCawley began to struggle and managed to free himself, producing a pistol from his jacket pocket. He pointed this at Constable Anderson and shouted, 'I'm not kidding copper, this is for you.'

McCawley discharged the pistol toward Constable Anderson and then ran off. Members of the public came to the assistance of the officer and

217

detained Robinson. Constable Anderson gave pursuit and blasted his police whistle to attract the attention of colleagues. These were the days long before personal radios became the norm.

Walking nearby was Policewoman Constable Isabella Rankine of Lanarkshire Constabulary (Cambuslang). She heard the whistle and saw Constable Anderson in pursuit of McCawley. She could see that McCawley was in possession of a pistol and without hesitation and regardless of danger, she ran across the street to intercept him. McCawley pointed the pistol at her and discharged it toward her face, she ducked to avoid the shot. McCawley continued running and discharged the pistol for a second time, again missing Constable Rankine.

The chase ensued along Florence Street and for a further hundred yards on to Crown Street. Constable Rankine pursued him into a close where he slammed a gate shut on her. She opened the gate and with the assistance of Constable Anderson overpowered McCawley, wrestling the pistol from his grasp. Both Robinson and McCawley were arrested and appeared at Glasgow Sheriff Court on the 27th of June 1955, pleading guilty to the incident. Robinson was sentenced to six months imprisonment and McCawley twelve months imprisonment.

Sheriff A.G Walker publicly praised the two officers for their courage and tenacity. Furthermore, on the 27th of September 1955 Constable Rankine was awarded the British Empire Medal and was cited in the London Gazette with the comment, 'Constable Rankine displayed courage and determination and acted in the best tradition of the Police Service.'

Isabella was not the first woman to be given a bravery award, but that does not make her story any less impressive. This event is unusual as there weren't many policewomen at that time and many of their duties were restricted to domestic or child abuse cases. Therefore, to have a policewoman involved in such an incident and chase was very unusual.

Isabella was promoted to Sergeant, not long after this incident, which indicates that she was a valuable and respected police officer. One of her roles as a Sergeant was to check the background of new applicants to the police and visit their homes, to interview the candidate and their family for their suitability to be a police officer. Unfortunately, these checks no longer exist.

Sadly, Isabella died in 1967, she was only 48 years of age.

PART NINE:

IN MEMORIAM

When police officers leave their loved ones, friends and families to go out on their tour of duty, they do not know what will happen during those coming hours. Every corner an officer turns, every call that they attend has unknown quantities attached. Every day is different and police officers have to be alert and flexible to deal with any given situation.

People join the police to serve their local communities without fear or favour. As police officers they are asked to perform duties and tasks that no-one else will do. On occasions this means putting their safety and their lives at risk to protect the public, with little thought of the consequences. The sense of duty comes automatically. But the price paid is often great.

Chapter 55:

IN MEMORIAM

There are many instances of police officers whose actions go above and beyond the course of their normal duties, where their lives are put at risk to protect and indeed save members of the public. Unfortunately, many of these officers' brave actions go unrecognised, sometimes this is because it is felt that they are only doing their duty. Unlike military personnel that serve in conflict, there are no campaign medals issued. Indeed, until 1952, when the Police Long Service and Good Conduct Medal was introduced, there was no formal recognition of the role of a police officer, other than a certificate of service to show prospective future employers and their families.

It has always been at the discretion of senior police officers whether or not acts of bravery or actions which go above and beyond the call of duty are recognised. As you will read in other chapters, this is something that is inconsistent, throughout the country, indeed today, no policy or process is in place to ensure such acts are properly recognised.

The feeling of loss is immense. Twice in my police service, police officers from my own force were murdered in the line of duty. Although I did not know these officers personally the feeling of loss is tremendous, because you know that at any time it could be you.

The impact and effect on the families of these officers is with them for life. No-one, unless they are in that unfortunate position, can understand or appreciate how difficult that must be.

We therefore have to publicly recognise the bravery of these officers in some way because they have put their lives at risk and paid the ultimate sacrifice, on our behalf.

The following Chapters describe the bravery of only a few police officers.

Chapter 56:

SERGEANT JAMES TAYLOR

LANARKSHIRE CONSTABULARY – 1858 to 1877

This story emphasises the bravery and commitment of police officers including Sergeant James Taylor, of Lanarkshire Constabulary, who showed total disregard for his own safety to save the lives of others.

James Taylor was born in the Barony Parish of Glasgow in 1828. On leaving school he was employed as a Weaver. And at the age of eighteen, he joined the army in Glasgow on the 25th of November 1846, attached to the 47th Regiment of Foot. He was posted to Ireland and in 1850 to the Ionian Islands, and then in 1853 to Malta. The regiment then travelled to 'Calamity Bay', where they landed to take part in the Crimea war. He fought at Alma, Inkerman and at the siege of Balaclava. He was severely wounded at the Battle of Inkerman, on the 5th of November 1854, sustaining a gunshot wound to his leg and in 1857 he was declared unfit for active service and discharged from the Army on the 30th of November 1857. He had attained the rank of Corporal and was awarded the Crimea medals with clasps.

James returned to Scotland and was one of the first to join the newly established Lanarkshire Constabulary. He was initially posted to Hillhead and later at Rutherglen. On the 5th of November 1858, he married a Rutherglen girl, Mary Cameron, in Tradeston, Glasgow, and they lived in Main Street, Rutherglen. James was a good and conscientious officer with his military experience being easily recognised. So much so that he was promoted to Sergeant around 1870 and transferred to Crosshill.

Just after midnight, on Sunday the 25th of February 1877, Sergeant Taylor was on foot patrol near to Allison Street, Crosshill. He was approached by Mr Wallace of the Crosshill Omnibus Company and alerted to a fire in a nearby building, the two immediately making their way there. Sergeant Taylor saw that it was a corner building with the large portion on Winton Terrace, which was on Victoria Road and the other portion on the east part of Allison Street.

It was a four-storey building with shops on the ground level and six large half-flat apartments on the upper storeys. At the time of the fire five of these flats were occupied. One of the shops was a general store which had several highly flammable liquids stored within. This was the seat of the fire. Sergeant Taylor looked inside the shop to find it well ablaze. It is doubtful that he could have made any impact on the blaze.

His priority was the people sleeping in the rear of the shop, as he knew from working the area that it was also used for accommodation. Sergeant Taylor managed to rouse them and get them free of the property. He then decided to evacuate the tenement property. Along with Mr Wallace, he made his way from house to house, floor to floor leading residents from the upper floors.

It was a stormy morning, the wind blasting at the front of the building. As windows cracked and openings were made by residents the flames were fanned, making the situation much worse. Sergeant Taylor then entered the upper levels. As he brought the occupants downstairs, he found their path blocked as the ground floor hallway was fully engulfed in fire. There was no way through.

Undeterred, Sergeant Taylor led the tenants onto a balcony on the first floor and was able to gain entry to the adjacent building. He lowered the occupants onto a shop canopy and into the arms of the crowd that had gathered below, allowing several the residents to escape. An elderly man, Mr Fulton was still in his flat on the top floor, he was frail and immobile.

Sergeant Taylor made his way to the flat and wrapped Mr Fulton in bed sheets.

With flames surrounding them, Sergeant Taylor carried him down to the first floor, so intense that some of the bed clothes were burned during the rescue. The initial escape route through the adjacent building by this time was impassable. People of the street gathered large planks of wood and placed them against the building. Ropes were found, placed around a bed, and Mr Fulton was secured to the bed, then lowered to the ground. All the residents were now clear of the building, however, Sergeant Taylor remained within.

The floors of the building then gave way, the flames worsened as the contents fell into the heart of the fire.

The Glasgow Fire Brigade had been summoned, however as fate

would have it, they were already dealing with four fires in the area and were unable to attend. The Crosshill Burgh fire hose (basically a hand cart) was brought out, but it only stretched for 180 yards and was too far away from the building to have any effect, plus the water supply quickly ran out. The Glasgow Fire Brigade eventually arrived at about 2 a.m. but by that time it was too late, and the building had basically gone. They made efforts to extinguish the fire, however it eventually burned itself out. So what happened to Sergeant Taylor?

During the rescue of the tenants Sergeant Taylor was severely burned as he carried and led people through the flames, returning several times to evacuate people. Once he had evacuated everyone from the building, and as the floors collapsed, he jumped from the first floor to the ground, falling badly as he did so. As a result, he suffered severe internal injuries in addition to his burns and was taken to hospital. Sadly, his internal and external injuries were so severe that at 6 p.m. on the 7th of March 1877, he died.

There was a great outpouring of sympathy for his family and for his brave and gallant actions. On the 16th of March 1877, a meeting was held by officials and local businessmen in the Crosshill Burgh Chambers. It was intimated by Superintendent Cornelly, of Lanarkshire Constabulary, that police funds only allowed a sum of £14 to be paid to the widow. It was agreed that this sum was insufficient so it was decided that a committee would be established to gather funds for the widow and her family. It was read out that one of the residents rescued from the fire had given £10. A collection was made amongst those present and £80 was gathered. Mr Kinloch of the City of Glasgow Bank agreed to open an account in the name of Mrs Taylor.

In addition to the collection, on the 20th of April, a Grand Ball and Concert was held in the Marie Stuart Hall, Crosshill, to collect funds for the family. It was attended by businessmen and celebrities from around the area. A charity football match was also played between Glasgow Rangers and Queens Park, raising £13 for the family. In total over £350 was raised by the committee (almost £29,000 at today's rates).

In August 1877, his wife had a memorial stone erected at the highest point in Cathcart cemetery. The inscription reads, *"Erected by Mary Cameron, in memory of her husband, James Taylor, Sergeant of Lanarkshire Constabulary, who died on the 7th of March 1877 aged 48."*

Despite the public's sympathy, Sergeant Taylor's sacrifice remained unrecognised until 2019 when his name was placed on the Scottish Police Memorial which is located at the Scottish Police College. The memorial stands in remembrance of those that have died on duty. His name remained unrecognised, as many do, until research uncovered the details and circumstances of his death.

Having discovered this story and act of exceptional bravery, we decided to find the memorial erected to Sergeant Taylor. One of our members, serving police officer Chief Superintendent Gordon McCreadie, found the grave at Cathcart Cemetery. It is in a state of disrepair with ivy and other weeds having concealed it from view. These have been cleared away making it obvious that it is irreparable. We are endeavouring to have a memorial laid at the site of his grave to make it more noticeable for people visiting the cemetery to recognise the bravery and sacrifice of Sergeant Taylor.

Chapter 57:

THE MURDER OF SUB-INSPECTOR JAMES ALLAN

RENFREWSHIRE CONSTABULARY – 1869 to 1870
LANARKSHIRE CONSTABULARY – 1870 to 1893

On the night of Monday, 4th September 1893, Inspector James Allan of the Lanarkshire Constabulary was fatally stabbed outside the Crow Tavern in the main street of Bishopbriggs.

His killer, a notorious criminal and fugitive from justice, narrowly escaped the gallows.

At the time of his murder, James Allan was forty-nine years of age. He was born in Newarthill and had been a police officer for twenty-four years, the last eleven spent at Bishopbriggs. He had joined Lanarkshire Constabulary on the 26th of February 1870, having served for a year in Renfrewshire Constabulary. He was regarded by all as a skillful and efficient officer. He was well regarded in the local community and his eldest daughter was a teacher in the local school.

In July 1882, he was transferred to Bishopbriggs as Sergeant and Sub-Inspector where he remained until the time of his death. He lived beside his small police station in Crowhill Road with his wife and eight children.

The fatal incident began whilst he was on a routine night patrol with Constable John Pirie. Just after 11:10 p.m. they were approached by a breathless railwayman who said he had seen two men robbing a drunk, lying on the ground, outside the nearby Crow Tavern. Running to the scene, the two officers encountered two men striding towards them.

Allan, suspicious, asked if they had seen someone lying on the ground and, when the men said they had, the officers escorted them back towards the gaunt stony towers of the pub. Allan took hold of one man while Pirie held the other. The group had only taken a few steps, however, when the man held by Allan suddenly broke free and bolted.

Allan pursued and caught him almost immediately but a struggle

226

ensued, quickly ending with the Inspector collapsing to the ground, groaning, 'I'm stabbed!'

His attacker ran off towards Glasgow. Pirie, still holding his own suspect, appealed to two men standing nearby who had witnessed the scuffle, asking them to hold what was now his prisoner while he pursued the escapee, but the men refused to help, not an uncommon situation, as people are reluctant to become involved in such incidents.

Pirie, frustrated, then hurried his prisoner to the nearby police station, pushing him into a cell and locking him in. Returning to Allan, he found him trying to rise to his feet. As Pirie helped him up, the injured man gasped, 'I'm dying!'

Allan then collapsed limply in Pirie's arms. Eventually, with some much-needed assistance from more helpful passers-by, Allan was carried to the police station where his distraught family gathered round his lifeless body.

A local doctor was summoned but there was nothing he could do.

Although he wanted to console Allan's family, Pirie was still on duty and tore himself away to return to the scene of the crime where he found a bloodstained knife lying on the ground.

In those days, Bishopbriggs was only a small village in the countryside and Pirie found himself totally alone in the chilly darkness with no means of summoning help.

He set out to walk to the nearest manned police station which was in Glasgow and soon after starting out on this long trek, he fortunately managed to hail a horse-drawn cab. The cab took him to St. Rollox Police Station where senior officers were made aware of the circumstances.

Constable Pirie then travelled to Rutherglen Police Station, the Divisional Headquarters, and alerted Superintendent Smith, who was in charge of the Division. Superintendent Smith, Inspector Fraser and Constable Pirie then returned to Bishopbriggs. The investigation began in earnest.

When more senior officers questioned Pirie's prisoner later that day, they found he was a thirty-eight-year-old former miner called Robert McGhee of no fixed abode. When his cell was searched, a knife was found below a chair. It was later identified as belonging to the drunk man who had been robbed, Daniel Elliot, an engineer from the neighbouring Springburn.

His coat, shoes, tobacco and ten shillings in cash had also been stolen.

227

McGhee, keen to save his own skin, willingly named his accomplice as William Coubrough.

He said he had been drinking in Glasgow with Coubrough and they had decided to walk to Kilsyth.

En-route, they had encountered the intoxicated Elliot and decided to rob him.

Coubrough was a familiar name to the police. He was a notorious criminal who had been sentenced in Septermber 1888, at Glasgow High Court, to five years imprisonment for breaking into a convalescent home in Kirkintiiloch. This sentence had been served at Peterhead Prison but on 17th June 1892, he had been released on parole. However, he had breached the conditions of his release by failing to inform the police of his whereabouts and, even before the murder, had been a fugitive on the run.

Born at Campsie village to the north of Glasgow in 1854, Coubrough had enlisted in the army as a young man and was posted to India, however he had found military discipline too harsh and had deserted. Living by his wits, he had made the long journey back home and had embarked on a life of crime.

Occasionally working legitimately as a miner, he more often survived by poaching and housebreaking.

Roaming the countryside around his birthplace in the Campsie Hills, he gained an intimate knowledge of the area and a fearsome reputation. Gamekeepers were wary of him. Caught poaching in the woods with his gun, Coubrough challenged one gamekeeper to duel.

Indicating the gamekeeper's gun, the criminal sneered, 'I'm loaded. If you're loaded, raise your gun and we'll see who's going to Hell first!' Wisely, the gamekeeper withdrew.

Coubrough was always threatening to shoot policemen, especially when they came too close to him.

But for all his violent bravado, he was cunning as well.

Having stolen some ferrets, he was visited at home by the police. He watched as they searched vainly for the missing animals. A few weeks later, one of the officers who had participated in this search offered the criminal a bottle of whisky to reveal how he had managed to successfully conceal the ferrets. No doubt this was a common crime for the police to investigate and the officer perhaps wanted an upper-hand for future investigations.

Mellowing, Coubrough explained that, on seeing the police approaching, he had wrapped the ferrets in pieces of flannel and had then placed them in an empty kettle on his fire which was burning low. As the officers carried out their fruitless search, the ferrets lay undiscovered in the kettle which the police naturally assumed contained simmering water.

At various stages in his criminal career, when he was in the money, he had his body heavily tattooed with vivid illustrations including ships, flags, horses, and crowns. Perhaps the most dramatic tattoo was a nude female in chains on his chest. He had over a dozen, showing just how extensive his criminal activities were.

Named as Allan's heartless killer, a widespread manhunt was now mounted for Coubrough throughout his old stomping grounds. Scores of policemen, gamekeepers and shepherds combed the hills and woodlands that were his usual haunts. Officers from Lanarkshire, Glasgow, Stirlingshire and Dunbartonshire assisted in the search.

For four days, the area between Kilsyth and Strathblane was thoroughly searched, but the fugitive evaded his pursuers by using the fieldcraft he had acquired as a poacher and his native cunning.

Meanwhile, a postmortem examination of Allan's body was held at Bishopbriggs Police Station two days after his death. There was no mortuary in the village and the officer's bloodstained corpse had lain there since the night of his murder.

A forensic examination revealed two severe stab wounds and three cuts on the body. The most serious wound was on the inner left thigh. It was three inches long and two inches wide and had also penetrated to a depth of three inches, severing two arteries. Profuse bleeding from this wound had caused the Inspector's rapid death. The other stab wound, beneath the left shoulder blade, had almost entered the chest cavity.

Both wounds had involved the use of considerable force. The cuts were on the dead man's hands. One had almost severed the little finger of his left hand; these had been caused when Allan had desperately tried to wrench the knife from his assailant.

Sub-Inspector Allan's funeral took place at Cadder cemetery on Friday the 8th of September. The cortege and mourners met at the police station. A large contingent of policemen attended along with crowds of local people who wanted to pay their respects to this popular officer who had served in so many parts of the County.

As the fruitless search for Coubrough entered its fourth day the police became increasingly convinced that he was hiding out in a place in the Campsie Hills called Haughhead for his aged mother lived in a cottage there and information had been received that the fugitive had appeared in her home one night, seized some bread and a knife and had ran out again.

It was also rumoured that he had been hiding up in the branches of a large tree, watching the police below searching for him. He certainly knew the area well and showed how capable he was at evading capture.

At about 3 a.m. on Saturday the 9th of September, Superintendent Simpson, of the Airdrie Division, in charge of a party of police officers with dogs, arrived at Blairtummock Farm near Haughhead. Acting on impulse or information received, they decided to search the area which had already been covered the previous evening.

They moved silently into the steading, searching the farm buildings which included an open hayshed. The officers entered quietly in the dark and one of them climbed the pile of hay stored there. Digging into the hay, he uncovered the slumbering form of Coubrough.

The fugitive was so exhausted with the chase that it took his captors some time to wake him up.

By chance, one of them was the policeman who had once offered him whisky to reveal how he had concealed the stolen ferrets.

Coubrough now stared at him and said wryly, 'It's good to see you again – but not on such an occasion as this!' There was no whisky on offer this time, only a journey under escort in a farmer's gig to Glasgow.

At the Central Police Office, Coubrough was securely locked into a cell known as 'The Cage,' used to contain difficult prisoners.

On the first day of his trial at Glasgow High Court before Lord Young, the accused was charged with the capital murder of Allan.

Asked how he pleaded, Coubrough replied loudly, 'I plead guilty to culpable homicide!'

This was, of course, a lesser crime than murder and, more importantly from his point of view, did not carry the death sentence. Mr Crabb Watt Q.C., representing the accused, explained, apologetically that his client had never intended to kill Allan.

After robbing Elliot, Coubrough had apparently taken his knife and tobacco from his pocket and, while cutting a piece off, had been violently seized by the Inspector. In the ensuing struggle, according to Mr Watt's imaginative account, Coubrough accidentally stabbed the policeman. All of this went directly against the irrefutable forensic evidence which pointed clearly to deliberate murder.

One might have expected the prosecution to robustly repudiate Mr Watt's wildly inaccurateversion of events. It was not to be.

Mr Taylor Innes, Advocate Depute for the Crown, meekly accepted the lesser plea. But the judge, apparently startled, expressed his doubts about this decision. He adjourned the court to consider the peculiar legal circumstances of the case.

It is not known what factors entered his deliberations but, when the court reconvened, he stated that, while considering the crime 'on the very edge of murder,' he now agreed with the Crown's decision. We can only wonder at the content of that deliberation!

He then went on to make matters worse (from the point of view of the police and Allan's family and friends) by stating that he had considered imposing a sentence of life imprisonment but had decided instead to make it ten years. This bizarre verdict was received with dismay in Bishopbriggs.

It was also felt in legal circles that, if the Crown had simply persisted with the murder charge, they would have won their case easily.

Coubrough returned once more to Peterhead Prison where his conduct was exemplary. After only seven years he was released and spent his remaining years roaming once more in the Campsie Hills until, in old age, his sight began to fail.

He was admitted to the Stirling Poorhouse where he lived until his death in 1923.

Mrs Allan, meanwhile, was awarded a pension of £47 per annum by Lanark County Council and devoted the rest of her life to successfully bringing up her large, fatherless family.

The grateful citizens of Bishopbriggs erected a memorial, financed by public subscription, to Inspector Allan at his burial place in Cadder Cemetery. This was decided at a public meeting held in Bishopbriggs on Monday the 13th of October 1893.

Located just inside the main gate of Cadder Cemetery in Bishopbriggs, Lanarkshire, stands one of only two memorials in Scotland, dedicated to Police Officers unlawfully killed in the execution of their duties. Fashioned from granite, the memorial displays two bronze panels, one of which depicts the likeness of the Officer to whom the memorial is dedicated, while the other is inscribed:

MEMORIAL TO:

Inspector James Allan Lanark Constabulary,
Who lost his life at Bishopbriggs, On the 4th September 1893,
While in the discharge of his duty.

The legal system may have undervalued his life and death, but at least the community he had served faithfully for many years honoured his devotion to duty in this tangible, public way.

With thanks to former Inspector Joe Craig who supplied some of the information above, published in an article he produced for the Scottish Memories magazine in August 2000. Other information was obtained from the Bishopbriggs News.

Chapter 58:

CONSTABLE JAMES MCCALL

LANARKSHIRE CONSTABULARY – 1874 to 1876

The police face all sorts of dangers on a daily basis. On many occasions they face these dangers head on without any consideration of the consequences. One such officer was Constable James McCall of Lanarkshire Constabulary, who was killed in an explosion at a Railway Works at Burnbank in Hamilton, on the 19th of June 1876.

The location of the explosion was a brick building on the railway line at Burnbank on the line to Hamilton Railway station running parallel with Burnbank Road. The line was being constructed for the Bothwell & Hamilton Railway Company and the building was for the use of three joiners and four blacksmiths in the employment of Charles Brand & Sons, the contractors for building the railway.

At about 10.30 a.m. one of the blacksmiths had left the building to go to Hamilton and obtain a bar of iron for use in the workshop. At about 11.00 a.m. there was the sound of a large explosion, which could be heard beyond Wishaw and Baillieston.

The building and adjoining structures were razed to the ground and all within were killed outright. The police were on the scene immediately and found chaos and destruction over a wide area. The bodies of the men were found scattered around the area. One man was found hanging from a tree.

From the investigation, it appeared that approximately 30lbs of dynamite, which would not explode due to dampness, had been laid out near to the building to dry in the sun. The dynamite was usually kept in a nearby store, built for that purpose. It was not established how it exploded.

Constable McCall was at the building on normal duties. Officers were employed by the builders to patrol the area and Constable McCall

233

arranged to meet his colleague, Constable Crichton at 11.30 a.m. at the building, which was the Headquarters of the operation and used to pay the workers. They attended there on a daily basis to ascertain if there had been any complaints or incidents over the previous twenty-four hours, which required their attention.

Constable Crichton was a couple of minutes late and about 200 yards from the building, when he heard the explosion and immediately rushed to the area and observed the devastation. He called out for his colleague and began to search through the ruins of the building. He was joined by Sergeant Cruickshanks and other men of the Blantyre and High Blantyre detachments.

Constable Crichton eventually identified Constable McCall, in the ruins of the building, by means of his shirt, leather belt and handcuffs, pieces of which had been found lying near his body. The connecting rings of his handcuffs were found embedded in a nearby block of wood 15 yards away.

CC McHardy together with Sheriff Spens and Procurator Fiscal Dykes attended at the scene to be met with a sight of total carnage. A Fatal Accident Investigation was immediately put in place.

In total six people were killed in the explosion:

- *Constable James McCall*
- *William Dick, Foreman Joiner, Burnbank*
- *David Black, Foreman Blacksmith, Burnbank Toll*
- *George Horn, Joiner, Greenfield, Burnbank*
- *John Fraser, Blacksmith, Almada Street*
- *William McLay, Hammerman, Townhead Street*

Sergeant Cruickshanks was instructed by CC McHardy to attend at High Blantyre to inform Mrs McCall before local gossip could do so. On the way he met the Reverend Wright and asked him if he would accompany him to deliver the dreadful news.

On approaching the house at High Blantyre, they could see Mrs McCall in the doorway. On seeing Sergeant Cruickshank and the Reverend Wright she collapsed in tears, screaming, 'He's dead, he's dead.' She later told them that she knew as soon as she saw them approach that a tragedy had happened.

Constable McCall was only twenty five years of age with eighteen months police service. He left his widow, Catherine, and four young children. She was also near to giving birth to their fifth child.

This was indeed a tragic set of circumstances. Unfortunately, for that era, they were very commonplace at mines, steel works, railways and other locations. The requirement for Health & Safety was not as stringent as it is now, resulting in many accidents and fatalities, which nowadays could be avoided.

Chapter 59:

CONSTABLE THOMPSON COURT

COATBRIDGE BURGH POLICE – 1910 to 1914

Thompson Court was born on the 9th of March 1891 at Old Luce in Wigtonshire. His father was a Railway Surface man. Thompson was the eldest of five children. By 1901 the family his family were living at 8B North Main Street, Kirkmabreck in Kirkcudbrightshire, near to Creetown, where his father was employed as a Domestic Gardner.

Thompson was educated in the area and on leaving school assisted his father as a labourer.

In 1910, at the age of nineteen, Thompson left home and travelled to Coatbridge where he joined Coatbridge Burgh Police. He lived in the Police Barracks on Muiryhall Street next to the Police Office. He excelled at sports, competing in the Lanarkshire Constabulary Sports events, particularly the 100-yard sprint, where he won several medals. In October 1913, he was presented with the Scottish Life Saving Association (SLSA) medallion for qualifying in advanced life saving techniques.

Like so many others at the time, he sought a better life and decided to leave for Canada to seek employment a policeman in Regina. He resigned from Coatbridge Burgh Police along with a colleague, Constable John Kane. On the 10th on May 1914, their friends and colleagues in the force bid them farewell with a party in the Police Barracks. On the 16th of May, the two friends left on their adventure, sailing on the SS Corsican from the Broomielaw in Glasgow, bound for Montreal.

On arriving in Montreal, they then headed for Regina, a distance of 1,760 miles. When they got there, they immediately attended at the Police Headquarters to apply for jobs as police officers, only to find that there were no vacancies.

John Kane had two brothers already in Canada, Charlie & Patrick, working in the mines at Hillcrest, Crowsnest Pass in Alberta. The Kane's

236

were originally from Carluke and had emigrated to Canada in 1906 with their wives and families.

This involved another journey of almost 500 miles for the two friends.

On arrival there, on the 16th of June 1914, they registered for work, Thompson being employed as a Timber Packer. Their plan was to raise money to travel further west to Vancouver and try to join the police there. Neither had ever worked in the mines.

Thompson's first shift was on Friday the 19th of June. He arrived early and at 7.00 a.m. descended the mine with Patrick Kane and other colleagues. John and Charlie Kane could not get a shift until later that day.

Shortly after 9 a.m. the village of Hillcrest was changed forever when an explosion ripped through the mine, at a depth of 1200 feet. Of the two-hundred-and-thirty-five men that had entered the Hillcrest Coal Mine for the morning shift, one-hundred-and-eighty-nine did not make it out alive.

Of the one-hundred-and-eighty-nine men, seventeen were born in Canada and of those only two in Alberta. The remainder were immigrants, the majority of whom arrived in Canada between 1910 and 1914. The men were from Great Britain, France, Belgium, Italy, Austria and other European countries.

John and his brother Charlie assisted with the recovery operations and recovered and formally identified the bodies of Thompson and Patrick.

The fatalities accounted for almost half of the mine's total workforce, which left ninety women widowed and about two-hundred-and-fifty children fatherless. Many of the victims were buried in a mass grave at the Hillcrest Cemetery.

The Government of Alberta held an inquiry into the circumstances surrounding the explosion in 1915. The majority of men were killed by a direct result of the blast, the others, including Thompson and Patrick, were killed by toxic gases in the mine caused by the explosion.

Patrick was survived by his wife and five children.

Condolences came from across the country, including a brief message from King George V, but the commencement of World War I soon overshadowed this event and it went largely unnoticed. The King said,

'I am grieved to hear through the press of the terrible disaster at Hillcrest coal mine by which it is feared hundreds have lost their lives. Please express my deepest sympathy with the sufferers and also with the families of those who have perished.'

The incident remains Canada's worst ever mining disaster.

Thompson, who was only twenty years old, was buried at the Masonic Plot of Hillcrest Cemetery.

Like many people of the time and many police officers, they travelled to far away places in search of a better life. He clearly wanted to be a police officer in Canada and if only the Regina Police had been recruiting, when they arrived, Thompson would have enjoyed that new life and perhaps even raised a family. A young and hopeful life, taken too soon.

Chapter 60:

CONSTABLE ROBERT MCBETH BREAKENRIDGE KPM

LANARKSHIRE CONSTABULARY – 1913 to 1943

The passage of time means that sometimes we forget the legacy our predecessors leave. However, families do sometimes keep mementos, newspaper clippings and other items which provide some background as to their family members.

The internet is now a valuable resource to find out additional information about people and particular events. The story of Constable Robert Breakenridge is one such instance where my research led me to relatives of the officer and to the items they have held close to them for many years.

Robert McBeth Breakenridge was born on the 24th of April 1892 at 53 Townhead Street in Hamilton, Lanarkshire. His father was a Railway Engine Keeper.

Robert grew up and was educated in Hamilton. On leaving school he worked as a coal miner, however, on the 25th of November 1910 he joined the Scots Guards at Hamilton, with the Service No 7763.

During his service he received further education, receiving his certificates on the 7th of February 1911. In July 1913 he was also awarded a medallion and certificate for proficiency in life saving.

Robert was retained on the Reserve List from the 25th of November 1913 and returned home to Hamilton where his family were living at 5 Wylie Street.

Shortly after his return Robert joined Lanarkshire Constabulary and after initial training was posted to Wishaw, living at 51 West Academy Street. His Collar No. was 'LC' 169.

However, Robert's police service was interrupted after less than a year when the hostilities of WWI commenced. He was recalled to 'The Colours' and re-joined the 1st Battalion, Scots Guards on the 6th of

August 1914.

At the beginning of November 1914, the 1st Battalion Scots Guards were in trenches between Veldhoek and Gheluvelt in the area north of the Menin Road. They were also holding a barricade on the Menin Road. Up to the 8th of November the enemy attacks continued and there was a real danger the line would be overcome. As they had feared, the enemy did get into trenches held by the French and Loyal North Lancashire troops but were driven out by a counterattack by the Scots Guards and the line was held.

The next day was quieter but on 10 November the shelling started again which, on 11 November, the War Diary records as 'Terrific shelling commenced at 6.30am and lasted for three hours, all trenches and dug outs were knocked in.' The enemy then attacked, the Prussian Guard leading the assault. This time the Germans broke through and the whole front was pushed back.

Men from the Scots Guards in forward positions became isolated and had to fight their way back. One of these men was Robert Breakenridge. The Germans got to within two-hundred metres of the artillery line before the attack was stopped and driven back.

He was involved in a bayonet charge against the Germans and was knocked unconscious, possibly by a shell or blow to the head. He lay on the battleground for a considerable time.

When he regained consciousness, he saw that he was surrounded by dead bodies and silence. He had bruises to his hand's and his forehead. He got to his feet and stumbled around for a period, unaware of the direction he was travelling. Fortunately, he found an Artillery Battery, which turned out to be the 2nd Battalion of the French Artillery.

Meantime, Robert was reported Missing in Action and communications travelled between his family in Hamilton and the regimental offices. The military authorities could not confirm whether he was missing or killed.

That is until his family started receiving communications from Robert, himself, telling them that he was with the French. They wrote to the authorities and it was later confirmed that he was indeed engaged in action with the French Artillery.

Robert returned to his unit until they returned to the UK on the 22nd of August 1915.

He returned to France on the 6th of April 1916 by which time the 1st Battalion was part of the Guards Division. Robert saw action on the

Somme at The Battle of Flers-Courcelette between the 15th and 22nd of September. Unfortunately, he became debilitated and suffered shellshock.

He was returned to the UK on the 24th of September and, following treatment, served the remainder of the war at home.

During home leave on the 24th of November 1916, he married Margaret McNeilly in Wishaw and they later had one son, John, born on the 2nd of September 1917 at Wishaw.

Robert survived the war, however, it took its toll on his family. His brother, William Breakenridge, was killed in action on the 22nd of December 1917, whilst serving in the Royal Navy aboard HMS Valkyrie. His brother-in-law, John H. Allan, was a Serjeant with the Scottish Rifles, also killed in action, on the 7th of April 1915.

On his discharge from military service, Robert returned to Wishaw where he re-joined Lanarkshire Constabulary on the 9th of April 1918. He was awarded three WWI medals and the silver wound badge. Robert was then transferred to Douglas, residing in the Police Station with his family.

Sadly, his wife Margaret, died at the age of 33, in the Police Station on the 31st of August 1919.

Following the death of his wife, Robert was transferred to Motherwell, to be closer to his family for support.

On the 10th of August 1921, Robert was on duty at Wishaw Cross. The area was quite unsettled as only a few days previously, Constable Peter Munro had been attacked and killed on Main Street, Wishaw.

During the late evening of the 10th, Robert was approached by a rather large and muscular local. For no apparent reason he became abusive, challenging Robert to fight. He was advised to go away, several of his friends giving him the same advice. He moved forward toward Robert, however the group with him restrained him.

He broke free of them and lunged at Robert, striking him on the face and causing him to reel backward. The male continued reigning blows with his fists on Roberts body. Robert defended himself well and reached to his pocket, producing his baton. Several well aimed blows struck the male on the head, causing him to fall to the ground. Robert quickly got on top of him and handcuffed him. With the assistance of the others, he removed the man to the police station.

The following day the man made an appearance at Hamilton Sheriff Court. The man admitted the charge of assault on Constable Breakenridge and was sentenced to thirty days imprisonment.

On the 14th of October 1921, Robert married Mary Martin, a Tram Car Driver from Hamilton. After the marriage Robert was transferred to Stonehouse. They had one daughter, Marion.

On the evening of Thursday the 23rd of March 1922 Robert was on nightshift duty along with Constable John 'Jock' Robinson. They had made a check of their property in the village and then headed for the Caledonian Railway Station on the edge of the village, between Lawrie Street and Vicars Road.

The station had four platforms, a footbridge, two signal boxes, two water pumps and a goods shed. Due to the size of the property, they split up and each took one side of the platforms.

It was now the early hours of the morning and quite dark. As Robert checked the platform offices and waiting rooms, he saw a man walking on the opposite platform. Initially he thought that it was 'Jock' Robinson.

He continued and then became aware of movement ahead of him. A closer look revealed three men crouching behind one of the water pumps. Robert moved closer toward them and challenged them, with no response.

The three got to their feet and Robert grabbed one by the arm. The other two ran toward Robert and a struggle started. On seeing them approach, Robert drew his baton and struck several blows at the two men as he held on to his prisoner.

One of the men, later identified as Arthur Friel, grabbed the wrist of the arm that Robert was holding his baton with. The third man shouted, 'Shoot for Christ's sake.' Robert thought this an idle threat to make him release his prisoner.

However, when he looked toward the other male, later identified as Magnus Petrie, he saw that he was holding a revolver, which was pointed at his face. Robert lashed out with his boot, striking Petrie as he discharged the revolver, fortunately sending the bullet away from his head.

Robert then called out for his colleague, 'Jock, Jock,' however he had already heard the commotion and gun shot and came to see what was happening.

By this time Friel had released himself from Robert's grip and struck two heavy blows to the back of Robert's head. It was later discovered that he had used a crowbar. Robert's scalp burst open with blood flowing down his neck, making him unsteady.

Robert could see that he was close to the edge of the platform and was losing his balance. He had the presence of mind to grab on to two of the

242

men, Friel and another, as he fell on to the track. All three landed with an almighty thud.

Jock Robinson was by this time running across the tracks to his struggling colleague. He could see Robert on the ground and the two men rose to their feet, they began to lash out at Robert with their feet, landing several blows on his body and head. Robert, unsurprisingly, lost consciousness.

As Jock closed in, the two made off, however, he caught up with them and he engaged them in a fight, drawing his baton and landing several excellent blows.

Robert came too after a few seconds and could see Jock with the two. He heard Jock shout, 'Grab your baton and we'll smash their heads in.' Robert staggered to his feet and headed toward his colleague.

As he did so, another shot was fired, and he heard it ricochet off the rail track. A voice shouted, 'Shoot the bastards.' The man with the gun was Petrie.

Petrie took aim again, Jock pulled his two prisoners around to face the gunman, he discharged the revolver toward them, narrowly missing all three.

Robert was clearly losing consciousness again and fell to the ground. Jock, fearing that he was losing his struggle released the two who immediately ran off. Jock ran toward Robert as a third shot rang out, again missing the target.

He also became aware of a fourth man on the opposite platform watching what was happening, he ran off when the others did.

Robert was losing a lot of blood and getting weak. Jock helped as much as he could and then ran to the Station Masters House and raised the alarm.

Police re-enforcements arrived but there was no trace of the criminals. The officers did find the crowbar used to assault Robert and other housebreaking implements. The bullets were also recovered.

Both officers managed to give good descriptions of the men before they were taken to hospital. Robert had numerous cuts which were stitched and a broken collar bone. Luckily, that was the extent of his injuries. Jock had cuts and bruises and had to have ten teeth extracted as he was also struck on the face by the crowbar.

As dawn broke the police search spread out, with officers coming from all over the County and Glasgow. One of the men, Richard Lennox was arrested quite quickly in the morning, near to Larkhall. He very quickly provided the names of his accomplices, setting in motion an extensive search for them.

Several reports were received at Motherwell Police Office about a man skirting the main roads and was last seen wading across the River Avon.

At about 4 p.m. the police observed a man near to the Holm Forge Bridge which crosses the River Calder at the Motherwell to Bellshill Road. He had managed to evade the chasing officers by clambering up the embankment and on to the road.

A car glided up behind him and stopped. The man thought the occupants were about to offer him lift. However, the vehicle occupants were Detective Jack of Lanarkshire Constabulary, Lieutenant Forbes and Detectives Mowat and McPhail of the City of Glasgow Police. The officers grabbed their man and placed him under arrest. He was searched but there was no trace of a gun. This man was Arthur Friel.

Both men came from the Shettleston area and a search of that location resulted in the arrest of Magnus Petrie. The fourth man evaded capture.

The three stood trials at the High Court in Glasgow on Tuesday the 13th of June 1922, charged with Attempted Murder of Constables Breakenridge and Robinson and having on their possession gelignite, detonators, cartridges and other items in Contravention of the Explosives Act 1883. The officers gave evidence and at the conclusion of the trial the final speeches were made. Lord MacKenzie charges the jury, and they were dismissed until Wednesday the 14th of June.

The jury did not take long to reach their decision and all three were found guilty on both charges. Lord MacKenzie said, 'In any civilised country it was essential that the police should be adequately protected in the execution of their duty. There is no doubt that the conduct of Constables Breakenridge and Robinson on this occasion was deserving of the Highest Commendation. They had loyally endeavoured to discharge their duty in spite of the determined attack upon them and did so to the best of their ability, even after they had been severely injured.'

Lord MacKenzie sentenced Lennox to ten years Penal Servitude while Petrie and Friel received eight years Penal Servitude.

In recognition of their bravery, the CC, Captain Despard, awarded both officers the Merit Star. At that time, it was the highest award that the force could give to officers.

Both were also nominated for the Kings Police Medal for Gallantry, which they were awarded in the New Year's honours list in January 1923.

Their investiture took place at Buckingham Palace on Thursday the 22nd of February 1923 where the medals were presented by King George V.

It was a unique occasion that day, as another two Lanarkshire Constabulary officers were also awarded the Kings Police Medal. Sergeant Alexander McKay and Constable David Gray received their award for tackling IRA gunmen at Bothwell on the 28th of October 1920.

Following the incident at Stonehouse, Robert Breakenridge was transferred to Morningside. He remained there until February 1924 when he transferred to Gartcosh, living with his family at No. 4 Whitehill Terrace.

In November of that year, he was involved in another exciting incident. On Sunday the 23rd of November, Robert was on duty in the village of Gartcosh when he was approached by some locals. They informed him that they had seen a male on some farm lanes leading from Gartcosh to Coatbridge. The man had stopped them and asked for directions to Airdrie. They thought they recognised him as 'Noble Dan,' wanted for the murder of a child in Stirling, from the descriptions they had read in the papers.

Robert obtained the details and recalled the incident from The Hue & Cry. He then headed off on his bike to try and find this man. He made enquiries at Whitehill Farm and was told that a male of the same description had earlier called at the farmhouse looking for some tea. He was last seen heading for Woodend Loch.

Robert made in that direction and observed a male answering the description crossing a field. He approached him and quickly formed the opinion that this indeed was the man he was looking for. The male gave the name Henry Bickerstaff, which Robert recognised as one of his aliases. He then made his arrest.

Bickerstaff was initially taken to Gartcosh Police office and then to Muirhead Police office, where the authorities in Stirling were notified. Detectives travelled to Muirhead with a witness and quickly identified their man as Bickerstaff. He was arrested by them and conveyed to Stirling.

Robert received the CCs High Commendation for this arrest.

Robert was later transferred again and by 1930 was stationed at Baillieston, living in the houses attached to the police office. In May

1935, he was awarded the Kings Silver Jubilee Medal for long and meritorious service. He remained at Baillieston for the rest of his police service, retiring around 1943.

In his retirement he worked for Whatlings Civil Engineering Company as a Security Officer at their London Road premises.

Robert died on the 14th of January 1958, at the Royal Infirmary, Glasgow at the age of sixty- five. His address at the time was 2414 London Road, Mount Vernon, Glasgow.

It can be said, with some confidence, that Robert lived quite a varied and interesting life.

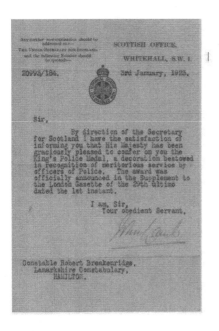

NOTE:
Thank you to Robert McBeth Breakenridge, the grandson of Constable Breakenridge KPM, for providing newspaper clippings and photographs of the Kings Police Medal, which he proudly possesses.

Chapter 61:

CONSTABLE PETER MUNRO

LANARKSHIRE CONSTABULARY

The early 20th century witnessed a period of unrest in Lanarkshire, particularly with regard to religious differences. The situation in Ireland being one of the main causes. The police had to deal with serious disturbances around the county, often resulting in injuries to police and protesters.

Police officers coming from other areas of Scotland were perhaps not familiar with these religious divides and were no doubt surprised by the intensity of people's differences.

Peter Munro was born on the 6th of March 1900 at Sanquhar Cottage, Gartly near Rothiemay in Moray. He was the son of a farm servant and grew up on a farm. On leaving school he worked on the local estate as a Forrester.

At the age of nineteen he left home and travelled to Lanarkshire where he joined Lanarkshire Constabulary and was stationed at Wishaw. He lived in the Police Barracks attached to the police station.

On the evening of Friday the 5th of August 1921, the Newmains Juniors Schools Cup Final took place between Park Road School, Motherwell and Carfin R.C. School. The Park Road School were the victors and were conveyed back to Motherwell in a Charabanc. The supporters marched back toward Motherwell led by an Irish Flute Band. This attracted quite a large crowd.

At about 9.30 p.m. the group and the band arrived at the East Cross in Wishaw. The crowd and become boisterous and some were chanting Irish slogans and referring to the recent events in Ireland. There were more than 150 in this march.

Constables Peter Munro and George Davidson were on duty at the junction of Kirk Road and Main Street. The band turned on to Main Street and at that point the officers made to arrest a male for Breach of the Peace. A struggle ensued as they walked him toward the police station. The officers were rushed by a large section of the crowd and Constable Munro was tripped by one of the group and he fell to the ground. A male, later identified as Edward Higgins, was seen to strike Constable Munro on the mouth and jaw. Constable Munro lay still on the ground.

Constables Stewart and Mclean, who had shortly before conveyed a prisoner to the police office by motor car, returned with additional police officers. Reports of the time put the crowds at about one thousand in total. The scene was described as a serious riot. The scenes would have been chaotic and difficult to control with lack of resources and equipment. Nowadays, with communications and public order training, the situation would be dealt with more rapidly.

After some time, order was restored, and several arrests were made. Constable Munro was found on the road unconscious and was immediately conveyed to the Glasgow Royal Infirmary. Sadly, he succumbed to his injuries on Sunday the 7th of August at 9.05 a.m. The cause of death was recorded as a fracture to the spine near the base of the skull. The injuries were described as a crushing to the upper part of the spinal column, following rupture of the ligament between the base of the skull and the first cervical vert ebra, these injuries were caused by violence to the back of the head.

Nine men were arrested and charged with Mobbing & Rioting, Police Assault and Attempting to rescue prisoners. One, Edward Higgins, was charged with the murder of Constable Munro.

The trial took place on Wednesday the 26th of October 1921. All accused pled 'Not Guilty.' Evidence was led identifying Higgins as the person that struck blows to the head of Constable Munro.

On Thursday the 27th of October guilty verdicts were returned against five of the accused for Mobbing and Rioting, Assault and Attempt to Rescue Prisoners. The others were found 'Not Guilty.' Higgins was found guilty of the Culpable Homicide of Constable Munro and received five years penal servitude.

The charge against Higgins was reduced to Culpable Homicide as it was difficult to prove that he had the intention to kill Constable Munro, which is required in a murder charge. Culpable Homicide is the term used in Scots Law for the crime of causing the death of another person without planning or intending to.

Constable Munro's funeral took place on Wednesday the 10th of August 1921.

CC Despard, Superintendent Walker and fifty officers of the Constabulary attended at the Glasgow Royal Infirmary to pay their last respects to Constable Munro. A short service was delivered by the Reverend Donald MacDonald of the Coltness Memorial Church, Newmains. Constable Munro's mother and father were also present.

The cortege then proceeded to Buchanan Street Station through streets lined with members of the public. Six Constables and one Sergeant of the Wishaw Division accompanied the family and the body of Constable Munro to Huntly.

They marched with the cortege to the grave and laid a wreath on behalf of Lanarkshire Constabulary bearing the words, 'Presented as a token of esteem and deepest sympathy by members of the Lanarkshire Constabulary in memory of Constable Peter Munro who died of injuries received on duty.'

Chapter 62:

DUNCAN WILLIAM MACINTOSH C.M.G., OBE, K.P.M., KStJ

ROYAL IRISH CONSTABULARY – 1920 to 1922
AIRDRIE BURGH POLICE – 1922 to 1929
STRAITS SETTLEMENT POLICE – 1929 to 1942
SINGAPORE POLICE – 1945 to 1946
HONG KONG POLICE – 1946 to 1954

Many police officers joining Scottish police forces in the early part of the 20th century made decisions to leave Scotland to pursue careers across the world. There was, no doubt, good reasons for this, such as a better lifestyle, better career opportunities or perhaps they already had family members in the country they were going to. Some countries specifically advertised in the United Kingdom for police officers as they were of the opinion that the criminal justice system here was something to be admired (which is a matter of opinion), therefore police officers could bring experience and knowledge of the system to their country. There were many success stories amongst the officers that left our shores to go on to bigger and better things and carve out a highly successful career. Duncan William MacIntosh is one of those men.

Duncan William Macintosh was the son of a Printer and Compositor, born on the 5th of May 1904, in Inverness at 22 Crown Street. His surname, on his birth certificate is MacKintosh though throughout his life his surname spelling differed on several occasions. He was educated in Inverness, attending Inverness High School.

In 1920, he left Inverness and travelled to Ireland. He was only sixteen years of age however, he provided an altered date of birth to join the Royal Irish Constabulary (R.I.C.). He made himself three years older, stating that he was born of the 5th of May 1901. The R.I.C. were recruiting from the mainland. The fact that Duncan worked in Ireland during the early part of the Troubles is also worthy of note as many police officers in Ireland, at that time, were targeted and murdered. Due to this, it was difficult to recruit locally, therefore the authorities actively recruited in mainland Britain.

Duncan was allocated the Registered No 77131. He remained there for two years and returned to Scotland in 1922.

He joined Airdrie Burgh Police in 1922 and lived in the Barracks attached to the police office. He spent seven years with the Burgh force performing beat duties in the town. It is worth nothing that Duncan and I share this experience of police work in Airdrie as I was also stationed there for a number of years. We would have both walked the same streets, sixty years apart.

He resigned from the force in 1929 to join the Straits Settlements Police (Malaya) as a Detective Inspector, departing from London on the 2nd of May 1929. The move from the UK to the Straits Settlements would have been a massive decision for Duncan. Although the job came with a promotion, it also came with great danger as drug smuggling was a major problem in the area and there were many gun battles with the police.

He had not been with the Force long when, on the 3rd of January 1930, he and a fellow officer received a tip that a gang from China were planning to commit a bank robbery that day. They gathered a group of local officers to intercept these criminals.

The team split into two groups and approached the vehicle being used by the robbers – it had been stopped, pre-arranged, by a Traffic Officer. The robbers, realizing what was happening, opened fire on the police officers. Duncan was shot through the throat and his colleague in the leg.

Undeterred, the officers regained their feet and with their colleagues, returned fire. The robbers made off on foot, pursued by Duncan and the others. All three robbers were caught, two of whom had been fatally shot (one by Duncan).

Following the incident, Duncan and his colleague were taken to hospital where they remained for some time. It was reported that Duncan narrowly escaped death, suffering from serious gunshot wounds. As a result of their determination and bravery, Duncan and his colleague were awarded the Kings Police Medal in the 1932 New Year's Honours List.

In his early years, Duncan was responsible for targeting and arresting numerous high-profile criminals who were involved in murder, drug

251

smuggling and other serious crimes involving firearms. A large number of criminals were deported to China.

In 1937, Duncan returned to the United Kingdom for a brief period and whilst there, he married Kathleen Jones in Monmouthshire, Wales. The couple returned to Malaya shortly after the wedding.

On the 1st of January 1941, Duncan was awarded the Colonial Police Medal for Meritorious Service to the Straits Settlements Police. At that time, he was an Assistant Superintendent of Police.

Duncan remained with the Straits Settlements Police until 1942, when he joined the Royal Air Force, in Singapore, as an Intelligence Officer. He was given the rank of Pilot Officer. Unfortunately, when the Japanese overran Singapore later in 1942, he was captured as a Prisoner of War and interred until 1945. He was imprisoned in Changi Jail and later, Sime Road Internment Camp. Also taken prisoner of war with Duncan was another former Airdrie Burgh Police Officer, Sydney J. Halkett, who was serving with the Malay States Volunteers. Luckily, his wife Kathleen was evacuated from Singapore in February 1942 arriving in Liverpool on the 19th of March aboard the Empress of Japan.

Also interred with Duncan was a Mr William Haxworth, Chief Investigator of the War Risks Insurance Department in Singapore. Mr Haxworth is famed for making three hundred small sketches and paintings of life in the camps using any materials he could find. These appear in many museums in the Asian continent and in online virtual collections – 'Colours Behind Barbed Wires: A Prisoner of War's Story Through Haxworth's Sketches.' One of such drawings was of Duncan MacIntosh which clearly shows the loss of weight and malnutrition which all the prisoners suffered at the hands of the Japanese.

On liberation, at the end of the War, Duncan joined the Singapore police and was responsible for re-building the force into an efficient entity. He was appointed Superintendent and then Deputy Commissioner of the force. His wife also returned to Singapore in May 1946 aboard the Salandia. In June 1946 Duncan was awarded an OBE. At the end of 1946, the British Government appointed Duncan as Commissioner of the Hong Kong Police. They said that he was a man of foresight and progressive instincts.

Through his tenure he improved the image of the Force, whipping the post-war Hong Kong Police Force back into shape. The police force he took over was decimated, its equipment lost or looted, and its stations largely destroyed. Its operating strength was down to under two thousand officers.

He was a truly formidable individual, unbending, determined and utterly professional. Upon his arrival, Duncan's main task was to rebuild the post-war Police Force. His first concern was for his officers. Pay rates were disgraceful. Housing in a society packed with refugees and ravaged by war was critically short and he battled the Government for increases in pay and better conditions for all ranks.

Firearms were in plentiful supply and armed robberies a common occurrence, with gun battles between police and robbers often resulting in death or serious injuries. Between 1948 and 1951, at least eleven police officers were killed whilst on duty by armed gangs.

Impressively, Duncan continued to climb the ranks. In June 1949, Duncan was made a Knight Grand Cross of the Order of St. Michael & St. George (C.M.G.). In June 1950, he was made a Commander of The Most Venerable Order of the Hospital of St. John of Jerusalem and in 1952, a Knight Of The Order.

In January 1948, Duncan returned to Airdrie where he attended the annual dance of the Airdrie Division of Lanarkshire Constabulary as a guest of his former colleague, Inspector David Bannerman of the Burgh force.

Just as the extensive reforms initiated by Duncan were paying obvious dividends, tumultuous events in China swept Hong Kong once more into its turbulent wake. A new police headquarters was underway in Arsenal Yard, thousands of new recruits had been signed up – many former soldiers or veterans of other forces – and morale was high. Then the climax of the civil war in China sent another wave of a million refugees pouring over the Shenzhen River or arriving from ports like Shanghai in crammed boats.

Among them were battle-hardened nationalist soldiers, bitter and vengeful in defeat, armed and highly dangerous. Policemen were ambushed and murdered for their revolvers. Kidnapping was endemic. Violence was acute.

The territory was tense. A string of fortified posts, still currently known as 'MacIntosh Cathedrals', named after Duncan MacIntosh, were built along the border. From these strategic vantage points, police could look down as communist soldiers took over checkpoints on the other side of the narrow waterway.

Commissioner MacIntosh laid strong foundations for a force meant to last. His redoubtable and forceful personality had transformed the disjointed, shattered police into an effective and stable force. This had happened just in time for them to cope with a calamity, both natural and manmade.

Duncan retired as Commissioner of the Hong Kong Police in 1954 having established the Hong Kong Police Pipe Band before he left. They adopted the MacIntosh tartan in his memory. He left the Force in a much improved and professional state than when he took up his post. Duncan suffered greatly by being interred during WWII and came through these terrible experiences to establish himself as a significant figure in the Far East, improving and developing policing for two decades. An amazing man.

His career did not stop there. The retiring Commissioner was appointed by The Colonial Office to be Police Advisor to the Government of Iraq. It was considered that he had a 'blend of astuteness and friendliness', which would 'earn the confidence, and goodwill of the Iraqi authorities.' Above all, Duncan was regarded as a 'first-class allrounder', who thus could manage not only the CID, but also the police post.

Although his appointment was delayed due to the dissolution of the Iraqi Parliament and general elections in Iraq, Macintosh finally arrived in Baghdad in October 1954 after the thirteenth government was formed under the premiership of Nuri el-Said.

Sir Robin Hooper, Counsellor at the British Embassy in Baghdad, observed two months after his appointment that:

'Macintosh was liked by the Iraqis and was making progress in the Iraqi Police and the CID: his advice is being sought and readily taken. He has made far-reaching recommendations for the re-organisation of the C.I.D. and the uniformed branches of the Police Force, including... the creation of a Special Branch and integrated reporting of political and subversive activities between the various districts... [and] there is a marked desire among junior officers of the Police Force to better themselves now that they see that the Government is taking steps to reform and improve the Police Force, which has for so many years remained stagnant.'

Duncan's post ended when the Iraqi Revolution occurred in July 1958.

He was later appointed by the British Government as Police Advisor to the Government of Jordan until he fully retired in 1964.

He died on the 14th of September 1966, at his home in Summerlea,

Hurst Green, East Sussex. He was survived by his wife. They did not have any children.

Several items of memorabilia relating to Mr MacIntosh, including his medals, are on display in the Hong Kong Police Museum.

As mentioned in the introduction to William Macintosh, some police officers, from very humble beginnings made a highly successful career for themselves, working in sometimes hostile environments with great danger. To become the Commissioner of the Royal Hong Kong Police was no mean feat and clearly shows the ability and passion to succeed. Even beyond policing, his skills and experience were highly sought after by governments.

Unfortunately, like many police officers of that era, he did not live long enough to enjoy retirement and reflect on his successful career.

Chapter 63:

SERGEANT RONALD IRVINE KPM

LANARKSHIRE CONSTA BULARY – 1926 to 1951
NEW ZEALAND POLICE – 1952 to 1966

At the end of each year, we are made aware of the many people who receive awards from the Queen in her New Year's Honours list. No doubt we all have our own opinion about these awards however, what we must recognise are those that are awarded for acts of bravery or sacrifice which go above and beyond the normal call of duty.

There have been many of these over the years and the following stories show the heroic acts of some of the many officers to be honoured with such awards. The KPM or QPM (Kings Police Medal or Queens Police Medal, as it is now known) is the highest police award available to serving police officers.

One of such heroic officers who received an award for outstanding bravery, the Kings Police Medal, was Ronald McBain Irvine.

Ronald McBain Irvine was born on the 30th of February 1906, at Dunecht in Aberdeenshire. His father was Constable Ronald Irvine who, at that time, was stationed at Berryhill in Sutherlandshire.

Like his father, Ronald built a career in the police, joining Lanarkshire Constabulary around 1926 and was stationed at Larkhall until around 1932. He married in Edinburgh on the 14th of June 1932, to Helen McGregor, a Post Office clerkess from Larkhall. Sadly, both Ronald and Helen had lost their parents by this time. After their marriage, Ronald was posted to Bishopbriggs where, in 1937, their son, also Ronald Irvine, was born at the police houses.

Ronald was later posted to Glenboig, where he later resigned in 1953 and the family emigrated to New Zealand, leaving the United Kingdom on the 30th of September 1953, from London aboard the SS Mooltan.

He was appointed Constable 5105 on the 15th of November 1954. He worked in Auckland, mostly in the Districts of Papatoetoe and Parnell and in 1960 his police number was changed to 2363T. Ronald was also a member of the New Zealand Police Pipe Band. In 1962 he was with the band when it attended Sydney for the centennial celebrations of the New South Wales Police.

On the 22nd of February 1963, Ronald was promoted uniform Sergeant and officer-in-charge of the 'Modus Operandi' section at Police Headquarters in Auckland. Three years later, he retired from the New Zealand Police on the 7th of April 1966, however, he did not fully retire as he found work as a clerk with a local Auckland company, finally retiring when he reached the age of sixty-five.

Ronald died in August 1987 aged eighty-one.

He was dedicated officer, with a long and distinguished career, and a true hero.

On Wednesday the 1st of January 1930, the London Gazette announced the award of the Kings Police Medal to Constable Ronald Irvine of Lanarkshire Constabulary.

The award related to an incident at Raploch Street, Larkhall, on the morning of Sunday the 18th of August 1929. Constable Irvine was on duty at Larkhall Cross when he was made aware of a fire at buildings on Raploch Street. He immediately left his post and took control of the situation.

The fire had taken hold in a tenement building and spread to four shops on the ground level. Constable Irvine ran to the rear of the tenements and entered the burning building. He found women and children in one of the houses and rolled them in blankets, escorting seven adults and eight children to the common landing and stairs where they were guided out of the building to safety. He carried one of the young children under his cape to protect her from the flames.

Constable Irvine remained in the building, which was now well ablaze, going from house to house. The wooden staircase was engulfed in flames as he made his way to the houses facing on to the street. He reached out of a window and, using his ingenuity, removed one of the sunshades from above a shop and lowered it to the ground. This allowed other occupants to scramble down to ground level. This time, Constable Irvine joined them on the street.

However, he was quickly informed that a Mrs Wilson was trapped within her house on the first floor. He immediately placed two trestles against the building and, using them as a ladder, entered the burning building once again. He found Mrs Wilson in her living room in a very distressed state. He calmed her and grabbed some blankets, damping them with water and placing them around her. He then guided her out of the living-room window to the trestles and assisted her to the ground, with the assistance of people that had gathered to watch.

He re-entered the building again as two other women were thought to still be within. He found one of the women and guided her to the ground via the trestles. The other woman had already jumped from the building, but missed the blankets being held to catch her and broke her leg. She was the only casualty.

One can only imagine how Ronald felt, entering a burning building and guiding everyone to safety. Feeling relieved to have removed the majority of people only to be told that another person was still within. Yet, without hesitation, he re-entered the burning building to remove the woman in an act of true heroism.

Shortly after he left the building the floor collapsed and the building completely gutted. It must have been a terrifying situation and one which brought him close to death.

In total, Constable Irvine was personally responsible for saving the lives of nine adults and eight children, without the loss of any lives.

To sum up the extent of the fire, it took the Larkhall, Cambuslang and Bellshill Fire Brigades over two hours to eventually extinguish the fire. It was clearly an intense fire which makes Constable Irvine's bravery even more incredible, entering the building several times without thought for his own safety.

On Monday 3rd March 1930, Constable Ronald Irvine attended an investiture at Buckingham Palace where he was presented with his KPM by King George V.

A truly remarkable feat of selfless heroism by a young constable. The award of the KPM cannot be underestimated. It was only awarded to officers who displayed extreme bravery in the face of danger. Ronald showed tremendous courage entering the building as he did, without regard for his own safety. One can only imagine how catastrophic this incident would have been, without the intervention of Constable Irvine.

Chapter 64:

CONSTABLE SYDNEY HUSSEY CRAIK

LANARKSHIRE CONSTABULARY – 1919 to 1932

When events happen in the presence of a police officer, there is an expectation by the public, that the police officer will act. Sometimes incidents happen so quickly that officers react without careful consideration of their surroundings. The adrenaline is flowing and the only thought on their mind is to deal with what is happening or arrest the person responsible.

When such incidents happen in busy streets, there are many hazards to consider, such as traffic on the road, pedestrian, obstacles and other things depending on the environment they are in. However, the police officer will forget about such things as their full attention is on the matter at hand. Sometimes with unfortunate and tragic results.

On Tuesday the 6th of September 1932, Constable's Sydney Craik and James Prentice were on duty in Cambuslang, keeping watch on a street bookmaker, near to 32 Glasgow Road. At about 2.50 p.m. they decided to make their arrest.

To ensure they weren't seen, they jumped on to a passing bus and as they neared their prey, they jumped from the bus. Constable Craik ran behind the bus with the intention of crossing the road to make their capture. Unfortunately, he did not see a bus travelling in the opposite direction. He ran into the path on the oncoming bus and fell under the front wheels.

Constable Prentice heard a loud shout and looked onto the road to see his colleague trapped under the front wheels of the bus. They carefully removed the vehicle to release Constable Craik, however, it was clear that he had received serious head and leg injuries.

An ambulance was summoned and he was taken to Glasgow Royal Infirmary, where he died of his injuries on Monday the 12th of September.

259

The cause of death was a Fractured Skull.

Sydney, who was thirty-one-years-old, was born in Arbroath and grew up in Carnoustie where his father was a Police Inspector. He served with the RAF, as a Fitter, from the 22nd of August 1918 to the 6th of March 1919 when he was placed on the RAF reserve list. He joined Lanarkshire Constabulary on leaving the RAF.

He served in Hamilton, Larkhall, Cleland, Rutherglen and Cambuslang and had also been the 'Black Maria' and fire engine driver. Evidently, his father's career impacted the family as Sydney's brother, George Craik, was also an officer with Lanarkshire Constabulary. Sydney left behind his wife Sarah Stewart whom he had married in 1925 in Larkhall while serving there.

In May 1932, Sydney won the Scottish Police Golf Handicap Championship played over Glasgow Gailes and Dundonald courses.

A Fatal Accident Inquiry was held on Monday the 31st of October 1932 at Hamilton Sheriff Court. Evidence was heard from all witnesses, including Constable Prentice. An open verdict was returned with an emphasis on the fact that no blame should be attached to the driver.

In all likelihood, the whole incident happened so quickly, with little time for the driver to properly react. The fact that the officer was knocked down by him, and killed, would have weighed heavily on his mind since the time it happened and would continue to do so. It must have been a terrible thing for him to experience.

Sydney left £253 in his estate. The equivalent value today would be approximately £17,700. Sydney's name is on the Scottish Police Memorial Wall.

Chapter 65:

PC DONALD JOHN MCLEOD

LANARKSHIRE CONSTABULARY

The role and responsibilities of a police officer should never be underestimated. Police officers leave their homes and loved-ones every day to go on duty, not knowing what the day ahead has in store. There is little or no routine to police work and it depends on the actions of others as to what a police officer will encounter and deal with.

An officer will never know in fact whether that particular day will be the last time that they see their families, as all sorts of dangers may be lying ahead for them to deal with. Every call they attend, every corner they turn and every door opened to them could have all sorts of dangers attached, which the officer will have to deal with in a split second, making life changing decisions for everyone present.

The day-to-day bravery of police officers is not something that is highlighted very often, nor is it recognised very often. Most police officers see their actions as 'just doing the job.' Some, unfortunately pay the ultimate sacrifice and some suffer the consequences for the rest of their lives.

Bravery also comes in many different forms and this story is one of those where the professionalism and driving abilities of an officer saved others from serious injury or even worse.

Donald John McLeod was born in the village of Urgha, in the Isle of Harris in 1931 the eldest of a family of five. Following schooling in Harris, and on completion of National Service in the RAF, Donald joined Lanarkshire Constabulary.

He served in various stations throughout Lanarkshire including Bellshill and Cambuslang. Notably, he was involved in the case of murderer Peter Manuel. He escorted Manuel into Glasgow and drove Manuel and senior Detective officers to the River Clyde where Manuel

261

indicated the spot in the River Clyde where he had deposited the pistol used in his crimes. The pistol was later recovered by divers and used as a production at the subsequent trial at the High Court in Glasgow.

McLeod would have been driving the car listening to every word spoken and no doubt feeling uneasy about having a serial killer so close to him. Not many police officers will have contact with serial killers and this would have been a unique occasion and the story will have been told endlessly to family and friends.

Most people would think that working on a serial killer case and being in close contact with one would be the most memorable moment of an officer's career but not for Donald.

In fact, one of his more memorable moments came just after midnight on Monday 10th September 1962, when he was working in the Lanarkshire Traffic Department, he was on patrol duties in his Jaguar Traffic car. He was accompanied by two officers, Constables William Bryden, based at Carmyle, and Eric Robertson, based at New Stevenston. The officers saw a vehicle which appeared suspicious and was later found to have been reported stolen.

The officers failed to stop the vehicle and a chase ensued, starting in Crawford through to Beattock and several other country roads, taking the officers into 4 different force areas: Lanarkshire, Dumfries and Galloway, Ayrshire and Lothians and Peebles for a distance of over 60 miles. At one point fifty police officers were involved in the incident.

The occupants of the stolen vehicle drove at speeds in excess of 100 miles per hour. During the pursuit they threw several items toward the chasing police vehicle including a hammer, a boring bit, a tyre lever, and a car seat. Having been involved in high-speed pursuits, I can visualise the scene, with adrenaline flowing and tight grip on the steering wheel whilst taking sharp corners or trying to maintain contact with the other vehicle. Donald would have had to be very alert to avoid all of the items being thrown at them, making quick manoeuvres to avoid a possible fatal error.

The skill and driving of Constable MacLeod avoided colliding with these items and he maintained a close pursuit of the vehicle until it was abandoned. The occupants bailed out of the vehicle close to Ettrick Water, near Selkirk and two of them were arrested following a search of farms and outbuildings in the area. The third was arrested sometime later.

The culprits were charged with seven crimes including attempted murder of the officers, three thefts of motor vehicles and housebreaking charges. One culprit received ten years imprisonment and the others received seven years imprisonment at the High Court in Glasgow. Lord Walker congratulated the three officers on their commitment and brave conduct.

On top of Lord Walker's congratulations, Constable MacLeod was officially commended for his bravery and driving skills. He was mentioned in the London Gazette of 6th October 1964, receiving The Queens Commendation for Brave Conduct.[1] Donald received his award from Lord Clydesdale at the County Buildings in Hamilton.

Latterly, Donald worked at Craigie Street Police Office where he finished his service as warrant officer. On retirement, Donald set up his own successful rubberising business in Cambuslang, catering for the fishing industry, before retiring to the Inverness area. He died on Friday 18th October 2019 at the age of eighty-eight.

Sadly, I never managed to meet Donald McLeod however, like many other officers in these stories I wish I had. I would have loved to have gotten a greater insight into the actual incident and his own personal feelings and emotions during and after the chase.

As mentioned at the beginning of this story, bravery and brave conduct can be in many forms. On this occasion, the driving skills of Constable McLeod were key to the situation the officers found themselves in. His tenacity and professionalism were incredible, maintaining the chase with all sorts of items and objects being thrown into his path and successfully apprehending those involved. At any point, one of the items could have struck the car or caused Constable McLeod to lose control and crash the police car, with possibly fatal consequences. His brave conduct was rightly recognised and his award could be worn with pride.

---

1   The Queen's Commendation for Brave Conduct, formerly the King's Commendation for Brave Conduct, acknowledged brave acts by both civilians and members of the armed services in both war and peace, for gallantry not in the presence of an enemy. Established by King George VI in 1939, the award was discontinued in 1994 on the institution of the Queen's Commendation for Bravery.

Chapter 66:

CONSTABLE JOHN MCNICOLL RAMSAY

MOTHERWELL & WISHAW BURGH POLICE

The role of police officer is a very unique one. In the very early years of the police service, a police officer was expected to be on duty on every day of the year. Indeed, it was not until the passing of the Police Weekly Rest Day (Scotland) Act of 1914, that police officers were actually allowed one day off every seven days.

Following the Desborough Committee Reports of 1919 and 1920, police Constables were awarded twelve days of annual leave. This has increased significantly in recent years.

That being said, when is a police officer actually off duty? The expectation is that even on an official day off or on annual leave, if a police officer observes any criminal activity or members of the public requiring assistance, the expectation is that the officer will place themselves 'on duty' and deal with the situation they have encountered. Therefore, a police officer is never really 'off duty.'

On the 11th of September 1938, Constable John McNicholl Ramsay, of the Motherwell & Wishaw Burgh Police was on a day off, enjoying a paddle steamer journey on the River Clyde on the LMS Caledonia.

He had been to Rothesay in the morning and then boarded the paddle steamer to Dunoon and was standing at the bow of the steamer, enjoying the view.

The steamer was passing 'The Gantocks', just off Dunoon, when the Captain noticed a motor dinghy in trouble. The waves struck the dinghy and it capsized, throwing the occupants, a male and female into the water. The Captain immediately sounded the distress signal.

The dinghy had just left the SS Caledonia, an 'Anchor Line' passenger ship which had just arrived from New York and was anchored in the Firth of Clyde.

John Ramsay heard the distress signal and looked out into the Clyde. He could see the overturned dinghy and the two occupants in the water, about 50 yards away.

Without a second thought, John removed his overcoat, jacket, shoes and socks and dived into the water, swimming toward the man and woman. Two other passengers followed him shortly after. John was first to get to the dinghy and quickly pulled it toward the pair. The male was really struggling, and John held on to him, keeping him afloat. The female laid on her back keeping herself afloat by holding on to the overturned dinghy.

The two other men were quickly on the scene, assisting him to keep everyone afloat.

A lifeboat crew had also heard the distress signal and launched their boat, reaching everyone within about fifteen minutes. John and the two men were returned to the LMS Caledonia and the pair from the dinghy were taken to shore by the lifeboat.

Fortunately, no-one was injured and the pair that had been in the dinghy were taken home to Glasgow following some medical attention.

John and his companions were given fresh clothes and dried off, completing their sight-seeing tour and later returning home, on their separate ways.

The pair in the dinghy were very fortunate as John was an exceptionally strong swimmer and had life-saving certificates gained through the Motherwell & Wishaw Burgh Police. One of his special feats was to swim two lengths of the Motherwell Baths underwater. At the recent police inspection display he had walked along the 'deep end' of the baths with another Constable seated on his shoulders. No mean feat, even for an experienced swimmer, taking great stamina and strength.

It's safe to say that John Ramsay had many accomplishments in his life.

He was born in Carnoustie in 1912, the family moving to Clydebank whilst he was still at school. He attended Clydebank High School, where he excelled at football, athletics and swimming.

In 1930, he joined the Motherwell & Wishaw Burgh Police in May of that year, shortly after it had been established. He worked for periods in both Motherwell & Wishaw.

Then in 1942, he joined the Royal Air Force, training in Canada and seeing active service in Palestine and the United Kingdom as a Wireless-Navigator. At the end of the war, he returned to the police, working at

Headquarters in Motherwell. However, shortly after his return he was seconded to the Civil Control Commission in Germany, in the Public Safety section.

After the defeat of Germany in 1945, a Control Commission was set up to support the Military Government, which was in place at that time. The Military Government was gradually phased out and the Control Commission took over the role of 'Local Government.' It was responsible for Public Safety, Health, Transport, Housing and Intelligence. The forward HQ was in Cumberland House, Berlin. Recruits had to be over twenty-one and were recruited from the Police, Civil Servants, the Foreign Office and demobbed Military Personnel. He served there until 1950, returning to the Burgh force.

John then served on street and traffic department duties in Motherwell until November 1957, when he was promoted to Sergeant at Headquarters in Motherwell. He was later appointed as the force training officer, where he remained until his retiral in August 1963, with thirty-three years' service.

John, a bachelor, lived in Motherwell following his retirement, at 20 Crawford Street. Sadly, he only managed just over two years of his retirement. He died, at home, on the 16th of November 1965.

His funeral, held at Daldowie Crematorium, was well attended by friends, colleagues and senior police officers.

Sergeant Ramsay was the holder of the Africa Star, WW2 Defence Medal, WW2 Medal, France & Germany Star and the Police Long Service & Good Conduct Medal.

PART TEN:

THE NEED FOR FORMAL RECOGNITION FOR TWO WHO DIED ON DUTY IN LANARKSHIRE

Chapter 67:

THE NEED FOR RECOGNITION FOR CONSTABLE GEORGE TAYLOR & DETECTIVE SERGEANT WILLIAM ROSS HUNT

We have discussed, in previous sections of this book, the bravery of police officers. As you may have noticed, on a few occasions that bravery goes one step further and results in the ultimate sacrifice of the officer, the loss of his or her life.

In this chapter we will examine the cases of Constable George Taylor & DS William Ross Hunt, where both were murdered whilst on duty and in quite horrific circumstances.

The murder of these officers were almost seven years apart in 1976 and 1983 respectively. Both incidents were in Lanarkshire and within the same policing division.

Both had joined Lanarkshire Constabulary and later transferred to the newly formed Strathclyde Police when it was established on the 16th of May 1975. They had also worked together for a short period during their service.

The circumstances of each case will describe the violent and ferocious manner of their murders. One would therefore be excused for believing that these officers would receive some form of recognition for their bravery, which is clearly evident in each set of circumstances. However, to this day, neither has received any form of recognition at a local or national level for their sacrifice, and the years of loss and pain caused to their families.

The only recognition the officers received was the erection of a small plaque at the public entrance to Hamilton Police Office, paid for by their colleagues through charity events and collections.

Why have these officers not been recognised? Lanarkshire Police Historical Society are presently involved in a campaign, together with the families of both officers, to have this reviewed and have their bravery and

269

sacrifice properly recognised. It will be a long fight however, we will not give up until the proper recognition has been awarded.

The words of Adrian Hunt, the son of William Ross Hunt, go some way to describing the pain that the families endure to this day:

The author has asked me, on behalf of my family, to provide a personal note concerning the legacy of my father's death. Before I do so, I'd like to offer some perspective, proffered by two professionals.

A prominent Politician once said:

'Of all the consequences suffered as a result of crime, the anguish experienced in those cases where a relative is killed, stands alone. The trauma of bereavement is no doubt made even worse by the suddenness of the loss, and the knowledge of the circumstances in which it occurred.'

In 2011, the first Victims Commissioner, Louise Casey CB, commented in a forward to a report on the effects of Murder:

'The impact of an individual homicide goes broad and deep, affecting particularly the surviving family but many other individuals as well. Profound changes are wrought upon these families and others as a result. It is something that many of us, thankfully, will only ever have to imagine.'

Sunday June 5th, 1983

Two in the morning, a date, etched into my family's memory.

There was a knock at the door... the nightshift Superintendent and a Woman PC stood on the doorstep. The Superintendent said, 'Something has happened, your husband has been seriously injured.'

My mother was stunned... 'Ross,' she said, 'How could this be, he's due to retire in a couple of months.'

I can still remember the red Slazenger jumper and blue Adidas jogging bottoms I was wearing. I wonder how many people can remember what they were wearing on a specific, date thirty-eight years ago! Such was the impact.

My father was dead. Ross lay in a theatre, cold, still, beaten and swollen from his injuries. Staff looked on in disbelief and the Night Shift Sister, Sister Blackie who had known Ross professionally, offered some words of comfort.

My mother was in a trance like state and kissed my father on the forehead. She told me it was okay to do the same. My family's lives had changed forever.

My brothers were already living their lives away from home, one in Canada the other in England. This significant, traumatic and life changing event undoubtedly affected their own mental health and inevitably the ripple effect will have cascaded down to their own respective families, to some degree.

My own mental health has suffered greatly and again its effects have sadly impacted heavily on my wife and no doubt affected the thoughts of my two sons.

Despite this, we have all tried to live honest and decent lives. We all worked, raised families and have contributed in certain ways for the good of society. I know this is something my father would have been proud of as he always promoted that type of ethos in our childhood.

On a personal level, one of the greatest hurdles some of us have found difficult to deal with relates to trust, a trust in your fellow being, a trust in a Society where evil has its influences. To cope and adapt to everyday pressures with that constantly in the back of your mind is not an easy task but when good people are found a faith is restored.

The friends we have all made over the years have been special to us in our lives, never intruding, always a constant, never judging and willing to listen. They no doubt find it hard to feel our pain but life has and will present them with their own trials and tribulations. The important thing for us has been their understanding.

Ross, the man and his life are lovingly remembered by us daily. Why daily? The circumstances of his death dictate that.

My family lost an honourable, principled, loving and caring man that day, a man who meant the world to his family and the community he served.

A man murdered in cold blood protecting the public.

The people of Larkhall turned out in their hundreds on the day of Ross funeral, to pay their respects. Shops closed and ordinary people openly wept, such was their attitude towards my father whose interaction had impacted on many of their lives.

Sadly Ross, the family man, would never know or experience the lasting love of his three daughters in law, his grandchildren and great grandchildren. We lost an anchor that day.

Away from Police work, Ross in his more active years enjoyed athletics, badminton, table tennis, golf, cricket, stamp collecting, reading, music and cooking.

He was also a member of a Bowling Green and a Professional & Businessman's Club (similar to Rotary) and supported many local causes.

271

Police colleagues and the general public will testify to a consummate professional, who would always go that extra mile.

Ross was of that 'Dixon of Dock Green era.'

He would help an elderly couple dig their allotment on his days off because their house had been broken into and their garden destroyed; he would chop wood for two spinster sisters who were blind and their home had also been broken into; he held the hand of a young girl involved in a road accident, comforting her as she died in the back of an Ambulance (an event remembered in the press, by the young girl's mother, following Ross' death); he would take the time to counsel the criminal fraternity, trying to set them on the straight and narrow; and he would offer support and assistance to colleagues on a personal basis, often when he saw someone struggling with life.

For this reason Ross was referred to as 'Faither,' by colleagues and criminals alike.

How do I know these things, I met many of them over the years and in some cases it has been documented.

Ross was truly a man for all seasons.

Official recognition, for Ross' actions on 5th June 1983 and his many years of Crown Service in the RAF, Merchant Navy and Police, never followed.

This is truly a sad indictment for one who gave the ultimate sacrifice.

My mother, Marjory, lived out her life in relative obscurity, save for close friends and neighbours, for a further thirty years following Ross' death.

She left Larkhall in the early 90's and spent twenty years in the small town of Biggar. She became more dependent on close family members, as a support mechanism. She never discussed the events of that terrible night and only reminisced about her marriage and earlier years with Ross. She once confided that if she did truly open up it would be like 'a Pandoras box' and she couldn't go there.

In later life Marjory fought and survived Cancer, one side effect however, left her suffering from Dementia and she passed away in a Care Home in 2013.

Marjory died with no formal State recognition for Ross. This would have meant a great deal to her in her lifetime and is something, as I have said, that my family still feel is an affront to Ross' life and memory.

I know that the author feels passionately about this cause as well as

272

the Murder of George Taylor, whose service and sacrifice, once again, was never recognised at the time.

George is working tirelessly to have these cases reviewed and I commend his book to the Police Family. Once again on behalf of the Hunt family, I thank George for all his efforts.

Adrian W Hunt

(Sgt retd., Strathclyde Police)

Chapter 68:

THE MURDER OF DETECTIVE SERGEANT WILLIAM ROSS HUNT

At about 11:35 p.m. on Saturday the 4th of June 1983, Constables Douglas Reid and John Limerick were on duty in the Larkhall area of 'Q' Division of Strathclyde Police, when they were instructed by their control room to attend at Larkhall police office where a man was reporting a serious assault.

On arriving at the police office they met Alexander Matusavage, a local man from Larkhall. Matusavage was bleeding heavily from a head wound and his white shirt and jacket were saturated with blood. He also had a dozen or so bleeding slash wounds to his back. An ambulance had already been called.

Matusavage told the officers that Hugh Murray Jnr. of 16 Earn Gardens, Larkhall, had inflicted these injuries on him whilst he was in the 'Wheels Inn' pub in Larkhall. Matusavage was taken to Law Hospital, Carluke.

Initial enquiries were made at the pub and a search of the general area was made, however, there was no trace of Hugh Murray Jnr. The officers made the local CID, DCs Wilson Gillan and Duncan Nicholson aware of the incident. These officers also made a search of the area and they too could not trace Murray. DCs Gillan and Nicholson had started their shift at 6 p.m. covering the Larkhall and surrounding areas of Lanarkshire, and they were shortly due to finish at 2 p.m.

Also, on duty within the division that evening, were DS William Ross Hunt, known as 'Ross', and DC John Hair. These officers worked from Hamilton Police Office and covered the Hamilton, Bothwell, Uddingston and East Kilbride areas.

These officers had started at 11 p.m. and were working the nightshift, finishing at 7 a.m.

Only four Criminal Investigation Department (CID) officers covered the division between 6 p.m. and 7 a.m. Their duties included the investigation of the more serious incidents in the division, such as serious assaults, robberies and rapes.

As there were only four officers to cover a significant area, it was not unusual for them to assist each other where an investigation required additional resources.

DS Hunt was the senior Detective Officer on duty within the division, however a DI was the senior 'on-call' Detective Officer, if required.

At about quarter past midnight on Sunday the 5th of June, DCs Gillan and Nicholson were patrolling the Larkhall area in their unmarked police car when they were contacted by the divisional control room and requested to attend at Larkhall Police Office and speak to the Bar Officer.

On their return the Bar Officer made them aware that a second serious assault had been reported, which had occurred a short time earlier.

A man called William Strang reported that he had been attacked on Victoria Street. Someone had attacked him, punched him on the face and attempted to stab him with a knife. He said that he struggled with his attacker, who threw the knife away into a garden. A statement was taken from Mr Strang at the end of which he identified the person responsible as Hugh Murray Jnr. who was well known to Strang as he was a close friend.

The officers took Mr Strang to the area where he was assaulted by Hugh Murray Jnr. They searched the gardens in the general area; however, they did not find the knife.

They returned to Larkhall Police office where DC Gillan contacted DS Hunt to make him aware of the two incidents and that the suspect for both was Hugh Murray Jnr.

DS Hunt knew Murray as he had worked for several years in the Larkhall area. Knowing that Murray was a violent individual, DS Hunt decided to attend at Larkhall and assist with enquiries. He and DC Hair arrived there at about 1:20 a.m.

DC Gillan made them aware of the investigation to that point. DS Hunt decided that all four officers should attend at the home address of Murray Jnr. in an attempt to trace him. He lived at 16 Earn Gardens, Larkhall, at the end of a long cul-de-sac.

All four officers left Larkhall Police Office at about 1:30 a.m. and attended at No. 16 Earn Gardens. On arrival at the street, they parked their unmarked vehicles and walked to the front door of the house, which appeared to be in darkness.

DC Gillan knocked on the door several times and eventually a young woman came to the door. DC Gillan and the other officers identified themselves as police officers by showing their photographic police warrant cards. He asked if she was the occupier of the house and she replied that her Mum and Dad were the householders. The girl was asked if she could waken them, she agreed and went inside the house.

A few minutes later an older woman, Jean Murray, appeared at the door. She was quite aggressive in her attitude, asking what the officers wanted. DS Hunt informed her that they wished to speak to Hugh Murray Jnr. regarding a serious assault which took place earlier in the evening. She told the officers that she knew nothing about it.

DS Hunt asked if they could come into the house to speak to her. She denied them access adding that her son was not at home. She asked, 'Do you have a warrant?'

DS Hunt replied, 'No' and the door was slammed shut as the officers stood on the doorstep. As police officers know, this was not an unusual occurrence as not everyone is willing to assist with police enquiries

The officers then walked away from the door and down the garden path. At that point they saw three people walking toward them, along Earn Gardens, two males and one female. DS Hunt informed the others that Hugh Murray Jnr. may possibly be one of them and nodded toward one of the males who was wearing spectacles.

The officers walked toward the three and as they approached each other, DS Hunt asked if any of them was Hugh Murray Jnr. The elder looking of the two said that Hugh was at home in bed, adding in a jocular manner, 'I will go and get him for you.' The three continued walking toward No. 16.

DS Hunt and DC Gillan walked alongside this male, talking to him. DCs Hair and Nicholson followed behind with the other male and the female. They walked along the garden path toward the front door. DC Nicholson could see that the door was open with Jean and Hugh Murray Snr. on the doorstep.

The first male (James Murray) entered the doorway of the house. The officers thought that he was going to get Hugh Jnr.

Slightly behind were DC Hair and Nicholson with the other male and female. As they reached the gate at No. 14, the female pushed the male into the pathway. He appeared startled and confused by this and returned to the footpath, looking puzzled at the female's actions.

She then took hold of his arm and said that he must be drunk. They then continued to walk toward No. 16, with the female pushing the male several times toward the door.

DS Hunt and DC Gillan, who were standing outside the door, were forced apart when the female pushed this male between them.

DC Hair realised that this man was indeed Hugh Murray Jnr. and that the female was trying to get him in to the house and away from the police officers. Just before Hugh Jnr. could enter the doorway, DC Hair grabbed the waist belt of his trousers and pulled him backwards onto the garden path. He then turned to face Hugh Jnr. and blocked his way back to the door.

DC Hair asked him for his name, taking hold of him by the arm but he refused to answer. DC Hair declared to his colleagues that this was Hugh Jnr. and informed him that he was being arrested.

At this point, James Murray, who heard what was being said, came out from the house and jumped from the doorway onto DC Hair's back, Hugh Jnr. took the opportunity to punch DC Hair, and by doing so pulled himself free of his grip. DC Gillon, responded by pulling James Murray off of DC Hair and then became involved in a fist fight with him.

DC Nicholson went to assist his colleague however he was forced into a garden hedge with James Murray jumping on top of him punching his face several times.

Meanwhile, Jean Murray had ran into the house and grabbed a poker. When she came out she ran at DC Hair striking him on the back of the head, causing him to fall into the hedge beside DC Gillan. Blood began to pour from a wound to DC Hair's head.

DCs Gillan and Hair recovered their composure and released themselves from the hedge, with the assistance of DC Nicholson. As they did so they could see Hugh Murray Snr. and DS Hunt fighting with each other. This fight appeared to stop abruptly and DS Hunt, realising the situation was getting out of hand and thinking about the safety of his officers, called to his colleagues to return to their vehicles. He realised that things were not going well and it would be best to re-group and summon additional officers to assist them.

As they ran down the garden path, DC Hair was struck across the head with a brush shaft wielded by Hugh Murray Snr. however he managed to stagger away. DC Nicholson ran to his police vehicle and at 2:03 a.m. used the police radio to call a 'Code 21 – RED,' (this means that police officers require assistance urgently.)

When the 'Code 21' emergency call for assistance was broadcast, officers from across Lanarkshire headed for the scene with blue lights and sirens, to the aid of their colleagues.

Back at the entrance to the garden, DS Hunt stumbled, falling to the ground and was immediately jumped upon by Hugh Murray Snr., who began striking him violently about the head and upper body with a large wooden pole. DS Hunt was now isolated and surrounded by Hugh Murray Snr., Margaret Smith and Jean Murray, striking him about the head and body with wooden poles. DC Hair tried to go to his assistance, however, he was driven back, being struck on the head by a wooden pole.

At one point Hugh Murray Jnr. joined in and was seen sitting astride DS Hunts body in a frenzied state. The other officers and members of the public who had come to their windows and doors to see the commotion, could see that Murray Jnr. was holding a knife and was stabbing DS Hunt on the chest and abdomen, whilst the others kicked him violently on the body and head with their feet and the wooden poles.

One witness, a local resident, watching from the window of her house recalls seeing DS Hunt's body rise in the air several times with the ferocity of the kicks. She witnessed Hugh Murray Jnr. sitting on top of DS Hunt with a knife in his hand. She also heard Jean Murray shout at Hugh Murray Snr. 'Gie me that fuckin' stick,' which she grabbed, hitting DS Hunt several times about the head.

Hugh Murray Snr. grabbed it back and continued the beating as DS Hunt attempted to crawl away from the onslaught. DS Hunt was heard to call out, 'Oh God, I've been stabbed. They've got knives.' DS Hunt didn't stand a chance and the violence used toward him was terrifying. It is impossible to imagine what was going through DS Hunt's mind as he was brutally attacked. Was he thinking of his wife and family, the safety of his colleagues or was this all just a horrible dream.

DCs Hair, Gillan and Nicholson tried in vain to reach DS Hunt. Each of them was beaten with a variety of weapons, including large wooden poles and metal pokers. This must have been a terrifying situation for all of the officers as they tried to control the violent attacks and reach their fallen colleague.

DC Nicholson saw James Murray and another run down the garden path brandishing large wooden poles. He and DC Gillan attempted to take them from the men. Margaret Smith also ran at him with a poker and the next thing he recalls is lying in a hedge with James Murray gouging at his eye, Murray also had his hand inside DC Nicholson's mouth, he responded by biting on his hand until it was released.

James Murray continued to punch DC Nicholson about the face and he recalls Hugh Murray Jnr. approach and attempt to strike him with a stick. DC Nicholson pulled James Murray across his body, causing Murray to take the full force of the blows, shouting, 'You've hit me ya stupid bastard.'

However, Hugh Murray Jnr. also had a knife and stabbed DC Nicholson on the leg and back, the wound to his back caused his lung to collapse and he lost consciousness.

As the police assistance began to arrive at the scene, the situation started to calm down, however, Hugh Murray Jnr. ran off.

Although the attacks only lasted a matter of minutes, for the officers involved, it must have seemed like an eternity.

Two of the first officers to arrive, Constables Fenwick and Limerick, arrived at Earn Gardens and saw total chaos. They could see DC Gillan struggling with James Murray, both with blood on their heads and faces.

They also saw DC Nicholson in the front garden of No. 16. His head and face was covered in blood, as was his shirt. He looked to be seriously injured and the officers called for ambulances to be sent.

Constables Fenwick and Limerick grabbed James Murray and as they did so, heard DC Gillan say 'They've stabbed Ross and Duncan.' James Murray struggled so violently that Constable Fenwick had to draw his wooden baton, striking him numerous times on the upper body. They eventually overpowered him and placed handcuffs on him.

As they placed him in the police vehicle, Hugh Murray Snr. walked down the garden path brandishing a wooden broom handle, he was clearly enraged, shouting, 'Leave him alone.' DC Gillan called to the officers saying that he too was involved in the incident.

Constable Fenwick went toward Murray and he threw the wooden broom handle into the garden at No. 14. Constable Fenwick took hold of him by the left arm and walked him toward the police vehicle, however, Murray became extremely violent, lashing out at Constable Fenwick with his free hand. DC Gillan saw this and went to the assistance of his colleague.

Once again Constable Fenwick had to use his wooden baton, striking Murray Snr. on the shoulder and as he was moving so quickly, the right side of his head. This seemed to have the desired effect and Murray Snr. calmed down. He too was handcuffed and placed into a police vehicle.

William Murray was standing in the street, naked other than the underpants he was wearing. He was aggressive, shouting and swearing at the top of his voice. DC Hair, who was tending to DS Hunt, called to other officers now in attendance to arrest him.

Constables Ritchie and Weir made their way over to him and he began to struggle with them as they took hold of him. They managed to control him and placed handcuffs on his wrists before he was placed in a police vehicle.

Jean and Margaret Murray ran into the house at No. 16, locking the door behind them. Officers pursued them, eventually forcing the door and smashing a window with their batons. They found them inside crouching in a downstairs room, not quite as brave as they had been earlier. Both of them were arrested.

Meanwhile, DC Hair was kneeling beside DS Hunt on the footpath outside 16 Earn Gardens. He could see that DS Hunt was seriously injured and unconscious. He placed him in the recovery position and stayed with him until the Ambulance crew arrived. The Ambulanceman, John Nelson, could see that DS Hunt had several stab wounds on his legs and body and was losing a large amount of blood. Along with DC Hair, the ambulanceman placed DS Hunt on a stretcher and took him to the ambulance. DC Nicholson, who had regained consciousness, was placed in the same ambulance and driven to Law Hospital.

On the way there the Ambulance crew contacted their control room to make the staff at the hospital aware that they had two seriously injured police officers on board.

On arrival at Law Hospital, DS Hunt was examined by Dr Alasdair Sneddon. His initial impression was that DS Hunt was dead. There was no breathing and no pulse. He was placed on an ECG machine which indicated that there was some heart activity. Every effort was put into trying to resuscitate him.

Dr Sneddon could see that DS Hunt had two lacerations, one on the right side of his chest, measuring about three centimetres, the second wound was on the right side of the lower abdomen, about two centimetres long. There were also multiple lacerations to his head and face.

At 5:40 a.m. it was decided that DS Hunt would require an operation to examine the extent of his wounds and he was rushed into the operating theatre. On opening his abdomen, Dr Sneddon could see that there had been a tremendous loss of blood, his diaphragm had been lacerated extending to the liver. This had been caused by a downward stab wound to his chest, probably caused by a sharp bladed weapon, such as a knife.

DS Hunt never regained consciousness, and despite every effort by the Doctors and nurses he died on the operating table at 6 a.m.

This was now a murder investigation.

The other officers had also been taken to low hospital and were treated by the Doctors and nursing staff. They were found to have numerous injuries:

Detective Constable Duncan Nicholson

- *Four, three-inch lacerations to the right thigh*
- *one inch laceration on the shoulder*
- *One inch laceration below the left eye*
- *Half inch laceration to the right thigh*
- *A punctured lung*

He was in a serious condition and admitted to a ward.

Detective Constable Hair

- *Numerous lacerations to the head and chin*
- *Severe bruising to the right thigh*
- *Severe bruising to the left eye*
- *Bruising to most parts of the body*

He was allowed home after treatment.

Detective Constable Gillan

- *Severe bruising to his left side*
- *Severe bruising to his left eye*
- *Severe bruising to his right hand*

He was also allowed home after treatment.

Earn Gardens was subjected to a detailed forensic and fingertip search with the entire area photographed. A large amount of weapons were recovered, highlighting the ferocity and intensity of the attack on the police officers.

These included:

- *Axe*
- *Hatchet*

281

- *Poker*
- *Metal Bar*
- *Hoover extension tube*
- *Spade handle*
- *Broom Head*
- *Broom handle*
- *Brush handle*
- *Clothes police*
- *Nine broken brush handles*

The majority of these weapons had blood on them. The list shows the extent of the attacks on the officers and the variety of items used to do so. In situations such as these, criminals will use anything that comes to hand as a weapon, not just conventional weapons

Hugh Murray Jnr. remained at large and an intensive search of the local area was under way, with uniformed and plain clothes police officers.

At about 4 a.m. DS Charles McArthur and Detective Constable Alan Fabian were touring the Larkhall area in an effort to trace Hugh Murray Jnr. They were driving their unmarked police vehicle on Robert Smellie Crescent, approximately half a mile from the location of the incident, when their attention was drawn to a man running on the footpath towards Strutherhill.

On seeing the vehicle, this man, who was partially undressed, attempted to conceal himself behind the hedge at No. 8 Robert Smellie Crescent. DS McArthur stopped the vehicle and the youth stood up, placing his hands above his head and shouted, 'Alright, it's me you're after. Don't hurt me.' DS McArthur and Detective Constable Fabian went over to this man and asked his name. He replied, 'Hugh Murray, I wish I could say it wasn't. How's my ma and da.' Clearly the severity of the situation had dawned on him.

Murray was cautioned by DS McArthur and informed that his parents were at the police office, having been detained for assaulting the police officers earlier that morning and it was believed he was also responsible. Murray replied, 'It was me, don't blame them. I don't know what made me stab them, I just went crazy.'

The officers detained Murray and placed him in the police vehicle. Whilst travelling to Larkhall police office, he sat in the back cradling his head in his hands, crying and repeating 'Oh Ma, I'll never drink again, never again, they shouldn't have touched you.'

He then stopped crying and quite rationally said, 'How is it that big Polis, will he live?' DS McArthur did not reply to this remark and Murray then said, 'I suppose you think I'm an animal,' and he then lapsed into silence. His comments revealed the fact that he knew how severe his attack had been on DS Hunt and the fact that he used bladed weapons would have caused life threatening injuries. However, it was too late for him to turn the clock back.

Murray was taken to Larkhall Police Office where he was detained on suspicion of assaulting the police officers.

At about five o'clock that morning, DS McArthur was informed that Murray had volunteered to show where he had discarded one of the knives. With other officers, and on the directions of Murray, they arrived at Birkenshaw playing fields where Murray took them to a part overlooking a gully leading into the River Avon. There he pointed, saying, 'I flung it down there when I realised it was covered in blood.'

He also showed the officers the route he took when he ran away from the scene. It was while showing the officers this route that he said, 'What do you think I'll get, four years maybe? I must be crazy to stab a Polis.' This is another example of Murray wondering how bad the injuries were to DS Hunt and now thinking about the possible outcome for himself.

Despite searches of these areas, in daylight, there was no trace of the weapons used.

Although DS Hunt and DC Nicholson had clearly been stabbed with knives or similar bladed weapons, none were found at Earn Crescent.

At 9:55 p.m. on Sunday the 5th of June, John Dickson was leaving his house at No. 32 Strutherhill, Larkhall, to take his dog for a walk around his garden, as he did every evening.

At the bottom of his garden, he had a privacy wall from the housing development at the rear of his house, measuring over 6ft in height. The wall separated his garden from a pathway on the other side which came from Roberts Melia Crescent and goes to Westerton Ave.

As he walked out into the garden, he noticed a paper handkerchief lying on the path which bordered the grass and wall. He looked at the paper handkerchief and found that it contained what looked like two knives. He didn't touch them as he realised that the police were searching the area for murder weapons which had been used in the murder of DS

283

Ross Hunt, whom he knew.

He immediately went into his house and telephoned the police.

Inspector Scott and Sergeant Dyer, who were on patrol in the area, were contacted by their control room and requested to attend at Mr Dickson's house. They attended and Mr Dickson showed them the knives and where they were lying. The officers examined the tissue and could see that it contained a small vegetable knife and a broken cook's knife, and it was lying on the footpath approximately 15 inches from the boundary wall. It appeared as if it had possibly been thrown over the wall from the path at the other side. The officers seized them and handed them to the Detectives investigating the case.

The knives were later forensically examined and found to have blood staining from both DS Hunt and DC Nicholson on the blades.

When serious cases of this nature occur, a Senior Investigating Officer (SIO) is appointed to lead the enquiry.

On this occasion the SIO was Detective Chief Inspector Alex Cowie. His deputy was Detective Inspector Wilson Bruce. These were the senior CID officers based in 'Q' Division at that time.

Both were contacted at home at about 2:30 a.m. that fateful morning. Both knew the officers involved, especially Ross Hunt, as they had worked with him at various points during their service. They attended at Earn Gardens, where there was a large police presence. They received continual updates, especially regarding the condition of DS Hunt and DC Nicholson.

Instructions were issued to have the location sealed off, forensically examined and photographed.

Both officers then attended at Law Hospital, where the news was not good for DS Hunt. They spoke to DCs Hair and Gillan who provided them with an update as to what had happened.

The suspects were at Larkhall Police office and Detective Chief Inspector Cowie instructed that they be moved to Hamilton Police Office to facilitate interviews and further investigations as there were bigger and better facilities there.

Detective Chief Inspector Cowie and DI Bruce then headed for Hamilton. This must have been devastating for both officers as they knew DS Hunt personally and professionally. For DI Bruce, this was the second murder of a police officer he had investigated. He was involved in the investigation into the murder of Constable George Taylor, at Carstairs, in 1976.

At 5:15 a.m. Detective Chief Inspector Cowie, in the presence of DI Bruce, cautioned James Murray Jnr. regarding the incident at Earn Gardens, he indicated that he understood the situation and then made a comment, saying:

'I was walking tae my mother's house with my brother Hugh and my sister Margaret. Hugh had been in trouble, fighting with a fella earlier and I was taking him to my mother's house. When we got there, we were stopped by four plainclothes police who said that they were looking for Hugh. I told them wait till I see my faither and we all went into the house. I heard my faither arguing with somebody. I was standing behind him. That's when the fighting started. I was fighting with a big bloke with a moustache and I got caw'd over a garden and I was fighting with another one. I don't know what I did then. The next thing I remember was sitting on McCluskey's doorstep and I asked him for a fag. A women Margaret, from next to door, came and gave me a fag. Uniform police arrived and I got lifted.'

Next, they spoke to Margaret Murray, who was cautioned and said that she understood what that meant. She said:

'The Polis grabbed oor Hugh. I ran into my Ma's house. They were all at the door and everything just blew up. I saw one of them hit my faither and jump on him. I wasn't having that so I had a go at the Polis. I tried to get him off my father but he wouldn't come off. Stab him, who says I stabbed anybody. You bastards prove I had a knife. Prove who did the stabbing. I'm saying nothing else. I couldn't see what was happening anyway, somebody smashed my glasses.'

All six were later charged with the murder of DS Hunt and other related charges. None of them made a reply to the charges. They were all remanded in custody.

The trial took place at the High Court in Glasgow. At the trial, supporters of the Murray family spat and cursed at DS Hunt's family and friends who had attended in support, as they entered the court buildings.

At the end of the trial, the family members were all convicted of varying charges.

Hugh Murray Jnr. then sixteen, was sentenced to be detained without limit of time for the killing. He was also sentenced to seven years for the attempted murder of DC Duncan Nicholson and a further two years for the serious knife attack on Alexander Matusavage. He was released after twenty-one years, having been detained at her Majesty's pleasure.

His father, Hugh Murray Snr. and married sister Margaret Smith were also jailed for life for murdering DS Hunt. Hugh Snr. was released after ten years and Margaret Smith after thirteen years.

Brothers, James Murray and William Murray were cleared of murdering DS Hunt. James Murray was cleared of attempting to murder DC Nicholson but jailed for three years for assaulting him to his severe injury. William Murray and his mother, Jean, were cleared of all charges.

At the time, the press reported, and it was confirmed by other residents in Larkhall, that the Murray family marked each release with a party to celebrate not only the release but also DS Hunt's death.

Hugh Murray Jnr. was freed from jail in 2004, living in Stonehouse, Lanarkshire. He developed a serious drug addiction and died of a drugs overdose in 2008.

The funeral of DS Hunt took place on Thursday the 9th of June 1983. The funeral service was held at St.Machan's Church in Larkhall and thereafter at Daldowie Crematorium.

Hundreds of serving and retired police officers attended the funeral to pay their respects to and show their support to the Hunt family. Uniformed officers provided a 'Guard of Honour' for Ross and lined the route for the hearse with the Strathclyde Police Pipe band leading the way. His coffin was carried into the service by six uniformed officers.

The attendance of so many people at the funeral emphasises how well-respected DS Hunt was. He was an outstanding husband, father, colleague and mentor to so many police officers, many of whom achieved great success in the careers due to his tutoring and guidance.

Many of those in attendance had never met DS Hunt but were there to show their support to the family and pride in the fact that they proudly served as police officers, just as DS Hunt had done.

We have described the tragic murder of DS Hunt, but who was the man?

Ross was born on the 30th of March 1927 in Bellshill. On leaving school he became an engineer to trade, both in civilian life and during National Service in the RAF (1946-1948). Following a brief spell in the Merchant Navy, he joined Lanarkshire County Constabulary on the 1st of March 1954.

In 1955, he married Marjory Kirkpatrick at Bellshill. They went on to have three sons, Adrian, Ross and Philip. Adrian became a police officer with Strathclyde Police and was a Police Cadet at the time of his father's murder.

During his police career Ross worked at Cambuslang and Caldercruix as a young uniform Constable and at Baillieston as DC. On promotion to uniformed Sergeant in 1968, he was posted to Larkhall and later as DS at Hamilton, where he remained, through the transition to Strathclyde Police in 1975.

Ross was a loyal, dedicated police officer who was extremely popular with his colleagues.

Sadly, DS Hunt never had the opportunity to enjoy his retirement after a long and distinguished career. Notably, Ross was due to retire from the police only a few months after his tragic murder.

His widow, Marjory, was left with three sons aged eighteen, twenty-four and twenty-nine at the time of his death. After her husband's death, life proved difficult. She lived in Larkhall, which compounded an already horrific situation. Marjory struggled with life and was eventually forced to leave the home where her family had grown up, due to illness and living in the same community as those that had taken the life of her beloved husband.

She tried to make a new life for herself whilst one after another, the Murray family were released from prison with the usual frenzy for media coverage and further revisiting of past events.

Her life was shattered and broken. She fought cancer for five years only to be diagnosed with Vascular Dementia. She passed away, in a nursing home in 2013.

DS Hunt's junior colleagues would often refer to him as 'Faither', such was his character as a person who could offer sound advice and was more than willing to go that extra mile in the care of officers on his watch.

It was also not uncommon for Senior Officers to seek DS Hunt's counsel with a particular problem. The wider community also recognised this officers' qualities and it did not matter what part of the country he worked in, he was always a willing ear, offering the appropriate advice and assistance whether on or off duty.

Within the criminal community, as many colleagues will testify, he was referred to as 'Mr Hunt' and very often those on the other side of the law would specifically ask for him by name. Such was the strength of feeling among certain criminals that following his death they either wrote, commented or attended his funeral (evidenced by letter, sent via a

Police Colleague, to the Hunt family, by an inmate of A Hall, Barlinnie Prison, Glasgow).

The CC at the time, the late Sir Patrick Hamill writing to the late Mrs Marjory Hunt, commented after the funeral that 'the very large attendance was a tribute to the respect which your late husband held both within the force and in the wider community.' He continued, 'May I also take the opportunity to let you know of the many personal messages I have received both from Police Officers and members of the public.'

An article in a newspaper (1984) sums up the qualities of DS Ross Hunt. The article commented that twenty years earlier, a young man had been at the scene of a road accident where a car had collided with a little girl on a bike. This young man had accompanied the little girl in the ambulance and was holding her hand when she died.

This affected the young man deeply and he would return to the children's ward to cheer up the young patients. He also devoted much of his time to road safety and cycle proficiency so that other children would not meet the same fate. That man was DS Ross Hunt.

He quickly became a pillar of the community, with strong Christian values. His work for the care of children was renowned and he was engaged in many areas of charity work. It is no surprise that a lot of his charity work and personal commitments went unnoticed as he was not one to seek the limelight. Not even his closest friends and colleagues were aware of the full extent of his charitable work. Following his tragic murder, it became apparent just how loved and respected Ross was.

Many professional people, members of clubs and societies in the community, approached the police to ask if there was anything they could do to keep his memory alive. It was suggested that a fund be established to provide a lasting memorial.

On the 19th of September 1983, a committee was formed and was named 'Ross Hunt Memorial Project Committee.' The Lord Lieutenant at the time, Lord Clydesmuir, agreed to be the patron for the project. Others on the committee were the Chairman, George Hall B.A., F.R.I.B.A., Treasurer Alan McGregor of the Bank of Scotland and the Secretary was Robert Carty, LL.B., N.P. and DC John Lowe, a close friend and colleague of Ross, represented the police on the committee. Initially the target was to raise £50,000.

It was agreed that the beneficiaries of the project would be children in the Lanarkshire area, as the needs of children were close to his heart.

The local Health Board agreed to the refurbishment of a children's ward at Stonehouse Hospital.

The generosity of individuals and organisations was astounding. The final sum raised was £82,107.62 The money was raised by police officers (locally and nationally,) community groups, societies and individuals. Horse Race Nights, Discos, Dances, Golf Competitions, Quiz Nights, Darts Competitions, Boxing Nights, Fashion Shows, Rallies, 'Jail Breaks', Fun Runs and many more events were held to raise the funds.

A 'Grand Charity Concert' was also held at Hamilton Town Hall starring local celebrities such as Sidney Devine, Ben Gunn, Mr Abie, Ann Williamson and others. The events brought people together in a common cause. Forging links between the police and communities, especially in Lanarkshire. It was a lasting tribute and memorial to a great man.

On the 28th of February 1985, a cheque for £80,000 was handed to Lanarkshire Health Board. Thereafter the children's ward at Stonehouse Hospital was named 'The Ross Hunt Memorial Ward.' Equipment was purchased, play areas built. Amazingly, other hospitals in the area benefitted from the remaining funds.

On Wednesday the 6th of March 1985, Mrs Marjory Hunt opened 'The Ross Hunt Memorial Ward.' She said, 'We are so overwhelmed by the generosity of people, the money came from people in all walks of life'.

The memorial project closed in 1985. Ross's local minister, Rev. Alec Ward M.A., B.D., S.T.M., of St. Machan's Parish Church, Larkhall was quoted as saying, 'Two years have gone by now. Even though wounds have healed, scars remain. He is not forgotten, neither by the police nor the criminals, certainly not by family and friends. The Memorial at Stonehouse Hospital will ensure that Ross Hunt will be remembered widely even by people who never knew him personally. Ross was an ordinary man who, in quiet and humble ways, tried to do good to serve the community. It is fitting then, that the Memorial Fund should be returned to the community through various medical services.'

Unfortunately, the children's ward at Stonehouse Hospital has now been closed for several years, however it helped so many families during the years it was opened.

In March 2010, the two commemorative plaques at the front entrance to Hamilton Police office, remembering Ross and his colleague, Constable George Taylor murdered on the 30th of November 1976, were replaced. The new commemorative plaque remembers both officers and remains on display at Hamilton Police office as a reminder to the officers that serve there and the public, of the ultimate sacrifice made by both officers.

Ross is remembered at the Scottish Police Memorial at the Scottish Police College, Tulliallan Castle, Kincardine, Fife, where his name is engraved on the memorial wall.

The murder of DS Ross Hunt remains uppermost in our thoughts together with colleagues who have fell in similar circumstances. It is tragic to note that Ross did not receive any official recognition of his service and sacrifice.

Chapter 69:

CONSTABLE GEORGE WILLIAM CHREE TAYLOR

George Taylor was born on the 26th of December 1948, in Edinburgh. His lifelong ambition was to join the police. On leaving school, George worked for a short time at Law Hospital, where his father also worked, before becoming a Lanarkshire Constabulary Police Cadet.

On the 26th of December 1968, his birthday, George married the love of his life, Sally, at Cambusnethan. Shortly after, on the 1st of January 1968, he was formally appointed as a police constable by Lanarkshire Constabulary. George was well suited to being a policeman, he was 6' 1" tall, well-built and a friendly affable man.

George was trained at the Scottish Police College, Tulliallan, and initially stationed at Larkhall for a brief period before he was transferred to Forth and then Carstairs.

Early in his service, George successfully passed an Advanced Driving Course at Tulliallan attaining the highest possible grade. This is a difficult course, which only a few police officers undertake, requiring great skill, determination and dedication.

When Lanarkshire Constabulary merged into Strathclyde Police on the 16th of May 1975, George was attached to 'Q' Division and allocated the shoulder number 'Q'167. He continued to work from Carstairs police station.

On the 1st of March 1976, George was selected for a six-month secondment to Lanark Criminal Investigation Department (C.I.D.) which ended on the 5th of September 1976. His Detective Chief Inspector, Duncan McKendrick, described him as 'A young and reliable officer who, prior to his secondment to the C.I.D. has been used to working on his own. He has adapted himself to C.I.D. duties and does not appear to have met difficulty in carrying out some. He is obviously keen to learn and get on with the job in hand. He could make a reliable Detective Officer given time and experience.'

George clearly had a promising career ahead of him.

At the end of his secondment to the C.I.D. George returned to work at Carstairs. George, his wife, Sally and their four young children, three boys aged between eight years and a baby girl aged only ten months old, lived at one of the police houses attached to the police office, at No. 5 St. Charles Avenue.

On the 30th of November 1976, George was rostered to work a 6 p.m. to 2 a.m. shift. He was to work, in police terms, 'single crewed', on his own.

Constable Gillies, who worked nearby at Forth, was rostered on a 2 p.m. to 11 p.m. shift. He had been working with his supervisor, Sergeant Iain Keith, until 5 p.m. when the Sergeant finished his shift. Constable Gillies busied himself with office duties until 5:30 p.m. when he took his refreshment break.

Constable Gillies required assistance to make enquiries into Road Traffic offences, on behalf of another force. At 6:15 p.m. he telephoned George at Carstairs and asked if he would assist him. This was not an unusual occurrence and George gladly agreed to help his colleague.

Constable Gillies drove the relatively short distance to Carstairs Police Station and picked George up in his marked police Ford Escort van Registered Number JGA 981 N. The call sign for this vehicle was 'Quebec Mike' 13 (QM13). This was quite clearly a police vehicle, white in colour with orange and blue reflective stripes along each side, a roof top illuminated 'Police' light with blue flashing light atop and klaxons on either side of the sign.

Constable Gillies drove the police van with Constable Taylor in the passenger seat, both were in full uniform. We can imagine both officers doing what all police officers do; engaging in small talk about overtime, who would be working the forthcoming public holidays (as these were lucrative duties,) who has been promoted and basically the usual small talk and chat that we all enjoy.

They drove from the police station on St. Charles Avenue, turning right onto Strawfrank Road, over the bridge which crosses the Glasgow to London railway and onto Carnwath Road in the direction of the State Hospital.

As they were about 150 yards away from the bridge, they saw a man walking on the road, toward the hospital. It was dark and they could only see that the man was wearing what appeared to be a dark three-quarter-length coat. His right arm was straight down the side of his body and he appeared to have something wooden tucked into his arm and close to his body.

George Taylor remarked that it was a cold night to be going fishing. They both thought that he was perhaps going to the nearby River Clyde, thinking that he had a fishing rod under his arm. They paid him no further attention. This wasn't unusual in that area however, being such a cold and wet night, it was noticeable.

They drove on a further distance of about 60 yards on Carnwath Road and were close to the entrance to the sewage works, when they saw a car stopped on the road, all of its lights were on. A figure could be seen standing beside the front passenger door. It was a man and he was wearing an anorak and a peaked cap, similar to those worn by staff from the state hospital.

Constable Gillies drove along the driver's side of the vehicle and stopped next to the driver's door. Constable Taylor lowered his passenger window and said, 'Can I help you, sir?'

Constable Gillies couldn't hear exactly what the man said in reply and thought he heard him say, 'Aye, a wee bit.' Constable Taylor opened his passenger door and exited the police vehicle. At the same time, Constable Gillies could see the headlights of a car approach from behind him. He shouted to Constable Taylor that he would pull in front of the parked car.

Constable Gillies put the blue flashing roof light into operation and drove in front of the parked car and stopped, applying the handbrake.

The parked vehicle, a Morris Marina, had been driven by Robert McAllan from Carnwath. He was returning home from work in Glasgow. As he drove on Carnwath Road, approaching the railway bridge, he saw a man lying in the middle of the road. The headlights of the car illuminated him in the darkness. There was a man standing beside this prone person and he was waving a torch from side to side. Mr McAllan naturally assumed that there had been some sort of accident. He drove past the standing man and stopped about 70 yards further along Carnwath Road.

He exited his car and walked toward the men on the road. As he did so he heard footsteps running and a short distance from his car he met a man wearing a dark jacket and a uniform cap. Mr McAllan didn't think anything was suspicious, at this point.

The man stated, 'There's been an accident,' and walked toward the passenger side of the car and said, 'Drive me up the road, there's an accident.' The man appeared perfectly normal.

At this point Mr McAllan could see the police van carrying Constables Gillies and Taylor approach from the direction of Carstairs. The man said, 'Let's go.' Mr McAllan pointed out that the police car was approaching and to let them deal with it.

The man started to become excited and said, 'Never mind the police, let's go.' Mr McAllan refused and said that he would wait for the police to stop.

Mr McAllan, when spoken to by Constable Taylor said, 'Look, this chap said he had an accident,' and pointed to the man standing with the peaked cap. Constable Taylor left the police car and walked up to the man, shining his torch in his face. This illuminated his face and the cap, which had a badge on the front above the skip. At this point, Mr McAllan began to get the feeling that something just wasn't right and thought that the man was from the nearby State Hospital, due to the cap he was wearing.

Constable Taylor asked the man, 'Where are you hurt?' The man motioned to the side of his face and Constable Taylor moved closer, shining his torch toward the man's face.

Mr McAllan then watched in horror as the man lunged at Constable Taylor grabbing his throat with both hands. Both then began a violent struggle and moved away from Mr McAllan. It was also clear that Constable Gillies did not see what was happening as he drove his car in front of Mr McAllan's.

As Constable Gillies got out of the vehicle, he saw a man standing with what appeared to be a male nurse's uniform at the front offside of the police vehicle. He also appeared to have a droopy moustache. Constable Gillies stood facing this man, who said, 'Look, your mate is in trouble, better go and help him.'

Constable Gillies looked toward the verge, about 8 to 10 yards away. He saw the man that had been standing beside the parked car in an intense and violent struggle with Constable Taylor. Constable Gillies saw that the man had a long-handled axe, which he swung in the air, the blade flashing like lightning, towards Constable Taylor.

The violent struggle was still ongoing and both Mr McAllan and Constable Gillies could hear Constable Taylor shout, 'Hurry up. This bastard's gone mad!' Constable Gillies then ran toward his colleague.

At this point, the second man attacked Constable Gillies, from behind, striking him on the back of the head and upper body, several times with a large wooden baton. It was clear that things were getting out of hand and Mr McAllan jumped into his car and drove off to get assistance.

Constable Gillies drew his baton and struck this man several times on the shoulders and neck. These appeared to have no effect whatsoever as the man was in a frenzy with enlarged eyes and spitting from the mouth.

Constable Gillies tried to get to Constable Taylor, however, the second male continued to strike him on the back and pushed him aside, running toward Constable Taylor.

Constable Gillies was confused and wondered why this man, dressed as a male nurse was attacking him and shouted, 'What are you playing at, we are on the same side.'

He could see Constable Taylor was still on his feet fighting with the man wielding the axe, he had his baton drawn and was striking at him. Both men then attacked Constable Taylor, striking him about the head and face.

Constable Gillies tried to pass a message over his personal radio to call for assistance, this did not appear to be working. He then tried to stop them attacking Constable Taylor by striking both with his baton, to no avail. Both appeared to stop attacking Constable Taylor momentarily, staring at Constable Gillies with enraged, glazed eyes. This must have been a terrifying sight to see your colleague being attacked in such a violent manner by two clearly deranged individuals. What went through Constable Gillies's mind?

They then turned their attention back to Constable Taylor. The axe could be seen thrust toward Constable Taylor's upper body, as it was raised Constable Gillies could see that the blade of the axe was covered and dripping with blood. He could also see that Constable Taylor's face and upper body was covered with blood and he screamed 'Get help, get help.'

Constable Gillies ran to the police van and tried to call for assistance via the VHF radio, shouting 'QM13 assistance…urgent.'

The time was now approximately 6:45pm, Constable June McCaw was on duty within the front office at Lanark Police Station. She heard a call over the radio and immediately recognised the voice of Constable John Gillies, whom she knew was based at Forth. She could tell that Constable Gillies was in a distressed state and listened as he said, 'Help, help me, they are after me. One has an axe and one has a knife. They have already got George.' She took this to mean that Constable George Taylor had been attacked. A further message from Constable Gillies identified the location as Carnwath Road near to The State Hospital.

Constable McCaw immediately broadcast a message over the radio for all available units to attend the area. Inspector Robert Clelland, Sergeant Thomas Anderson and DS Douglas Mortimer, who were all within Lanark Police office, were made aware of the messages received over the radio. The three officers, along with other officers immediately headed for The State Hospital, unaware of the severity of the unfolding events.

Meanwhile, back at the location of the attack, the male that had been wielding the axe ran toward Constable Gillies. He did not have the axe but did have a knife in his right hand. The male was shouting something that he couldn't make out and lunged at his chest pushing the knife toward him. Fortunately, Constable Gillies avoided being struck, however, the knife did graze his tunic several times. He defended himself by striking out with his baton.

Constable Gillies attempted to get past this man to assist his colleague, however, he was unable to do so. He vaulted a wire fence to try and get behind Constable Taylor, to help him. However, he lost his footing and fell into what he described as a bog, covering his uniform in mud and water.

When he managed to regain his composure, after a few minutes, he returned to the road to see that Constable Taylor and the police van were gone. This part of Constable Gillies's statement is vague and how long he was in this area is unknown. A later search of the surrounding area could not locate a bog as described by the officer.

During the period that Constable Gillies had been over the fence, the two men had driven off in the police vehicle, leaving Constable Taylor lying on the road, severely injured with numerous serious head and body wounds.

At the same time a bus, being driven by George Baxter, with five passengers on board, was travelling along the Carnwath Road, near to Lampits Road, toward Carstairs. He could see a police van in the distance with its Blue Light flashing.

As he approached the van he could see two police hats on the ground, he slowed when he saw the figure of a policeman, Constable Taylor, staggering on the road, signalling the bus to stop.

As he did so, he opened the doors of the bus and could see that

Constable Taylor's face was covered with blood. The policeman tried to speak, however, no words came out and blood gurgled from his mouth. He collapsed beside the driver's seat. It is hard to imagine this horrific scenario, however George Baxter remained as calm as he could and closed the bus doors.

One of the women on board shouted that the officer was 'Sally Taylor's man' and they should head to a Doctor. Mr Baxter drove to Doctor McClements nearby home. The Doctor tried to treat the horrendous wounds on Constable Taylor's body, however, he had great difficulty stemming the flow of blood.

In the meantime, Mr McAllan had driven to the main gate at The State Hospital and spoke to the officer on duty, informing him that two policemen were being attacked further along the road, by persons wearing male nurses caps. It would appear that this officer did not believe the report being made. He did not call the police or have the State Hospital checked to see if inmates were missing. *Why would he not believe Mr McAllan? It is difficult to imagine someone making up such a story and he should have taken some initial actions to test the accuracy of the report.*

Mr McAllan looked toward the road to see a police van, blue light flashing, speeding west on Carnwath Road. He ran toward the road to try and stop the van but it sped past. He formed the impression that the policemen had arrested the two men and were taking them to Carnwath police station. Mr McAllan drove to Carnwath Police office to report what he had seen, but the station was closed.

The staff at the Gatehouse had also seen the police van and formed the opinion that whatever had happened had been dealt with by the police. In actual fact, the police van that they had seen was the one used by Constables Gillies and Taylor, which had been stolen by the two men (Mone and McCulloch).

Also travelling on the Carnwath Road was James Martin, who was on his way to visit his mother at 11 Carnwath Road. As he drove toward the spot where Constable's Taylor and Gillies had been attacked, he noticed a lit torch lying on the road. He slowed down and as he got closer could see two policeman's caps also on the road. He slowed to a stop on the grass verge and got out of his car.

He stood on the road and listened. He could not see or hear anything. He picked the torch up and shone it toward the fields on either side of the road but still could not see anything. He then switched the torch off. He picked up the police caps and laid them on the verge to the left (north).

As he did so he saw another torch, which appeared to be a cycle lamp, also lit. He picked it up by the edge of the casing and could see blood staining on it. He placed it back to where it had been. About three feet away, toward the direction of Carnwath, he saw another cap. This one appeared black and looked as if it had been squashed. He did not touch it.

Mr Martin realised something wasn't right and got into his car, driving to his mother's house. When he got inside, he asked his mother and aunt for the telephone number of Carstairs Police Station. They gave it to him, and he called the number.

A woman answered the phone, it was Sally Taylor, the wife of Constable George Taylor. She was holding their youngest child when she took the call. James Martin told her what he had seen on the road and she said that she would pass this on to her husband. *What went through Sally's mind at that time? Did she think it was George or could it have been a malicious call?*

Mr Martin then looked at his watch and noted that it was 6:45 p.m. He told his mother and aunt what he had seen on the road before he went outside to move his car to the rear of the house. As he walked out the door, he saw a figure walking up the path toward the house. As the figure got closer, he could see that it was a policeman, it was Constable Gillies and he asked to use the telephone.

Both went inside the house and in the light, Mr Martin could see that Constable Gillies was in a wet and muddy state. The mud covered the front and side of his uniform and water was running from his trousers over the top of his boots. There were also traces of blood on his face.

Constable Gillies told Mr Martin to lock all the doors and windows of the house. He then telephoned Lanark Police station to report what had happened.

Meantime Mr Martin went to move his car and as he did so realised that he had lost his spectacles. He thought he might have dropped them when he stopped on Carnwath Road earlier. A police car stopped at the gate, and he told them that Constable Gillies was inside.

He then drove his car back to the spot, parking his car, leaving the headlights on. He found his spectacle case and walked back to his car. As he did so he saw a knife lying on the road near the opposite verge. He nudged it onto the verge with his foot. He also saw a set of police handcuffs on the verge but left them where they were. There was also a black clip-on tie, which belonged to Constable Taylor, on the verge.

He also saw what appeared to be a pool of blood, about two feet in diameter, near to where the knife was. At that point a police van arrived and Mr Martin told them what he had seen, pointing out the various items to them. He then returned to his mother's house.

Around 7p.m, Sergeant Thomas Anderson and Constable Thomas Jackson were travelling on Station Road, Carstairs. They were responding to the call for assistance at the State Hospital. As they did so, they saw Dr McClymont outside his house waving at them to stop, which they did. Dr McClymont informed the officers that an injured policeman was in his front garden.

The officers saw their colleague, Constable Taylor, lying on his right side on the grass in front of the house. They could see that he was seriously injured to the head with blood flowing from his wounds. Constable Jackson tried to speak to him but there was no response.

Sergeant Anderson instructed Constable Jackson to remain with their colleague whilst he attended at 11 Carnwath Road, in response to Mr Martin's telephone call.

An ambulance arrived at about 7:05p.m. and Constable Taylor was placed within. Constable Jackson accompanied him to Law Hospital.

Whilst in the ambulance, Constable Jackson could see, through his unbuttoned tunic, a stab wound to Constable Taylor's stomach. This appeared a deep injury with blood pouring form it. He tried to find a pulse from Constable Taylor's right wrist, there was no trace of any. This was at 7:11p.m. Shortly after this, a frothy mucus came from Constable Taylor's nose.

The ambulance arrived at Law Hospital at about 7:15p.m. Constable Taylor was rushed into the Casualty Department Theatre, where Dr Roddy tried to provide what medical assistance, he could. Unfortunately, at 7:38p.m. Dr Roddy pronounced that Constable Taylor was dead.

Constable Jackson was given the tragic news and immediately contacted Lanark Police office by personal radio.

As other officers were dealing with Constable Taylor, DS Mortimer and Constable Joseph Watson had attended at Carnwath Road, approximately 70 yards west of the sewage works entrance, where they saw two police hats, a bloodstained bicycle lamp, a small white card which had written on it the name of a patient from the State Hopital, James Ferguson.

DS Mortimer then attended at the State Hospital at about 7:05pm,

299

Constable Robert McKillop was already there and requested that checks be made to establish if any inmates were missing. DS Mortimer spoke to the officer on duty and explained what was happening. At that time the staff had still not established if any patients were missing, and checks were still ongoing.

DS Mortimer informed the officer about the card with the name of the patient called Ferguson. The officer confirmed that there was a patient called Ferguson in Ochil Block of the East Wing. His cell was checked, and he was found to be inside. By this time, it was about 7:10 p.m. Neither the officer at the gate or DS Mortimer were aware of anything untoward within the State Hospital.

As this was happening, Mary Hamilton, a Nurse within the State Hospital, was compiling a Christmas party list and found that one name was missing, that of Ian Simpson, a patient. Knowing that he was a patient in the hospital block, she telephoned Charge Nurse McGuire. She told McGuire that she required Simpson's hospital number for her list and to find out if he was attending the party. She explained to McGuire that she had earlier left Simpson with Nurse Neil McClellan and two other patients, Robert Mone and Thomas McCulloch, in the nearby hospital social club, but had received no reply from the telephone at MacLellan's office. Both she and McGuire telephoned on external and internal telephone lines at the same time, which meant that the two phones were ringing simultaneously in Nurse MacLellan's office. Still no reply was obtained, which was very unusual.

McGuire then sent Pupil Nurse Finlayson to the social club to find out what was wrong. Finlayson ran there immediately.

When Finlayson arrived, he entered from the rear of the hospital block, walked along the corridor towards the communicating door leading into MacLellan's office to the right, and the recreation room to the left. He found MacLellan lying face down on the corridor floor between his office and the recreation room. There was blood everywhere and MacLellan was badly injured about the head and lay there, apparently dead.

Meanwhile, McGuire got the feeling that something was seriously wrong and telephoned all other blocks in the West Wing, instructing staff to lock up all their patients and send any available staff to the social club. He also telephoned Mary Hamilton and told her to go immediately to the female block in The West Wing and lock herself in there along with the nurse in charge.

300

Finlayson returned to the hospital block and reported what he had found to McGuire. McGuire ordered him to return to the social club along with Nurse Hughes.

They headed back to the social club and carried out a systematic search of the area, in the event that the culprits were still there. Both must have been terrified as they made their search. However, there was no trace of three inmates, Robert Mone, Thomas McCulloch or Ian Simpson.

The nurses then noticed the door of Nurse MacLellan's office was slightly open. As they tried to open it they discovered that something heavy was lying behind it. As they pushed harder and finally opened it enough to look inside, they saw the body of Simpson lying on the floor, badly mutilated, he too appeared to be dead. He had suffered severe head injuries and stab wounds. Only then was it definitely established that the two missing patients were Robert Mone and Thomas McCulloch.

On receiving this information, McGuire informed the Central Administration office and the alarm in the hospital was sounded, alerting staff and local community of an escape. This was at 7:25 p.m. approximately forty minutes since the attack on Constable Taylor.

Sergeant Thomas Anderson had arrived by this point and on receiving this information, he DS Mortimer and Constable Watson, headed for the old administration block, which they were told was now the Patients Social Club.

They entered the building and headed to Neil MacLellan's office – MacLellan was well known to DS Mortimer from previous official visits. They were met with a horrific sight.

The officers then entered the office where they saw the inmate Ian Simpson, lying on the floor in a pool of blood.

A knife, covered in blood was seen lying on the floor of the recreation room.

DS Mortimer instructed that the area be sealed off and Constable Watson tasked to ensure that no-one entered until it had been forensically examined. DS Mortimer then relayed this information to the Police Control Room at Hamilton.

The murder investigation was now under way with officers being called upon for assistance throughout the force area. Senior officers, including the Chief Constable, Sir David McNee, were all informed and called out to duty.

A few miles away from the State Hospital, at about 7 p.m. two men,

William Lennon and John McAlroy, were travelling in their works Ford Motor van, on the A702 Glasgow to Peebles Road at Melbourne crossroads, when they saw a police van in a roadside ditch.

They thought the van had run off the road and been involved in a road accident so they stopped to see if they could assist in any way. As they approached the police van, they saw a man wearing a uniform type of cap, whom they thought was a policeman come from behind the van.

They had almost reached him when he turned toward the van, pointed and said something about checking that a prisoner in the van was alright. Suddenly a second man appeared and they could see that he was carrying an axe. They had just encountered Mone and McCulloch.

The one wearing the cap began brandishing a knife and jumped at Lennon, stabbing him six or seven times in the back. Lennon fell to the ground.

McAlroy seemed to think that he and Lennon were being mugged and he made to run off. Lennon called out to McAlroy to come back as he had been stabbed, and realizing that Lennon was seriously injured, he did so.

The man with the knife, then threatened McAlroy whilst the other struck him on the head with the axe. He too fell to the ground injured. Mone and McCulloch then began shouting and waving their weapons, demanding the keys to the van.

Lennon told them that the keys were in the van, which belonged to their employers, Motherwell Bridge Pollution Control limited. McCulloch and Mone jumped into the van and drove off towards Biggar, McCulloch driving as he had done with the police van. Lennon and McAlroy were left injured and bleeding at the roadside.

Passing motorists stopped to assist the injured men. Meanwhile, Mr Brodie Hewitt who lived nearby, telephoned Biggar Police station to report that a motorist had called at his house to say that a police van was on its side at Melbourne Cross. He also reported that someone had been stabbed and was sitting beside the van.

Sergeant Robert Archibald and Constable William Stewart attended from Biggar, arriving about 7:30 p.m, shortly after the alarm was being raised at the State Hospital.

They saw Lennon and McAlroy at the road verge, both with what appeared to be serious injuries. An ambulance was called, and the two men made the officers aware of what had happened.

Sergeant Archibald immediately recognised the police van as being that belonging to the Forth Section. He contacted the control room by radio and circulated the details of the second stolen van which had last been seen heading for Biggar.

The Control Room staff were now beginning to piece together the sequence of events. Details of Mone and McCulloch were circulated with warnings regarding how dangerous they were and not to be approached until armed officers were present.

As this was happening Firearms were being issued to plain clothes and uniformed officers who began heading to the area of the rapidly developing situation.

Lennon and McAlroy were taken to Law Hospital where they too were treated by Dr Roddy. Constable Jackson was still at the hospital and waited until they were treated to interview them.

Sergeant Archibald made an examination of the police van and found a large knife and an axe on the passenger floor footwell. A bloodstained road atlas was lying on the ground beside the passenger door. The two seats were also covered in blood as was the offside panels of the van.

Sergeant Archibald then drove to Biggar High Street to take a position and check passing vehicles for those responsible for these incidents.

The second van was later found abandoned further along the A702 near to Woodend Farm, Roberton. The rear of the vehicle was against a fence with the front across the carriageway. It transpired that McCulloch mistook a railway light for a police light. He pulled off the road and attempted a reversing manoeuvre, bogging the van down in the mud. When the police found the van, the keys were in the ignition and a gent's bloodstained and muddy jacket was found on the driver's seat.

Mone and McCulloch were nowhere to be seen as they had set off on foot in search of another vehicle.

Around 7:35 p.m. Rennie Craig was papering a door in the rear vestibule of his farmhouse at Townhead Farm, Roberton. His wife Catherine and four children were in the lounge. They were totally unaware of the events unfolding in the area.

Mr Craig heard a noise at his rear door and went to see what it was. He thought it may be his sister-in-law who was due to visit that evening.

As he opened the door, he was confronted by two very agitated, blood-stained men, he was facing Mone and McCulloch, Mone brandishing a knife and McCulloch an axe. His wife and children heard the commotion and came to see what was happening. They were confronted by a terrifying sight.

The men forced their way inside, Mr Craig grabbed at the handle of the axe and struggled with McCulloch who said shouted, 'Don't do anything and everyone will be all right.'

The pair demanded guns and car keys, threatening to kill him, his wife and family if he did not co-operate. He was in no position to argue and in hindsight their threats were no doubt genuine.

The blood covered their hands and faces, and both appeared wild and evil, with staring eyes, particularly the one carrying the axe. The family were unaware that this blood was from the murdered prison officer, patient and policeman.

Mr Craig told them that he did not have any guns but willingly volunteered the car keys. As they walked through the kitchen, one of the men grabbed the telephone, ripping it from the wall and its socket.

However, a very astute twelve-year-old, Catherine Craig, saw what was happening and went back into the lounge and then through to her bedroom, where there was a telephone with a separate connection to the one ripped from the wall. She didn't like what was happening and dialled '999', being put through to the police. She explained what was taking place giving her name and address. The officer on the telephone told her that he would send the police straight away. She then went back to the living-room. The officer clearly linked the incident to the escape and murders at Carstairs and broadcast the urgency of the call over the police radio networks.

Mone, McCulloch and Mr Craig went outside and into his garage. He showed them the family car, a Gold Colour Austin Maxi, registration number RVD858M, handing McCulloch the keys. McCulloch tried to start the car, unsuccessfully. He demanded that Mr Craig start it. Mr Craig realised that McCulloch had not pulled the choke out, which he did, and the car started immediately.

McCulloch reversed the car out and Mone made to go in the passenger door, as he opened the door, he said to McCulloch 'I think he should come with us,' nodding toward Mr Craig however, McCulloch disagreed and Mone got into the car and they drove off. Mr Craig had a very lucky escape.

Mr Craig ran into the house and telephoned the '999', he told the police what had happened and passed the details of his vehicle. Mr Craig and his family were in a terrified state, having no doubt that their lives had been in danger.

Meanwhile, Constable James Muir, of the Crawford Section, was on duty in the area and heard the wireless broadcast relating to the stolen van. He headed for Beattock Summit, on the A74, and took up a position to look out for the vehicle.

Constable Muir was made aware of the call at Townfoot Farm and began to drive in that direction. However, as he made his way there, he was informed that the men had left the farm and were in possession of the Gold colour Austin Maxi and the registration number was provided. He was told to go back to Beattock Summit and keep a look-out for the car. He attended there at speed.

At about 7:45 p.m. Constable Muir saw the Austin Maxi being driven south on the A74 near to Beattock Summit railway cottages. He drove onto the A74 and followed at a safe distance. He sent a radio message to the Hamilton Police Control room making them aware of his position and that he was now in pursuit of the Austin Maxi. He was instructed to follow the vehicle but under no circumstances was he to try and stop it until assistance was with him.

At the same time, Control Room staff contacted Dumfries & Galloway Constabulary to make them aware of the circumstances and that the stolen vehicle was heading in their direction.

Constable Muir followed at a safe distance, with speeds reaching 95 miles per hour. Unfortunately, as he approached the Dumfries & Galloway boundary with Strathclyde, he lost radio contact, as the systems at that time were very limited in range.

Sergeant James Stevenson, Constables Valance Robison and David Proudfoot of Dumfries & Galloway Constabulary, were on duty in Lockerbie Police Station when they received the information relating to the stolen Austin Maxi, driven by Mone and McCulloch. They attended at the A74 near to Coatesgate Quarry, with Constable Proudfoot driving the Traffic Rover motor car. Shortly after their arrival they spotted the Austin Maxi and pursuing Strathclyde Police vehicle containing Constable Muir. They pulled onto the A74 and joined the chase.

The look-out had also been heard by Superintendent Angus Irvine and Constable John Graham of Dumfries & Galloway Constabulary and they too headed for the A74, joining the chase at an area known as Castlemilk, south of Lockerbie.

At Castlemilk, the carriageway was being repaired and the southbound carriageway was being used for both north and southbound traffic. Superintendent Irvine and Constable Graham had entered this section of the road ahead of the Austin Maxi and were positioned in front of it, with Constable Proudfoot and colleagues behind. All police vehicles had their blue flashing lights illuminated.

The Austin Maxi made a violent swerve onto the northbound lane into the face of oncoming traffic and sped past the lead police vehicle making a violent manoeuvre back to the southbound carriageway narrowly missing the oncoming traffic. They headed on toward the English Border with varying speeds, slowing to 30 mph and then increasing to 95mph.

Cumbria Police had also been made aware of the ongoing car chase on the A74. Constable Andrew Gardner of Cumbria had received a radio message and took up a position at the Guards Mill Interchange of the M6, just over the border at the end on A74 and start of M6. He was joined by two other Cumbria traffic vehicles, driven by Constables Brough and Miller, all cars were singled crewed.

At 9:08 p.m., they saw the Austin Maxi travelling south pursued by the two Dumfries & Galloway Rover traffic cars and the Strathclyde Police patrol car. They too joined the pursuit.

Sergeant Irving Lyon, of Cumbria, had also heard the call and joined the pursuit just before Metal Bridge near to the border.

As the chase drove past Metal Bridge and on the approach to the Greymoorhill Interchange, Constable Gardner managed to overtake the front Rover Traffic car and come in behind the Austin Maxi. Constable Brough managed to overtake the Maxi and pull in front of it.

McCulloch unsuccessfully attempted to overtake Constable Brough on his inside and the two cars weaved between the outside and inside lanes with speeds recorded at 90mph.

As they approached the Rosehill slip road, leading to the A69, Constable Brough moved his car toward the Maxi, forcing McCulloch to drive up the slip road toward the A69 and a large roundabout. Constable Brough had to overshoot this junction; however he travelled on making a U-turn onto the on-bound slip road, against the flow of traffic, heading for the roundabout junction with the A69.

Constables Stevenson, Miller and Sergeant Lyon followed the Maxi up the slip road. As the Maxi approached the roundabout junction the pursuing officers saw the brake lights illuminate, however the vehicle did not stop. It shot through the junction, swerved slightly and came to an abrupt halt, colliding with a barrier and a lamp standard, finally stopping on the grass verge.

Mone and McCulloch leapt from the crashed vehicle, McCulloch, who had been driving, was seen brandishing an axe above his head. They ran towards a mini motor car which had stopped when the crash occurred.

Running after them Sergeant Lyon grabbed one man, Mone, who had entered the car and was sitting on the lap of the passenger in the vehicle. Mone immediately lunged at Sergeant Lyon with a knife, thrusting it toward his chest. Sergeant Lyon quickly grasped the knife by the blade and held it firmly while his assailant struggled violently, fortunately he was wearing gloves which took most of the impact, although he could feel the blade tear at the leather gloves.

With the assistance of Constable Brough and Miller, Mone was disarmed and, still violently struggling, removed from the car, overpowered, thrown to the ground and handcuffed.

Meanwhile McCulloch was partially on the floor of the car behind the front seats and threatening the driver with an axe, held at his head, shouting, 'Get this fucking car moving.'

While the McCulloch's attention was momentarily diverted, Constable Gardner grabbed hold of his weapon, struggled with him and after a short while was able to pull the axe away from his hand and out of his grasp.

He was joined by Constable Proudfoot and Sergeant Stevenson of Dumfries & Galloway Constabulary and between them they overpowered McCulloch, pulling him from the car and arresting him. Constable Muir, who had arrived on the scene after the crash, seized the axe, noticing that the handle of the axe was bloodstained about six inches from the blade.

Finally, this series of tragic events had come to a very dramatic and violent end. Mone and McCulloch now safely secured were taken to Carlisle Police office.

On the evening of the 30th of November 1976, officers of the Strathclyde Police Serious Crime Squad, DI John Fleming, DS Joe Jackson and DC Donald Maul were at East Kilbride Police office in Lanarkshire when they were made aware of the ongoing incident at the State Hospital. They had been in East Kilbride assisting with another enquiry.

Having been made aware they tried to draw firearms from the safe at East Kilbride Police office, however local officers had beat them to it! They had to return to their own office at St. Andrew's Square in Glasgow to obtain firearms from there.

Once they were armed, they headed, at speed, down the A74. They were continually updated by the police control room on the way. DS Jackson, who was driving, recalls the journey being one full of mixed emotions and uncertainty. He was tense and remembers DC Maul massaging his shoulders on the way. He recalls that this was a strange journey. A colleague had been murdered and they knew they were in pursuit of his killers who appeared to be heavily armed. DS Jackson and his colleagues were armed, but what would they do if they encountered them?

Other officers, including Detective Superintendent John Blincow and DC Graeme Pearson were amongst other Serious Crime Squad officers heading down the A74.

They received the good news that Mone and McCulloch had been stopped and arrested near to Carlisle and were instructed to attend at Carlisle Police office, arrest the pair and return them to Lanark Police office. The officers arrived at Carlisle at about 10:30 p.m.

Detective Superintendent Blincow instructed that Mone and McCulloch, who were still handcuffed and in separate cells, be examined by Dr Jolly, the Cumbria Police Casualty Surgeon, which he did at about 10:50 p.m. He noted a few minor injuries to both, as follows:

McCulloch:

- *Cut at base of the right thumb*
- *Minor scratches on left hand*
- *Scratches below both ears*

Mone:

- *Numerous superficial cuts to his scalp*
- *Abrasion to upper lip*
- *Bruise below right nipple*
- *Scratches to upper left thigh*

Their injuries were nothing in comparison to the brutal wounds they had delivered to their victims. Both were found to be lucid and fit for arrest and interview.

Both men were arrested and taken in separate vehicles on their journey to Scotland. As it happens in these situations, the suspects become talkative, and these two were no different.

DS Jackson drove and DI Fleming sat with Mone in their vehicle. Early in the journey, Mone wanted to talk and said, 'I have got remorse for what I've done.'

At this point, DI Fleming immediately cautioned Mone and asked if he knew what it meant. Mone said, 'Of course, Do you think I am that bloody stupid?'

Mone continued, 'It was Tommy (McCulloch) that done the butchering, he went berserk with the axe.'

Then Mone shouted, 'Tommy's a bloody fool, we intended to use the weapons as frighteners only. Nurse MacLellan put up a bit of resistance, and Tommy lost the head. It's too easy to get out of that place. We were supposed to get a day out at Biggar soon, but we couldn't wait, we had been planning this for months now. We were in the drama group. There was only four of us there, McCulloch, Simpson, Nurse MacLellan and myself. We had the weapons planked. We made the knives. I can't remember why we attacked Simpson. We still have more weapons planked in the paint shop where we work. There is a black painted board and we have garrottes concealed there. There is also a sword planked behind a board against the wall beside the shelves. We have an imitation gun about there somewhere and an impression of the master key concealed in a block of wood in the toolbox.

After we attacked Simpson and Nurse MacLellan, we took the keys from McClellan and got out to the fence and used a rope ladder to get over it. I laid down on the road and the car came along and I pretended to be injured. There was also a police car and two policemen were in it.

One of the policemen came over towards me and Tommy went for him with the axe. The other one was talking into something and I went for him with a knife. We took the car away and tried to work the wireless but couldn't get through.

We crashed the car along the road and then we got another one. There was either two or three in this car and we frightened them off and took it away. We crashed this one along the way and then crossed the river and went to a farm where we saw a man and we demanded car keys from him.

This man started the car and we drove away. When we got along the main road, I knew that police cars were following us. There must have been four or five cars after us. After a long way along the road, we crashed again and the police came and took us away. Tommy was always driving the cars.'

Detective Superintendent Blincow conveyed McCulloch back to Lanark along with DCs Kirby & Pearson.

McCulloch too wanted to talk, he mentioned stealing the police van and assaulting the police.

Detective Superintnedent Blincow cautioned McCulloch and when asked if he understood what that meant, McCulloch replied, 'Look. I have been studying law. It is not me to blame for killing these three people, but society. They should have shot me when they had me at the hotel in Clydebank (a reference to the case that saw him sent to Carstairs). They know I have a personality disorder, so I am not sorry I killed them because it is not my fault. I used the axe. Mone only had a small knife and it was me that killed them.'

McCulloch then went silent and later started to talk about stealing the police van. He was again cautioned. He said, 'It was easy. The police thought it was an accident. I crashed the van three times before we got another one off two men. The police should never have interfered.'

McCulloch then went silent and at one point began shaking. He was asked if he was cold and he replied, 'We walked through a river, and I was soaked.'

Further along the journey he started to talk of events in the prison earlier, and once again he was cautioned. However, he continued, 'I have told you before. I am not an idiot. Simpson should never have tried to stop us. Imagine, he has just got a degree too. We scalped him. It is a pity about Mr MacLellan. He was a nice fellow, but he had to go. He was in the way. If the policeman had not interfered, I would not have had to use my axe on him.'

McCulloch and Mone were both taken to Lanark police station. At 1:05 a.m. on Wednesday the 1st of December 1976, DS Mortimer was within Lanark police station when both were brought in by the Serious Crime Squad.

In the presence of Detective Chief Inspector McKendrick, DS Mortimer cautioned and charged both Mone and McCulloch, with the murder of Neil MacLellan. McCulloch replied, 'No comment until I see a lawyer.'

Mone replied, 'I don't wish to say anything.' Both were then locked up in the cells.

Both accused were charged with a total of nine other crimes, including the murder of Constable Taylor. Neither made any reply to the charges.

This ended a tragic and terrifying series of events and trail of devastation, leaving families with the lifelong consequences of their actions. Three lives lost for what reason.

Sally Taylor had the unenviable journey to Law Hospital, to identify the body of her husband, Constable George Taylor, whom she had seen off to his work only a few hours earlier, not knowing that her life was about to change for ever.

Mone and McCulloch later pled guilty to the charges and were sentenced to life imprisonment. However, although Mone remains incarcerated, McCulloch was released into society in May 2013, the parole board deeming that he was no longer a threat to society. An incredible decision with no thought for the victims or their families who have to live with the loss of their loved ones. In my opinion, McCulloch should never have been released.

So, what happened at the State Hospital on the lead up to that evening and on the 30th of November 1976, which led to the deaths of three people?

Mone and McCulloch were both long term inmates of the institution.

Robert Francis Mone was remitted to the State Hospital on the 23rd of January 1968. He was a member of the British Army at the time and was on leave from Germany. He travelled to Dundee and held a female teacher and some schoolgirls hostage in their classroom, ultimately shooting and killing the teacher.

He was deemed unfit to plead and was remitted to the State Hospital. He was described by staff as 'arrogant, supercilious and argumentative.' Dr Loweg, his responsible Medical Officer noted that he had a 'sadistic, schizoid psychopathic personality.'

Although his attitude and demeanour did change during his time at the State Hospital it was noted that his potential for aggression was always evident. He eventually achieved certain levels of parole and became Editor of the hospital magazine. He was given full internal parole on the 7th of October 1976.

Thomas Neil McCulloch had been remitted to Carstairs on the 20th of July 1970 following two charges of attempted murder in Clydebank. He showed no signs of violence during his time there and appeared to be co-operative and mature in his behaviour. He was a qualified painter and decorator and had other practical skills. He was employed in the Paint Shop and Woodworking Department from 1971.

McCulloch was given various levels of internal parole and was finally given full internal parole on the 10th of June 1976.

Mone and McCulloch became close friends and lovers in 1973.

[The following sections are from the official public inquiry, which was released by theScottish Home & Health Department in November 1977.]

Although Mone presented himself as the planner of the escape, it was McCulloch's energy, his ability to make weapons and escape equipment, and his skill in concealing them that made the escape possible. And by making this possible, drove them to attempt it. McCulloch accomplished so much so easily that they must have thought that there was nothing in which they could not succeed.

During the six months up to the end of November 1976, McCulloch manufactured or obtained escape equipment and a number of weapons. A motoring map of the area around Carstairs and a flashlight were brought into the hospital by some person or persons permitted to visit him. At that time the search regime was very poorly managed and virtually non-existent.

It was not possible to identify the visitors and it is possible they knew nothing of

McCulloch's intention to escape. His normal method of obtaining materials was to request them for an innocent purpose.

Mone had obtained money from unidentified visitor to the sum of at least £25. He carried it on his person to avoid being found during searches of this room.

McCulloch made a rope ladder with cord stolen from equipment which he was making for the drama group. The rungs were made by him in the woodworking shop. Attached to the ladder was a length of strong sash cord stolen from the woodworking department and weighted by a piece of lead which he obtained from a floor polisher sent to the woodworking department for repair and discarded as unfit for use.

The rope ladder was concealed for part of the time in a loudspeaker cabinet in the woodworking department and in his room at other times. It was carried from the woodworking department to his room and from there to the social club on the 30th of November 1976.

McCulloch made false identity cards for Mone and himself. The outer cover of Mone's card was made from an academic certificate in his possession. McCulloch had among his own property; a blue card issued to him when he qualified as a tradesman painter.

McCulloch worked in the paint shop, which opened off one end of the woodworking department. It was part of his work there to make, paint and notice boards and he was given Letraset sheets for that purpose. He

312

used the small type on these sheets to make printed card for Mone and a printed false inner sheet for his own card. Mone was permitted to have a Polaroid camera with film and flash cubes. He was allowed to take his camera to the woodworking department to take photographs of articles made there. However, he managed to conceal it in the paint shop, telling members of staff who enquired that it was in someone else's possession. This was never checked.

Mone and McCulloch took photographs of each other, suitably disguised with false moustache's and used these to complete their false identity cards. The false moustaches were found on them when they were arrested after their escape.

The pair had obtained nurses caps of an obsolete pattern for a play produced by the drama group. McCulloch also obtained a large canvas sheet and some pieces of rexine from the Occupational Therapy Department. These were intended to help Mone and himself to surmount the barbed wire on the top of the perimeter fence. These caps and materials were kept openly amongst the props of the drama group and were collected by them on the evening of their escape.

McCulloch made a number of weapons. Their use turned the attempt to escape into a tragedy, the process of making them aroused or renewed in McCulloch a homicidal intention, which might have led to killing, even if there had been no resistance to his escape. It erupted at the first hint of resistance and resulted in the murders.

The original plan had been to disable the nurse or nurses is in charge of them by using ammonia and then by intimidating them with weapons and to lock them in a large wall safe in MacLellan's office.

McCulloch stated in his evidence, that as he made the weapons, a desire to use them to kill anyone who stood in his way increased, so that when the time came to make the escape attempt, he was possessed by an intention to kill.

The number of weapons and the care with which they were manufactured, demonstrate the strength of McCulloch's obsession with them, and to that extent support his account of the growth of his intention to use them. It does not appear that he told Mone about his growing homicidal intent.

McCulloch made three knives from flat mild steel, which he had used in the woodworking shop for the runners of sledges manufactured there. The blades were sharpened to a fine edge on a power buff in the

313

woodworking shop. Metal guards were made for the lower end of the handle of each knife. These were also manufactured from mild steel. They were buffed into an Oval shape and slotted for the blade. The slots were made by using the vertical boring machine to make a row of holes, the divisions between which were battered through using a hammer and screwdriver and trimmed with a file.

Well finished wooden handles, in one case covered with cord, or then fitted to the tang of each knife. The blades were concealed in whole pieces of wood, screwed to the bench so as to appear part of it. One knife used in the occupational therapy department for cutting leather was taken from a drawer.

Whilst the evidence is not entirely clear, it appears that the slot in which the knife should have been placed was filled by a dummy knife which had been made in the woodworking department as a stage prop. But it was very different in appearance from the knife it replaced.

McCulloch made a small axe from a sharpened piece of metal, which he had stolen from the office in the occupational therapy department. He attached it to a hammer handle with screws riveted to it to prevent them slackening. The axe was light and small enough to be hidden easily, but its blade was very sharp and it proved a frighteningly effective weapon up to the day of the escape. It was hidden in a space between panels, forming the side of a workbench, which McCulloch used for hiding weapons. Because staff were so used to seeing it no one thought of searching it.

McCulloch made sheaths for the knives and a holder for the axe, so that they could be carried on a belt. The sheaths were made on a sewing machine which he had been allowed to bring into the hospital to enable him to pursue his hobby of making soft toys. This machine was kept in the paint shop. Material from which sheaths were made was obtained in the occupational therapy department.

McCulloch began to make a sword, but never finished it. It was made from a long metal bar which had been part of a joiner's clamp for holding joints under pressure while they were being glued. One end was roughly sharpened to a point. At the other end, McCulloch had begun to cut a tang using a hacksaw. The sword was concealed in a whole piece of wood.

This piece of wood was made by running a white rectangular groove in two pieces of wood in a machine and gluing these pieces together to form a sort of scabbard. The piece of wood and the sword it enclosed were incorporated into some shelving so skilfully that they were only discovered in the course of a second search of the paint shop, after the escape. The sword was not used in the escape attempt.

Two garrottes were also made by McCulloch. One was made from a violin string and had two handles made of a brass covered rod, neatly bored to receive the wire. The other was made of thicker wire obtained from the occupational therapy department fitted with central cylindrical wooden handles, made in the woodworking shop.

The sword and garrottes were concealed in a space in a bench in the paint shop shortly before the escape. They were not used in escape attempt and were discovered when the paint shop was searched after the murders.

McCulloch also obtained wooden replicas of pistols which had been used as stage props and painted them to make them appear more realistic. They were not used in the escape attempt and were left in the paint shop. He also stated that he made a crossbow, using a leaf from a discarded motor car suspension spring, but had broken it up because they could not hide it. He was thinking about the problems involved in making a simple but effective gun at the time of the escape.

As previously stated, McCulloch and Mone had intended to throw ammonia into the faces of their nurses to disable them. They were unable to obtain ammonia, but McCulloch obtained a quantity of Nitromors, a strong caustic paint stripper used in the paint shop. The Nitromors was transferred to plastic bottles which, when squeezed, emitted a jet of caustic liquid.

The weapons made by McCulloch, the sources of the materials from which they were manufactured and the method of the manufacture have been set out in detail, not because of any intrinsic interest, but because they throw light upon and raise questions about, the variety of materials available to him, the extent to which he was able to use machines in the woodworking department for manufacturing weapons and using the wood working department itself for their concealment.

There was clearly a lack of supervision in the woodworking department and an absence of effective searches of the premises in which the weapons were concealed.

Mone and McCulloch had the ability to win the trust of doctors and nurses, to such an extent that their motives in acquiring material of various kinds was never suspected.

Mone and McCulloch had decided to make their escape from the social club on a Tuesday evening. They chose the social club because the building was unoccupied and stood in an isolated position and because they knew that, at worst, they would be there with only MacLellan and Simpson to overpower.

They chose a Tuesday night because they had determined to make their getaway by stopping a car on the road which, at that time, ran through the hospital site and Mone had discovered, by observing the road, that the volume of traffic on it was at its greatest between 6:00 and 6:30 p.m. on Tuesday evenings.

They had first decided to make their escape on Tuesday the 23rd of November, but that attempt was called off because MacLellan expected a telephone call, and they feared that it might result in attempts to trace MacLellan, which would cause their escape to be discovered. They then fixed on the following Tuesday as the date on which they would make their attempt.

On the afternoon of the 30th of November 1976, McCulloch packed the axe, knives, Nitromors and other escape equipment in his hobbies box, at the end of the working day. He walked with it from the woodworking department to his room, in Tweed Ward. The box was not searched on his leaving one place or entering the other.

On the same day, nursing officer Neil MacLellan, the recreations officer at the state hospital, was required among his other duties to organise two activities, a badminton tournament in the East Wing and a meeting of the drama group in The West Wing. The first involved the transport of fourteen patients from The West Wing to the East Wing.

During the early afternoon of that day, he went to the Central Nursing Office and saw nursing officer, David Brownlie, who was in charge of the office for the whole of the day shift. The holding of recreational activities in the evening depended upon a sufficient number of nurses being available to supervise them. These nurses became available only if released from Ward for other duties, so that there was always a certain amount of last-minute planning. On occasions, activities required to be cancelled because of insufficient numbers of staff to escort and supervise patients, but that did not happen on this occasion.

MacLellan ascertained the number of members of staff available for supervision and in accordance with normal practice, allocated them between the two activities. He made no request for additional staff.

He allocated the available ward staff and two members of his own staff, Coulter and Mortimer, to the Badminton tournament. That left

316

himself and Nurse Mary Hamilton, to supervise the Drama Group.

On that night the group was to be a small one, consisting of McCulloch and Mone, although Simpson joined it later. The group was at that time engaged in producing tape recorded readings from books and plays for illiterate patients.

At about 5:45 p.m. MacLellan went to Clyde Ward and took custody of Mone from the charge nurse, and walked with Mone to Tweed Ward, where he collected McCulloch.

Mone carried a brown paper folder, and McCulloch had two boxes, he had been permitted to use one box for toy making equipment. He sometimes used the other box to carry an extension electrical lead, to use for the tape-recording equipment. Neither of these patients nor the boxes were searched by the respective Charge Nurses before the patients left their wards.

On arrival at the social club, McCulloch went into the club room and Mone went into the kitchen. McCulloch had not expected Mrs Hamilton to be present and expressed surprise at finding her there.

Mrs Hamilton took the comment amiss and answered sharply, but at this stage an event occurred to remove Mrs Hamilton from the social club.

The patient, Ian Simpson, asked that a call to be made from his ward, to ask if he could come and speak to MacLellan in the social club. Mrs Hamilton took this message when Mr MacLellan was away collecting Mone and McCulloch and related to MacLellan when he returned with them.

MacLellan then telephoned Charge Nurse McGuire, who was in charge of the hospital ward where Simpson was and asked that Simpson be allowed to come to the social club. Simpson was then taken under MacLellan's escort to the social club.

In addition to any supervisory duties she may have had on that evening, Mrs Hamilton was engaged in making up lists of patients who had expressed a wish to attend a Christmas party. She wanted to be free of interruptions while she did so and she did not like Simpson.

Accordingly, she asked Nurse MacLellan if she might go to her office in the Recreation Hall to prepare the lists.

The Recreation Hall was in another building, some distance from the social club. MacLellan gave her permission to go to her office and before leaving the social club, she collected some sweets from MacLellan's safe, for an elderly patient. As she was leaving, she asked MacLellan to remember to lock the safe.

She also noticed a Garden Fork and Spade, which were standing in MacLellan's office. They had been borrowed by MacLellan from the Garden Department a fortnight earlier, in order to enable some work to be done on flower beds near the office.

Mrs Hamilton then left the social club. There is no doubt that she owes her life to the fact that she did so. McCulloch later stated that in the frame of mind in which he then was, he would have killed her if she had remained.

The events thereafter depend on the evidence of McCulloch and Mone, but there is no reason to doubt their account. They had no opportunity to compare notes after their recapture and gave little appearance of concealing or reconstructing parts of their evidence.

The account they gave was that McCulloch opened the boxes in the clubroom, put on the belt carrying the knives and the small axe and put on part of his disguise. He was joined by Mone.

Each had a container of Nitromors and they went into the office where MacLellan and Simpson were standing. Mone threw Nitromors in MacLellan's face and rushed at him. McCulloch attacked Simpson in the same way.

The Nitromors did not appear to have had any immediate effect, and it is not possible to say what effect it had on the ability of MacLellan and Simpson to defend themselves in the ensuing struggle.

Simpson resisted violently and McCulloch immediately drew a knife and stabbed him on the head. This surprised Mone and galvanised MacLellan into efforts that enabled him to break away from Mone and go to Simpson's help.

There was a general struggle during which Simpson gained possession of the knife and MacLellan, who may have seen this, ran out of the office, followed by McCulloch, who caught him in the corridor between the office and the clubroom. MacLellan attempted to lock the door of the office, presumably because he was the only nurse present and his first thought would have been to lock up as many patients as possible.

He failed to lock the door due to the ferocity of the attack by McCulloch, who was, by then, armed with the axe he had made. They struggled for possession of the axe and MacLellan temporarily wrested it from McCulloch, who drew another knife and stabbed MacLellan thereby recovering the axe.

Meanwhile, in the office, Simpson had attacked Mone, who screamed for help. McCulloch and MacLellan were struggling nearby, and McCulloch, furious with Mone for failing to help him, struck Mone a glancing blow on the back of the head with the axe. Mone picked up the Garden Fork which had fallen to the floor in the struggle and attacked Simpson with it, stabbing him until he collapsed.

Mone then went to help McCulloch who was fighting with McClellan in the corridor. He squirted Nitromors at MacLellan without much success.

MacLellan had been seriously injured on the throat by McCulloch's knife and collapsed down on the floor with McCulloch on top of him, punching and stabbing him, rendering hum unconscious. There was no further resistance from either MacLellan or Simpson. The time was then about 6:20 p.m.

Nurse MacLellan acted with great courage and in accordance with the highest traditions of the nursing service. He was a powerful man and had he counter attacked with the weapons he took from McCulloch or attempted to make his escape, the result of the night's events might have been different.

These were easy and obvious courses and he took neither. Instead, he attempted to secure Mone and Simpson and to disarm McCulloch, presumably hoping to overpower McCulloch without causing him serious injury. However, he could not have known that McCulloch had a number of weapons in his possession.

There is also the nightmare quality in the way in which McCulloch was able to produce one weapon after another and to attack MacLellan until he was no longer able to defend himself.

Mone had been dazed by the blow on the head but was sufficiently in charge of himself to remember to cut the wires of the internal and post office telephones. He was slow in collecting the escape equipment, and McCulloch gathered it together and put it in Mone's arms.

McCulloch pushed Mone outside the door of the social club and told him to keep watch. McCulloch then went back into the social club and murdered the unconscious and seriously injured MacLellan and Simpson, by striking each of them repeatedly on the back of the head with the axe.

He cut MacLellan's belt and removed his keys. He opened the safe in the office and took from it a large fire axe, which was kept there for MacLellan's use as Fire Officer, and re-joined Mone outside.

Both put on the old-style nurses' caps which they had obtained and

319

walked across the lighted area of The West Wing, into the unlit open ground beyond it to a point about halfway along the southern side of the perimeter fence.

The weighted rope was thrown over the fence and secured to a horizontal rail near the ground, bringing the top of the ladder, which was fastened to the rope in line with the top of the fence. The canvas sheet was thrown up to cover the barbed wire but landed some feet to one side of the ladder in a position in which it could not be used.

They climbed over the fence and barbed wire, leaving the pieces of Rexine lying inside the fence. They crossed the railway line in its deep cutting and carried on across some fields, reaching the road at a point some hundreds of yards from the main gate and headed in the direction of Carstairs Junction. The time was then about 6:30 or 6:35 p.m.

No-one within the State Hospital knew that they had escaped, nor was it possible to contact the social club by radio or telephone. MacLellan possessed a two-way radio, issued by nurses, but was not wearing it at the time he was attacked. The cutting of the wires of the telephone handsets did not register on the types of telephone switchboard to which they were respectively connected, with the result that there was nothing to indicate to the telephone operator at the exchange in the Administration Block that anything was amiss.

Mone and McCulloch had planned to get away from the vicinity of the hospital by stopping a car and intimidating the driver into handing it over to them. Their plan, although not in its precise form was successful.

Constable's George Taylor and John Gillies faced a terrifying and frightening ordeal when they came face to face with Mone and McCulloch. Unknown to them, and anyone else at that point, they had already brutally taken two lives and had the taste for more blood.

The officers were taken by surprise and the savage attacks on them meant that they didn't really stand a chance against the weapons Mone and McCulloch possessed. The police officers were only equipped with their wooden truncheons.

Constable Taylor faced the full force of the attack by both monsters. He fought bravely but didn't stand a chance. Constable Gillies and Mr McAllan are testament to this.

Constable Gillies tried in vain to help his colleague and was beaten back with blows to his head and shoulders and an attack with a knife. He escaped and went for help as did Mr McAllan. It is possible that the actions of Constable Taylor saved both lives.

One would think that Constable Taylor would receive the highest bravery award available in the United Kingdom because of this violent and brutal attack. He gave his life in service to the public. Being a policeman was all he ever wanted to be and he loved his job and serving his community. He and his family received nothing from the Government and to this date the situation remains unchanged.

His wife Sally and four children were left without a husband and a father, all at a very young age.

In fairness to Strathclyde Police, the local Divisional Commander, Chief Superintendent John Lauder, wrote a report recommending Constable Taylor and many other people who came face to face with Mone and McCulloch that evening, for bravery awards. This report was endorsed by the Chief Constable, Patrick Hamill.

On the 28th of April 1977, following the conviction of Mone and McCulloch, The Chief Constable wrote to the then Scottish Secretary, Mr Bruce Millan, recommending Constable Taylor posthumously for the highest Queens Bravery award.

He wrote:

'Constable Taylor displayed exceptional gallantry and courage in attempting to overpower these two dangerous and violent armed men. His bravery and determination were in the highest traditions of the Police Service and it is considered that his heroism is such as to warrant recognition from Her Majesty.'

Did Constable Taylor receive this recognition, the answer is no, he did not. What happened to this letter after it arrived at the Scottish Home and Health Department is not known.

Indeed, the family of Constable Taylor were unaware that such a recommendation was made. This revelation was only discovered in 2021, when papers retained by Chief Superintendent Lauder were discovered by his daughter following his death.

The subject has now been raised with Police Scotland and the Scottish Office and we await an appropriate response.

Strathclyde Police also nominated many of the people, who came face to face with these evil killers, for Strathclyde Regional Council Bravery Awards. I can find no trace of any of them receiving an award.

We shall continue to campaign for the recognition that Constable

Taylor and other officers, who suffered the same fate, so rightly deserve, for giving their life in the service of their queen and country.

Three officers did receive Bravery Awards for their actions whilst arresting Mone and McCulloch. On the 25th of August 1978, it was announced that Sergeant Lyon and Constables Brough and Gardner of Cumbria Constabulary had been awarded the Queen's Gallantry Medal. No-one can doubt their bravery in the face of such evil individuals and their award was deserved.

Constable George Taylor is remembered at the Scottish Police Memorial at the Scottish Police College, Tulliallan Castle, Kincardine, Fife, where his name is engraved on the memorial wall.

A plaque is also displayed at the entrance to Hamilton Police office, which remembers the sacrifice of George Taylor and Ross Hunt.

Ultimately there was a significant failure in the operation and management of the establishment which resulted in the tragic and horrific events of the 30th of November 1976. Although many of the enquiry recommendations were implemented this meant very little to the victims or their families.

At the very least, the Government of the day should have recognised the bravery of all of the police officers, State Hospital staff and civilians who came into direct contact with Mone and McCulloch.

They have failed to do so, despite the appropriate recommendations being made by senior police officers, which is a very sad indictment of our Government. Even as recently as 2022 there has been a refusal on the part of the Honours Committee of the United Kingdom Government to correct this situation.

We hope that we can convince the appropriate people in Government to do the right thing and make posthumous awards to these brave people.

Together with the Hunt and Taylor family we are at the beginning of a campaign to correct this terrible situation, not only for Ross and George, but for other officers, who deserve to be recognised by the country they served without hesitation. It will not be easy; however, we are determined that these officers receive the recognition they so thoroughly deserve.

Farewell

I hope you have enjoyed reading these real-life stories of policing in Lanarkshire, some with very serious and sad endings. The purpose of the book is to raise awareness of the role of a police officer, the dangers, the community spirit, kindness and humane aspect of their job.

Most importantly, the book seeks to highlight the failure of our Government to recognise the bravery of police officers who give their lives to protecting our communities and their families who have to face the loss of their loved one on a daily basis, with little or no assistance or support. The very least our Government can do is to properly recognise the bravery and sacrifice of these officers and their families and award them the appropriate honour for doing so.

Appendix One:

A Brief History of Policing in Lanarkshire

Lanarkshire

Lanarkshire is a county located in the Central Lowlands of Scotland. It is the most populous county in Scotland, as it contains most of Glasgow and the surrounding towns. In earlier times it had considerably greater boundaries, including neighbouring Renfrewshire until 1402.

Lanarkshire is bounded to the north by the counties of Stirlingshire and Dunbartonshire, to the northeast by West Lothian and Mid Lothian, to the east by Peeblesshire, to the south by Dumfriesshire, and to the west by Ayrshire and Renfrewshire.

The County grew in stature and size in the mid-19th century with the expansion of industry and coal mining in the area, bringing people and their families, from across the United Kingdom and Ireland in the pursuit of work and a better life.

The Police Forces Of Lanarkshire

There is no formal history of policing in Lanarkshire and this section of the book will identify the police forces that existed in the County and Burgh's from the early 19th century.

Airdrie Rural Police – 1846 to 1857

The District of Airdrie had a police force in existence, since an Act of Parliament in 1846, instigated by local businessmen. The force operated in the Northern part of the County including Old & New Monkland, Shotts and part of Bothwell. The Rural force operated very successfully, with one Superintendent, 44 Sergeants and Constables. This police force was separate from the Airdrie Burgh Police.

The County force initially occupied premises in Anderson Street,

Airdrie, now a solicitors office and the Staging Post Public House, from 1846 to 1849.

A new County Police office and cells was erected in Callon Street, Airdrie around 1849. The force remained at that location until it moved to the new Sheriff Court House and Police office in Bank Street, Airdrie.

The force ceased to exist when it was amalgamated into the newly established Lanarkshire Constabulary on the 13th of October 1857.

Airdrie Burgh Police – 1835 to 1967

Airdrie Burgh Police was established in 1835 and ceased to exist in 1967 when it amalgamated with Coatbridge Burgh, Hamilton Burgh and Motherwell & Wishaw Burgh to become part of Lanarkshire Constabulary.

The first officers were recruited from the Calton area of Glasgow, and all had previous policing experience. A Superintendent and four Constables were appointed.

The first recorded numbers of officers in 1859, showed that the force had eleven officers. This increased to twenty-three in 1900 and twenty-six in 1910. The final establishment in 1967 was sixty-six officers.

The Burgh Coat of Arms is a silver shield with a two headed eagle below a crescent that has a five-point star with a central hole (known as a mullet) on either side and on top of the shield is a cockerel. The Burgh motto is 'Vigilantibus' meaning 'Forever watchful.'

Through time modern inventions were now beginning to be employed by the police and the first of these, a telephone, was installed in 1889. The second, a typewriter, was purchased in 1902. The typewriter, however, appeared to be kept in the nature of a secret weapon inasmuch as it was kept under lock and key. Only a favoured few were allowed to use it and then only under the supervision of a senior officer. If any other officer or constable made application to use the typewriter this was flatly turned down as the Chief Constable was apparently afraid that the improvement in the education of members of the force in any shape or form would usurp his authority.

In 1908 Alexander Wesley Christie was appointed Chief Constable and was responsible for various improvements in the conditions of service of the police and the manner of policing. Mr Christie was particularly interested in traffic problems and, as a result of his efforts, the first set of traffic signals in the West of Scotland were erected at the Car Terminus, Airdire, to be followed in 1932 with traffic signals at the New Town Cross and Old Town Cross.

Mr Christie appointed Mrs Waddell, who later endeared herself with the police officers and public – so much so that she was known as 'Auntie Waddell' – as Police Matron in 1912. The retirement of Mrs Waddell took place in 1932 after twenty years of faithful service and another matron, Mrs Wilson, succeeded her.

In 1930, the King's Police Medal was awarded to Chief Constable Christie for his outstanding work in police service.

Chief Constable Christie demitted office on 29th May 1933 after forty-three and a half years of service - twenty-four years of which he had served as Chief Constable of the burgh force.

To succeed Mr Christie, the Town Council unanimously agreed to appoint Inspector James Turner as Chief Constable and on 30th May 1933 he took up the position.

After his succession to the Chief Constableship, Mr Turner was ever alive to the need for the improvement of methods for combating crime and he was instrumental in having the Ericcson Police Pillar Telephone, Two-way Wireless Communications and Telex Communications Systems introduced.

On 13th June 1946, Chief Constable Turner was awarded the King's Police Medal for his meritorious police service. He retired on 15th April 1951.

Mr Turner was succeeded by Chief Constable Robert M. Clark who received the Queen's Police Medal in 1970 and the OBE in 1971.

Mr Clark became assistant Chief Constable in Lanarkshire Constabulary on amalgamation of all the Lanarkshire Forces in 1967. He retired in March 1971 and died on 18th August 1971.

Coatbridge Burgh Police – 1894 to 1967

Coatbridge Burgh Police was established on Tuesday the 15th of May 1894, eight years after the town of Coatbridge was given Burgh status. Until that time Coatbridge had been policed by Lanarkshire Constabulary.

On the 14th of May 1894, the Chief Constable of Lanarkshire Constabulary, Wallace McHardy paraded the officers of the County force at Coatbridge in their county uniform taking stock of their uniform and equipment. He then handed over responsibility of policing to the local magistrates.

At midnight, the proper exchange took place and all officers transferred to the new Burgh force. The Lanarkshire Superintendent in charge at Coatbridge at that time was John Anderson who was appointed Chief Constable.

At 10 a.m. on Tuesday the 15th of May 1894 the officers once again paraded at the Burgh Courtroom, in their new uniforms, where they were formally sworn in as officers of the Coatbridge Burgh Police. Having taken the oath, they then signed a declaration of affirmation, which was also signed by Councillor Chisholm, who has administered at the swearing in ceremony.

The Burgh force remained in existence until 1967 when it amalgamated with Airdrie Burgh, Hamilton Burgh and Motherwell & Wishaw Burgh to become part of Lanarkshire Constabulary.

The first recorded numbers of officers, in 1894, showed that the force totalled thirty. In 1900 this had increased to thirty-six and the final establishment in 1967 was one- hundred-and-two officers.

The Helmet/Cap badge displayed the Burgh Coat of Arms has a tower in a centre square. Above in a rectangle is a water pump and to the right in a rectangle is the top of a mine shaft with its wheel. Below is another rectangle depicting hills. To the left, again in a rectangle, is a saint holding his left hand in benediction. In the northwest corner are what appear to be four arrows while in the northeast corner are four columns and in the southeast is a cog wheel and, in the southwest an anvil.

Hamilton Burgh Police – 1858 to 1967

Hamilton Burgh Police was established in 1858, headed by a Chief Officer who was designated as 'Superintendent of Police.' The strength of the force is believed to have been six Constables in addition to the Superintendent.

In 1901, the designation of Superintendent was discarded and rank of Chief Constable was given to the Chief Officer. In that same year the force was thirty-one strong.

Due to financial constraints, in 1949, the force came under the control of Lanarkshire Constabulary. For operational purposes it remained a Burgh force. By this time the force had introduced policewomen and civilian employees. Police Cadets were introduced in 1959.

In 1958 a new Chief Constable was appointed, Robert B. Gordon, of Lanarkshire Constabulary, with an establishment of sixty-seven officers.

The establishment in 1965 had risen substantially to one-hundred-

and-one, consisting of eighty-seven male and five female officers, three cadets and six civilians.

It remained a Burgh force until 1967 when it amalgamated with Airdrie Burgh, Coatbridge Burgh and Motherwell & Wishaw Burgh to become part of Lanarkshire Constabulary once again.

The Burgh coat of arms has three silver coloured and pierced cinquefoils (a full faced flower with five petals and no stalk). Above the shield is a helmet and above that is a flat wreath upon which is a pierced cinquefoil. The motto is 'SOLA NOBILITAT VIRTUS' (Virtue Alone Ennobles or Virtue Alone is Nobility).

Motherwell & Wishaw Burgh Police – 1930 to 1967

It was agreed, in 1914, that Motherwell should have its own Burgh Police Force. The Chief Constable was named and badges, buttons and first-aid badges were made but never issued as the 1914 war interrupted the formation plans. The town had to wait another sixteen years until the subject of a Burgh police force was once again discussed in earnest.

Motherwell & Wishaw Burgh Police was established in 1930 having previously been policed by the Lanarkshire Constabulary. It had seventy officers when established. In 1967 it amalgamated with Airdrie Burgh, Coatbridge Burgh and Hamilton Burgh to become part of Lanarkshire Constabulary once again. At that time the force had one- hundred-and-fifty-four officers.

The force adopted the national cap badge in 1930 with collar badges bearing the roped and intertwined letters MWP.

Lanarkshire Constabulary – 1857 to 1975

On Tuesday 13th October 1857, seventy-five of the Commissioners of Supply for the County of Lanark, under the chairmanship of Lord Belhaven, met in the County Hall, Hamilton, at a General Meeting specially convened to implement the provisions of the Police (Scotland) Act 1857, which required the setting up of the Police Forces.

For police purposes, the County was divided into four districts, namely:

- *Hamilton District .*
- *Lower ward District*
- *Airdrie District*

- *Lanark District*

The establishment of the force was fixed at:
  - *One Chief Constable*
  - *Four Superintendents*
  - *Seventy-six Sergeants and Constables*

Early Years

H.M. Inspector of Constabulary for Scotland reported that during the years 1868-1869, the force was being maintained in a good state of efficiency and discipline. All police forces in Scotland were not then in the same happy position of being reported in a state of efficiency, far less being described as in a good state.

The County had been fortunate in having George McKay as its first Chief Constable. Not only was he an efficient administrator, but he was supported by a committee of gentlemen who appreciated the value of a good police force.

Throughout the years, the force would appear to have borne a high reputation among other forces in Scotland, for on numerous occasions the Lanarkshire policemen were asked to serve outside their own district.

Centenary

To mark the centenary of the inauguration of the Lanarkshire Constabulary, on 13th October 1957, a church parade and service was held in the Old Parish church, Lanark.

During the centenary service, the County Council of Lanark presented the Constabulary colours, consisting of the Queen's colour and the Constabulary standard to commemorate the Centenary. It is believed that the Lanarkshire Constabulary was the only police force, at that time, to possess a County Council standard or colours. The flag was devised and authorised by the Lord Lyon, King-of-Arms.

The flag consists of a purple background with a white saltire cross in the upper left. In the centre, a yellow circle bearing the legend, 'The County Council of the County of Lanark,' was encircled by a total of eight thistles, slipped at the second, and the whole surmounted by a green crown of five points, with a bound sheaf enclosed between each two points.

The centre of the circle has a white background to the wedge of the bottom third, being the red heart of Douglas, and the upper two thirds bearing two lilies. It is scrolled on the left 'Lanarkshire 1857' and on the right 'Constabulary 1957' with the force motto 'Vigilantia' (Vigilance) enscrolled along the bottom, below the centre piece.

Amalgamations

On 16th August 1967 the former forces of Airdrie Burgh Police, Coatbridge Burgh police, Hamilton Burgh Police, Motherwell & Wishaw Burgh Police were amalgamated to form a new larger Lanarkshire Constabulary.

Mr J.K. MacLellan C.B.E., Q.P.M., M.A., B.Sc., F.R.I.C. former Chief Constable of Motherwell & Wishaw Burgh Police was appointed as Chief Constable of this new force.

The Lanarkshire Constabulary remained in that format until 16th May 1975 when, on Regionalisation, it became a part of the new Strathclyde Police.

Strathclyde Police – 1975 to 2013

Lanarkshire Constabulary ceased to exist on the 16th of May 1975 when, on Regionalisation, it became a part of the new Strathclyde Police.

Lanarkshire became three divisions:

- *'N' Division – Airdrie, Coatbridge, Cumbernauld & Kilsyth and surrounding villages*
- *'P' Division – Motherwell, Wishaw, Shotts Bellshill and surrounding villages*
- *'Q' Division – South Lanarkshire*

Some boundary and divisional merges took place over the intervening years, in each of these, adding some small parts of Strathclyde, such as Cambuslang, Rutherglen, Moodiesburn, etc. to the Lanarkshire divisions.

In 1998, 'P' Division ceased to exist and became part of 'N' Division.

With effect from 1st April 2013 Strathclyde Police ceased to exist and became part of 'Police Scotland', the new national police force.

Lanarkshire once again became a single police command known as Lanarkshire Division of Police Scotland, in effect covering the same geographical area as Lanarkshire Constabulary in 1975. However, the officers of today can rely on better methods of communication, more resources and advancements in the investigation of crime.

Although it has to be said and as these stories will show, the police are still dealing with the same types of crime they did over a century ago and sometimes involving the same families!

Appendix Two:

Lanarkshire Police Historical Society

I have had an interest in police history and collecting police memorabilia for several years, however never really thought about bringing this together into any sort of publication. Having been a police officer, I was always fascinated about those that walked my beats before me, what they experienced, the high's and lows of policing and the hardships they faced. I began to research these officers and their cases to bring them back to life and remember their service.

It wasn't until the 23rd of March 2013 when having been contacted by Strathclyde Police, to assist with an open day at Motherwell Police office, that I brought my collection of police memorabilia out from my loft, clearing a very large space and putting it on display for the very first time.

The open day was to mark the end of Strathclyde Police and the beginning of Police Scotland, which was taking place on the 1st of April 2013. I wasn't sure how the display would be received as the weather was particularly poor around that time. My colleagues and I braved the weather and set up the display in the old canteen of the police office.

However, any doubts were soon dispelled, as over 3,000 people attended the event, the majority spending time looking at the memorabilia we had on display, including uniforms, insignia, photographs, equipment and many other items. Members of the public, retired and serving police officers all showed a keen interest in the display, which was of course very satisfying. There were many positive comments and it was amazing the amount of people who told us about their family members that had served in the police over the years.

My colleagues and I decided to discuss the event and, following an excellent lunch in Uddingston, on the 22nd of May 2013, the Lanarkshire Police Historical Society was established. I was elected to be Chair of the

Society, a post that I still hold today.

Since then, the Society has gone from strength to strength, providing numerous displays, presentations and exhibitions.

At the beginning of the Covid pandemic, in 2020, I decided to create a Facebook page to keep in contact with our members and post photographs and stories of policing in Lanarkshire. This has been incredibly successful with over 800 people now members of our group.

The stories were well received with many positive comments. Former colleague, Simon McLean, /suggested that I should perhaps consider publishing these stories and facilitated discussions with Ringwood publishing which have resulted in the publication of this book.

I hope you enjoy the stories, some funny, some serious and some sad which depict the changing face of policing in Lanarkshire and beyond, over the past decade and a half.

Appendix Three:

Glossary of Abbreviations

CC – Chief Constable

DCC – Deputy Chief Constable

ACC – Assistant Chief Constable

Chief Sup' – Chief Superintendent

Sup' – Superintendent

CI – Chief Inspector

DCI - Detective Chief Inspector

PI – Police Inspector

PS – Police Sergeant

DS – Detective Sergeant

PC – Police Constable

DC – Detective Constable

Acknowledgements

A massive thank you to my wife Catherine and my family for their patience and support whilst writing this book. Without that, I could not have completed the project.

The Taylor and Hunt families for their courage, strength and pride in George Taylor and William Ross Hunt. They have been very badly let down by those in authority, maintaining their dignity, with many disappointments and difficult times, over the many years since the loss of their loved one. They are an excellent example to us all. Thank you all for agreeing to your stories being told.

Former police officer Joe Craig for providing the research and story of the murder of Sub-Inspector Allan. His attention to detail and description of events is first class.

Thank you to former officer Margaret McLean for the information relating to the police and military service of Jeremiah Shannon.

Former colleague, Simon McLean, suggested that I should perhaps consider publishing these stories and facilitated discussions with Ringwood Publishing, discussions which have eventually resulted in the publication of this book. Simon, now Managing Director of Ringwood, has been very supportive throughout this process. Thanks are also due to Hana Kennedy, my Editor at Ringwood, Reine Fernando, my Ringwood Support Worker, and to Skye Galloway the Ringwood Designer for her work on the cover.

About the Author

I was born and brought up in Airdrie, Lanarkshire. My ambition, from a very young age, was to be a police officer.

In 1978, I successfully applied to join the Strathclyde Police Cadets. My first day was on Monday the 19th of June 1978, I was dropped off by my parents and walked through the doors of the Strathclyde Police Training School at 71 Oxford Street, Glasgow. I walked through that door countless times over the coming years and even worked as a member of staff there between 1995 and 1997

In 1980, when I was eighteen and a half, I became a fully-fledged Police Constable. My acceptance letter informed me that I would be posted to 'N' Division, which was my local area, this was unusual as single officers were commonly sent well away from their home district.

After my initial training at the Scottish Police College at Tulliallan, I was posted to Coatbridge Police office, where I spent the next six years, working the beat and in patrol cars. A great place for any aspiring police officer to learn, as you experienced every aspect of life, happy and sad, dealing with the public.

I worked in the division until 1998 when I was promoted uniform Sergeant at Maryhill. Between then and my retirement in 2010, I served in every rank up to and including Superintendent in uniform and in the Criminal Investigation Department.

One of my more prominent roles was in 2003 when I was appointed Detective Inspector at the Serious Crime Squad, based at Helen Street in the Govan area of Glasgow. This was a role which covered the whole of the Strathclyde area responding to serious incidents such as murder, armed robbery and terrorist investigations. We would also support local divisions where they required additional resources to investigate serious crimes in their area.

I was involved in many high-profile investigations including the kidnap of an Asian gentleman from the southside of Glasgow by armed criminals. This particular investigation took us to the Manchester area where we arrested a number of criminals responsible for the kidnapping and managed the safe recovery of the victim. I also spent six months in charge of the Serious Crime Squad in 2006 as Detective Chief Inspector.

In 2006, I was promoted to Chief Inspector and Staff Officer at the Scottish Police College. This role gave me the responsibility for the management of the college on a day-to-day basis including VIP visits.

Three years later, in 2009, I was appointed Superintendent in charge of a national project to develop and deliver a major training programme. I remained in this post until August 2010, when I retired from the police.

I established my own training and consultancy company, with my wife, also a retired police officer, and since then I have delivered investigation training to organisations in the United Kingdom, who have a responsibility to investigate criminality, such as Local Authorities and Government Agencies. I also delivered investigation training to police officers in the United Arab Emirates and latterly Qatar.

Through the consultancy side of the business, I have provided expert opinion and services to several solicitors and Queens Counsel with regard to high profile criminal cases, looking at things from a different perspective.

I have been Police Advisor for three TV dramas,

- *In Plain Sight*
- *Deadwater Fell*
- *Shetland*

I was one of the drivers of the police cars used in the recording of the new Indiana Jones movie filmed in Glasgow City Centre.

I am married and have four grown up children and two grandchildren.

Other Titles from Ringwood

All titles are available from the Ringwood website in both print and ebook format, as well as from usual outlets.
www.ringwoodpublishing.com
mail@ringwoodpublishing.co

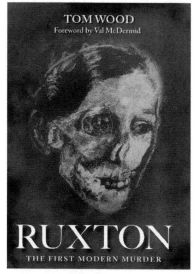

Ruxton - The First Modern Murder

Tom Wood

It is 1935 and the deaths of Isabella Ruxton and Mary Rogerson would result in one of the most complex investigations the world had ever seen. The gruesome murders captured worldwide attention with newspapers keeping the public enthralled with all the gory details.

But behind the headlines was a different, more important story: the ground-breaking work of Scottish forensic scientists who developed new techniques to solve the case and shape the future of scientific criminal investigation.

ISBN: 978-1-901514-84-1 £9.99

The Ten Percent

Simon McLean

An often hilarious, sometimes scary, always fascinating journey through the ranks of the Scottish police from his spell as a rookie constable in the hills and lochs of Argyll, through his career in Rothesay and to his ultimate goal: The Serious Crime Squad in Glasgow.

We get a unique glimpse of the turmoil caused when the rules are stretched to the limit, when the gloves come off and when some of their number decide that enough is enough. A very rare insight into the world of our plain clothes officer who infiltrate and suppress the very worst among us.

ISBN: 978-1-901514-43-8 £9.99

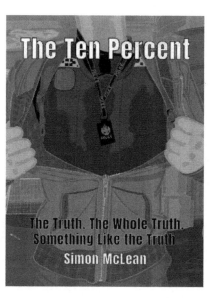

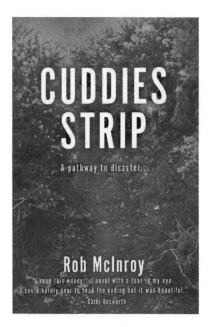

Cuddies Strip

Rob McInroy

Cuddies Strip is based on a true crime and faithfully follows the investigation and subsequent trial but it also examines the mores of the times and the insensitive treatment of women in a male-dominated society.

It is a highly absorbing period piece from 1930s Scotland, with strong contemporary resonances: both about the nature and responsiveness of police services and the ingrained misogyny of the whole criminal justice system.

ISBN: 978-1-901514-88-9
£9.99

Barossa Street

Rob McInroy

Set in Perth, Barossa Street offers, not only a look at the mishandling of justice in the face of 1930's prejudice, but also serves as a commentary of the British public's response to the government's shortcomings. Set on the backdrop of King Edward VIII's abdication and the threat of war Barossa Street is as much a critique of the times as it is a thrilling murder mystery.

With twists and turns down every street, follow Bob Kelty in this suspenseful thriller to see whether he can solve the latest who-done-it and find that much needed relief from the trials of life.

ISBN: 978-1-901514-41-4 £9.99

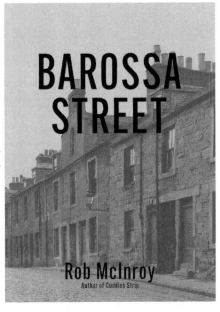

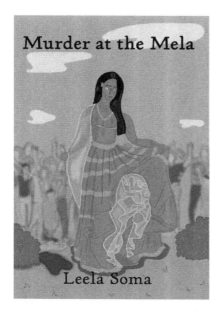

Murder at the Mela

Leela Soma

DI Alok Patel takes the helm of an investigation into the brutal murder of an Asian woman in this eagerly-awaited thriller. As Glasgow's first Asian DI, Patel faces prejudice from his colleagues and suspicion from the Asian community as he struggles with the pressure of his rank, relationships, and racism.

This murder-mystery explores not just the hate that lurks in the darkest corners of Glasgow, but the hate which exists in the very streets we walk.

ISBN: 978-1-901514-90-2

£9.99

The Carnelian Tree

Anne Pettigrew

A dead body, a disappearance, and an epic lost in time. Unrelated incidents on the surface. Judith Fraser's Oxford sabbatical quickly takes a sharp turn when she gets tangled in the mysterious murder of a colleague. With threads leading nowhere, conflicting impressions about people around her, and concern for increasing risk to her loved ones, whom can she trust?
The Carnelian Tree follows the journey of Judith Fraser as she unravels mysteries of locked doors, missing computers, cat's collars, and Reuter's reports, with the help of DCI Keith Steadman, her potential love interest. Judith probes into people, power, politics, and sex, only to discover that some things remain unchanged.

ISBN: 978-1-901514-81-0

£9.99